Evaluating
Development Aid

Evaluating Development Aid

Issues, Problems and Solutions

Basil Edward Cracknell

SAGE Publications
New Delhi • Thousand Oaks • London

First published in 2000 by

 Sage Publications India Pvt Ltd
M-32 Market, Greater Kailash, Part 1
New Delhi 110 048

Sage Publications Inc.
2455 Teller Road
Thousand Oaks, California 91320

Sage Publications Ltd
6 Bonhill Street
London EC2A 4PU

Published by Tejeshwar Singh for Sage Publications India Pvt Ltd, phototypeset by Line Arts, Pondicherry and printed at Chaman Enterprises, Delhi.

Second Printing 2001

Library of Congress Cataloging-in-Publication Data
Cracknell, B.E.
    Evaluating development aid: issues, problems and solutions/Basil Edward Cracknell.
        p.   cm.
    Includes bibliographical references and index.
    1. Economic assistance—Developing countries—History. 2. Economic assistance—Developing countries—Evaluation. I. Title.

HC60.C668   338.91'09172'4—dc 21   2000   00–024738

ISBN: 0–7619–9403–3 (US-HB)   81–7036–907–X (India-HB)
        0–7619–9404–1 (US-PB)   81–7036–908–8 (India-PB)

Sage Production Team: Abantika Chatterji, Mathew, P.J. and Santosh Rawat

*To fellow evaluators everywhere,
who share the task of making the there and then,
speak to the here and now.*

Contents

Part 1   A Brief History of Aid Evaluation

Part 2   Basic Issues: Purposes, Techniques and Methods

Part 3   Monitoring, Learning and Feedback

Part 4   Impact, Empowerment, Stakeholder Analysis and the Participatory Approach

Part 5   The Wider Horizon and the Way Ahead

List of Figures

List of Boxes

List of Acronyms and Abbreviations

ADB	Asian Development Bank
BMZ	Bundesministerium fur Wirtschaftliche Zusammenarbeit
CBA	Cost-Benefit Analysis
CDIE	Centre for Development Information and Evaluation (USAID)
CFTC	Commonwealth Fund for Technical Cooperation
CIDA	Canadian International Development Agency
DAC	Development Assistance Committee (of the OECD)
DANIDA	Danish International Development Assistance
DFID	Department for International Development
DGIS	Directorate General for International Cooperation (the Netherlands)
DPPC	Development and Project Planning Centre, University of Bradford
EADI	European Association of Development and Research Institutes
ECU/EUR	European Currency Unit
EDI	Economic Development Institute (of the World Bank), now called World Bank Institute
EEC	European Economic Community
EVSUM	Evaluation Summary
FASID	Foundation for Advanced Studies on International Development
FINNIDA	Finnish International Development Agency
FMI	Financial Management Initiative
GAD	Gender and Development
GTZ	Deutsche Gesellschaft fur Technische Zusammenarbeit
HMSO	Her Majesty's Stationery Office

IBRD	International Bank for Reconstruction and Development
IDB	Inter-American Development Bank
IDRC	International Development Research Centre (Ottawa)
IDS	Institute for Development Studies (University of Sussex)
IFC	International Finance Corporation
IMF	International Monetary Fund
ILO	International Labour Office
JIU	Joint Inspection Unit
KFW	Kreditanstalt fur Wiederaufbau
LFA	Logical Framework Approach
M & E	Monitoring and Evaluation
MIS	Management Information System
NGO	Non-Government Organisation
NORAD	Norwegian Agency for International Development
ODA	Overseas Development Administration (UK)
OECD	Organisation for Economic Cooperation and Development
OED	Operations Evaluation Department (World Bank)
PCR	Project Completion Report
PEC	Projects and Evaluation Committee
PIMS	Policy Information Marker System
PRA	Participatory Rural Appraisal
R & D	Research and Development
RRA	Rapid Rural Appraisal
SIDA (now Sida)	Swedish International Development Cooperation Agency
TC	Technical Cooperation
UNDP	United Nations Development Programme
UNEP	United Nations Environment Programme
UNFPA	United Nations Population Fund
UNICEF	United Nations Children's Fund
UNIDO	United Nations Industrial Development Organisation
UNIFEM	United Nations Development Fund for Women
USAID	United States Agency for International Development
WFP	World Food Programme
WHO	World Health Organisation
WID	Women in Development
ZOPP	Zielorientierte Projekt-planung (Objectives-oriented Planning)

Foreword

In development aid, as in other domains of development, we are living in an era of self-critical reflection and of rapid methodological change. In the evaluation of development aid, the rate of innovation and change has been fast and seems to be accelerating. This presents challenges which are personal, professional and institutional. At the personal level, and depending on their positions and orientations, those professionally engaged in the field find themselves variously left behind, bewildered, threatened or exhilarated. For all of them this book has something to offer.

For those who feel left behind, here is a summation of much of the state-of-the-art at the end of the twentieth century. The historical section outlines where we have come from. The remainder of the book summarises and synthesises where we are now, including aspects and approaches which have only recently come into prominence.

For those who are bewildered, this magisterial review will be a helpful guide. For it covers the field with comprehensive authority. It presents and examines a whole range of methods and methodologies related directly or indirectly to evaluation. A selection of these can illustrate this. In alphabetical order, they include: automated data bases, baselines, cost benefit analysis, fourth generation evaluation, impact analyses, logical frameworks, participatory monitoring and evaluation, peer group review, policy-level evaluation, PRA, problem trees, project cycle management, qualitative and quantitative evaluation, rating and scoring systems, stakeholder analysis, evaluating sustainability and ZOPP. It also covers applications in a variety of contexts such as governance, NGOs, organisations and organisational dynamics, policy, poverty alleviation, programme aid, R & D projects, sector aid, small countries, structural adjustment and technical cooperation.

For those who feel threatened, here is a balanced presentation of where we have come from and where we are. All development professionals have been trained into certain mindsets and methods. When these are challenged, it can be natural to react defensively. I have done this myself. Thirty years ago we were struggling with formal positivist evaluations. Like others I thought we could learn from baseline questionnaire surveys, with controls, followed by later similar surveys. I applied for funding for an impact evaluation of the Zaina water scheme in Kenya. This was to use a questionnaire survey. The results were to be compared with an earlier baseline study. When funding was refused because any 'findings' would be worthless, I was hurt and angry, and felt humiliated. My professional competence had been questioned. I was not willing to learn and change. Yet I came later to see that the proposed approach was fundamentally flawed, with many problems of comparability, unknown causal linkages and magnitudes, multiple causality, and the counterfactual, not to mention the costs and shortcomings of questionnaires and their analysis. What I should have done, and what I commend to myself and others now, is to accept and welcome critical debate, to enjoy change, and to embrace new ways of doing things as a normal and positive condition.

For others today who may feel similarly affronted when faced with, say, critiques of the logical framework and proposals for participatory monitoring and evaluation, there is comfort and inspiration in Basil Cracknell's own example. As an evaluation professional with long experience in a donor agency, he has himself lived and worked through the phases and fashions for evaluation which he describes. He has been part of the process of learning and change. He has been able and willing to adopt and adapt what has seemed good in what was new. As he stresses, the way forward is not rigid adherence to any one doctrine or methodology, but openness to diversity, innovation and change.

So this book can be read as an invitation to all who feel left behind, bewildered or threatened to join the growing band of those who find the current creative pluralism exhilarating. Some of the older approaches and methods seemed to promise a security and certainty which with hindsight we can see was hollow. We can now mingle, modify and replace them in a manner which is eclectic, flexible and adaptive. There is no methodological monoculture. There is no one solution. But there are recommended approaches and attitudes—self-critical awareness, inventiveness, learning from errors and successes alike, welcoming and managing change, and freely sharing information.

So the frontiers and challenges now are many. Above all they are to get it right about what has happened, and to make a difference.

On getting it right, we can now see that the old-style two or three week mission sent from a donor organisation to evaluate people-centred projects or programmes is deeply flawed. However well-intentioned and hard-working they are, outside evaluators are trapped in an epistemological cocoon. Their vision is blurred and bent. What is perceived and reported cannot reflect accurately the complex and diverse realities of people and institutions. Many conditions and interests combine to select and distort what is said, shown, and seen. In consequence, evaluation reports based on brief missions regularly mislead.

On making a difference, as Basil Cracknell points out, feedback is the Achilles'heel of evaluation. How, where and between whom it takes place are critical. The implications for process and reporting of his view that 'an ounce of face-to-face dialogue is worth a pound of automated data' are little short of revolutionary. They have yet to be worked through into common practice. Process and ownership do indeed seem to be key. So we can ask not just what methods should be used, but

- Who evaluates?
- Who analyses?
- Whose evaluation is it?
- Who feeds back to whom, where and how?
- Who gains experience and learns, and where and how?
- Who is empowered?
- Who changes?
- Who gains?

More and more we are learning that the answers can and should be 'poorer and local people' as well as or even instead of outside evaluators.

So it is that this book points to participatory monitoring and evaluation by local people as the major frontier. Evidence is accumulating that it has a huge potential both for empowering local and poor people and for improving aid. Again and again, participatory evaluations by local people are revealing a quality of insight and information inaccessible by other means. Moreover, such evaluations can have an authority and credibility that are otherwise inaccessible.

For participatory monitoring and evaluation to become widespread requires reversals and reorientations. These include shifts—of role from evaluator to facilitator, of style from judgement to learning, of mode from extractive to empowering, and of focus from one-off report to on-going process. Accountability tilts in its balance from upwards to donors to more downwards to poor local people.

The prize to be claimed is projects and programmes which are better for local people, especially the poorer. To achieve that prize demands vision, courage and commitment on the part of evaluators. Many of them will have to struggle against the personal, professional and institutional inertia to be found in donor agencies, NGOs and governments. But those who see the need for continuous learning and change should not despair. Their allies are growing in number and influence. And they have authoritative support in this book.

Basil Cracknell tells us that we are at a crossroads. The territory ahead is uncharted. If we are serious about poverty, we have to explore the diverse paths towards which he points us. For those setting out to evaluate development aid in the twenty-first century, he has done a signal service. For he has provided a comprehensive and forward-looking reference point and perspective based on personal experience. To this book, future evaluators and facilitators of evaluation will be able to turn for practical enlightenment and for an understanding of the state-of-the-art at the turn of the century. Above all, they will be able to read in it a challenge to be bold, creative and courageous, as the author has been, in finding better ways of making a difference.

Robert Chambers

Acknowledgements

If ever a book sprang directly from the rich soil of experience it is this one. So my first acknowledgements must go to the many evaluators with whom I have worked over many years in carrying out over 100 evaluations all over the developing world. Then I wish to acknowledge the tremendous support I have received from colleagues in the Overseas Development Administration, notably Bob Porter, John Healey, Richard Browning, Douglas Williams, Bob Ainscow, Rosalind Eykben, Ian Buist, Sir John Vereker, Johnnie Morris and many others. I have also benefited greatly from the professional expertise of fellow members of the DAC Expert Group on Aid Evaluation (recently renamed a Working Group), especially: Bob Berg, Haven North, Klaus Winkel, Hedy Von Metzsch and Niels Dabelstein.

I have worked closely with the European Commission over many years and I wish to acknowledge the inspiration I have received, especially in the field of project cycle management, from Dr Hellmut Eggers, one time Head of the Evaluation Unit of Directorate General VIII. The World Bank has been a leader in evaluation, as in so many other areas, and I am particularly grateful for the inspiration I have received from such people as: Mervyn Weiner, Robert Picciotto and Pablo Guerrero of Operations Evaluation Department; Bill Stevenson of the International Finance Corporation; John Oxenham and Ray Rist of the World Bank Institute; and Frank Rittner and Jarle Harsatd of the Global Environmental Facility.

For the last 14 years I have felt myself to be a part of the very stimulating community at the Institute of Development Studies, University of Sussex. As an Associate I have had free access to the splendid development library which I gratefully acknowledge. I have also enjoyed much intellectual stimulus from working with so many of the Fellows at the Institute, including Mike Faber, John Toye, Gerald Bloom, Mick Howes, Sir Hans Singer, Chris Colclough, Simon Maxwell and others.

In recent year, my interests have expanded into the area of organisational learning, and this has brought me into contact with a lively group of Scandinavian evaluators who have had a considerable influence on my mode of thinking; they include: Kim Forss, Knut Samset, Jerker Carlsson, Henrik Nielsen and Claus Rebien. Also in recent years I have profited greatly from the opportunities opened up by the formation of the UK Evaluation Society which has brought me into contact with a much wider circle of evaluators, including: Elliott Stern, May Pettigrew, Philip Hills, Helen Simons, Libby Cooper and Ian Davies.

Finally, my approach to aid evaluation has been transformed as a result of the close contact I have had with Robert Chambers and his group promoting participatory methods based on the Institute of Development Studies. I am particularly grateful to Robert for taking time from his incredibly busy schedule to write the Foreword to this book.

Introduction

'We are much beholden to Machiavel and others, who write what men do and not what they ought to do'
(The Advancement of Learning, *Francis Bacon*)

'The past at least is secure'
(Daniel Webster, Second Speech on Foot's Resolution, 6 January 1830)

'We learn from experience that men never learn anything from experience'
(George Bernard Shaw)

Evaluation—A Fast Growing Discipline

Evaluation must be one of the fastest growing disciplines in the world. In the United States, where there is a well-established professional evaluation society (The American Evaluation Association) with 2800 members, every agency in the government already has, or will soon have, its own evaluation unit. In recent years, new evaluation societies have been established in the United Kingdom (UK) and Europe. National evaluation societies already exist in France, Germany, Italy, Switzerland, Australia, Canada, and Central and South America, and others are in the pipeline. The first International Conference on Evaluation was held in Vancouver in the autumn of 1995. In addition to the *The American Journal of Evaluation* and *New Directions for Evaluation*, the journals of the American Evaluation Association, there has been a steady growth in the number of professional journals devoted to aspects of evaluation methodology and practice (the latest being the British journal *Evaluation*), while each year more institutions are offering specialised training in evaluation techniques.

Within the broad field of evaluation in general, the evaluation of development aid had an early start, and for many of the largest aid agencies its main period of development was the 1970s and 1980s (Cracknell, 1988a). It is an indication of the importance attached to this subject that increasing resources were being applied to it throughout the 1980s, even though aid funds during that period were subject to severe cuts. For two of the largest agencies, the European Commission and Japan, the most rapid period of growth of their evaluation capability has been the 1990s (when the evaluation budget of Directorate General VIII [DG VIII] of the European Commission, handling development aid, almost tripled), whilst rapid growth is still taking place in the main non-government organisations (NGOs) specialising in overseas aid. Aid evaluators meet twice a year under the aegis of the Development Assistance Committee of the Organisation for Economic Cooperation and Development (OECD), and those in the European Community also meet annually to share experiences and to plan joint activities. In 1994, the World Bank organised a major conference on evaluation which it hoped would be 'a small first step toward a global alliance for improved development evaluation' (World Bank, 1995).

A Favourable Climate

A number of factors have combined to produce a climate favourable to development evaluation. These include: the strengthening of democratic institutions and the decline of authoritative regimes; the gradual drying up of resources for aid, forcing donors to maximise the utility of the remaining aid funds; the growing complexity of development problems, highlighting the need for more feedback from experience; and the trend towards privatisation, leading to pressure for evaluation of how public funds are being spent. One might also add that evaluators have been able to prove their worth through the quality of the work they have done, so that the demand for their services has grown.

It is not only the donor organisations that have developed their evaluation capabilities—many of the developing countries have too. For example, India has had a large evaluation service, one of the largest in the world, for many years (ADB, 1995). Pakistan also has a substantial evaluation capability, as do Indonesia and other countries in Asia and elsewhere. These evaluation units in the developing countries seem destined to play an even more important role in the future as the main emphasis in development evaluation continues to shift from the aid-delivery concerns of the donor towards the development impact on the recipient, and as the donors take more serious steps to strengthen the evaluation capacity of the recipient countries. This book has been written mainly from the viewpoint of the developed country agencies giving development assistance, but most of the principles and practices apply equally to the developing countries' evaluation of their own public sector investments, and I hope that the book will be as useful (indeed perhaps even more useful) to the evaluators in the developing countries as to those in the developed countries.

The Stakeholder Approach

When I began writing, I envisaged a wide-ranging review of aid evaluation issues in general, and that is still the main purpose of the book. However, as my research for the book progressed, I became aware that there was one theme which kept on appearing again and again—almost as if it were another book struggling to get out—and this was the role of the respective stakeholders (i.e., anyone who has a role in the project or programme being evaluated, whether on the donor side or the recipient) in the evaluation process, especially the beneficiaries of the aid projects; and also the way in which participatory methods are being developed to ensure that the beneficiaries take a full part in both project implementation and evaluation. I even contemplated making this the main theme of the book, and changing the title to something like: 'Empowerment and the Stakeholder Approach'. However, I realised that this would be giving too great an emphasis to just one aspect, important though it is. So, in the end, what might have been the main theme of the book has survived as the title of one of its chapters (Chapter 19) and as the principal subject matter of Chapter 20. Nevertheless, it is still a key topic and one which recurs again and again throughout the rest of the text.

Principal Themes of the Book

My main aim in writing the book has been to contribute to the current discussion on the key issues involved in the evaluation of development assistance, from the practical as well as the theoretical point of view. There is now a growing body of literature on evaluation theory, as a glance at any of the various professional journals on evaluation will confirm. Although I fully appreciate the importance of this theoretical underpinning, and have made every effort to familiarise myself with the literature, my direct experience has been that of the practitioner rather than the theorist, and that is the perspective from which the book has been written. I have spent nearly 30 years as a development economist specialising in the evaluation of development aid. I count myself particularly fortunate in that I have experienced evaluation from two different sides—First, as a commissioner of evaluation studies (when I was Head of the Evaluation Department of the ODA[1] for a good many years), and second, as a consultant. For the last 14 years I have been engaged directly in evaluation work for clients. For a period, whilst I was in the ODA, I was Chairman of the OECD/DAC Expert Group on Aid Evaluation and this gave me many valuable insights into what was happening in the evaluation field outside the UK. Since then I have worked for many bilateral and multilateral aid agencies, and NGOs, as well as for recipient country institutions, and this has further extended my experience in the aid evaluation field worldwide.

While I was working for the ODA I played a role in the introduction of the logical framework technique of project planning into that organisation, and since I left the ODA I have continued to retain a keen interest in all aspects of project cycle management by running many training courses and preparing guidelines and manuals for various aid agencies. Experience has shown that it is very difficult to evaluate a project for which objectives were never clearly stated at the outset and which has not been regularly monitored during implementation. To quote the old saying, 'If you don't know where you're going any road will get you there'. Thus evaluation and project cycle management are intimately related, and exploring the implications of this linkage is one of my main aims in the book.

This book does not seek to prescribe specific solutions to specific problems, but rather to explore and discuss the main issues, and to critically examine some of the solutions that have been adopted in an attempt to address the common problems that all of us, who work in the aid evaluation field, face. There are many different approaches to evaluation and what may be right for one institution may not be right for another. Inevitably my approach is coloured by the fact that my experience has been mostly gained from my work with a donor agency, but I have made a conscientious attempt to see the issues and the problems from the standpoint of an aid recipient, and a separate chapter is devoted to this topic (Chapter 18). This was one of my principal concerns long before the stakeholder approach became fashionable. Indeed, one of the underlying themes of the book is that evaluation is essentially a subjective exercise and the results will be greatly influenced by the cultural background of the evaluator. This topic becomes crucially important once it is accepted that all the stakeholders (i.e., not just the donor) need to have a vital role in the whole process of evaluation.

Another important theme is that an evaluation report in itself does not mark the end of the evaluation process, but almost one might say the beginning of it—certainly the beginning of the hardest part! Most evaluations are meant to result directly in improved performance, and unless there is effective feedback, the whole process may be more a cosmetic than a really effectual one. Feedback has up to now been the least discussed topic in evaluation, but it is surely one of the most important, which is why three chapters are devoted to various aspects of it in the book (Chapters 10, 11 and 12). Moreover, I feel that my experience in a government department has given me a greater opportunity to practice feedback than most academics or consultants would have, so I can perhaps claim to speak with some experience on the subject.

Another neglected area is the whole question of organisational dynamics, and the processes by which organisations learn (vitally important for successful feedback). Several evaluators, notably in Scandinavia, have made this a principal theme of their research, and in recent years I have been privileged to be able to collaborate with them. They have apparently found my practical experience useful, and I have certainly learned an enormous amount about organisational learning through working with them. The articles and reports that have emerged from this body of research have been drawn upon heavily in the book, notably in Chapter 9.

Finally there is a special emphasis in the book on the topic of sustainability, that is, the extent to which a development activity survives once the aid comes to an end. This is now recognised as a critical criterion for aid evaluation, and it is so important that it cannot just be left to chance—it has to be planned for from the very beginning. The slogan 'sustainable benefits to target groups' is now seen as one of the keys to effective project cycle management, so the emphasis today is on 'building in' sustainability as a key element of all project and programme funding. I would go so far as to say that no aid evaluation can be satisfactory if it does not take sustainability into account.

In addition to these principal themes, the book also covers such practical aspects as: the role of monitoring; how evaluation results feed into management information systems; the importance of impact evaluation; the special problems associated with the evaluation of the activities of non-government organisations; the evaluation of research and development; and the evaluation of such aspects as gender, environment and good governance. There is also a chapter on international cooperation in aid evaluation, which has been one of the most encouraging aspects of the way the subject has developed over the last 20 years.

The book concludes with a look ahead at some of the new trends in evaluation methodology, especially the concept of the evaluator as a facilitator, mediator, or even negotiator, embodied in what has been called in America 'fourth generation evaluation' (Guba and Lincoln, 1989). An attempt is made to assess the extent to which these new ideas will replace the more traditional approach to aid evaluation. The opportunity is taken, in the closing chapter, to set aid evaluation in the broader context of evaluation generally, and to assess the relevance of the 'paradigm wars' that have characterised the development of the subject in the United States over the last two decades.

Building Bridges

Whereas until recently evaluators tended to work in their own separate fields, with little cross-fertilisation taking place between them, that is now rapidly changing, thanks largely to the formation of the new UK Evaluation Society and the others mentioned earlier. It is coming to be realised that although the subject matter may be different, the methodologies of evaluation are often similar, and similar problems are being encountered. As Elliot Stern wrote in the editorial of the first volume of the new journal, *Evaluation*, 'What we are now seeing is a blurring of the boundaries between different evaluation traditions which have often existed in relative isolation and even ignorance of each other' (Stern, 1995). I sincerely hope that this book helps evaluators working in other sectors become more familiar with what has been happening in the field of aid evaluation, and to share the insights they may have gained.

Another bridge that needs to be built is one between the community of professional evaluation researchers on the one hand, and on the other the evaluators working in aid agencies (often in the public sector) who sometimes commission evaluations to be carried out by others, and sometimes engage in them themselves. In the newly formed UK Evaluation Society, the different interests of these two groups rapidly became apparent, and there was even some doubt about whether they could satisfactorily be served within the same society. Fortunately it was decided that they have so much to learn from each other that there is merit in togetherness. University-based evaluation researchers have developed a jargon-laden language of their own, and hard-pressed officials, trying to meet their agencies' needs for an action-oriented evaluation programme, with tight time schedules, must sometimes feel that the academic evaluation researchers are living in another world. Yet, evaluation is nothing if it is not practical, and the researchers have to relate to the real world if they are to be effective, just as the official in the sponsoring agency has to master the ideas and concepts that are coming out of academia if the evaluations he/she commissions are to be of high quality. Again, I hope that this book will act as a bridge between the two sides.

As I was writing the book, I became acutely aware that evaluation has now become so multi-faceted, with many different approaches being adopted according to the circumstances of each case, that few generalisations would be valid universally for all aid agencies. At one extreme is the World Bank, with a relatively small number of very large projects, and at the other extreme are the NGOs with large numbers of very small projects. Obviously the circumstances of the latter are completely different from those of the former, and different evaluation techniques would be appropriate for each. Much of my own experience has been with a middle-sized bilateral donor, and that has inevitably coloured my perspective. However, where I was aware that markedly different practices would be followed in aid agencies of a different type or size (and fortunately I have worked, as a consultant, with agencies of all sizes) I have tried to indicate this in the text.

Evaluation as a subject is still in a state of flux. New methodologies and new approaches are still being tested, and there is now a growing willingness to find out from each other how and why different evaluation methods are used, and how successful they have been. For evaluators of all hues it is a good time to be alive. We now have the stimulus of a professional society and a professional journal, and more opportunities to learn from each other than ever before. There are few entrenched positions (in Europe at any rate) and a great willingness to enter into fruitful dialogue with each other. Virile debates are taking place on the directions which the future thrust of evaluation work should take, and I hope that this book will make a contribution towards that on-going process.

Note

1. The Overseas Development Administration (ODA) was renamed the Department for International Development (DFID) in 1997, but I have retained the old title where the context requires it. A similar problem arises with regard to other aid agencies that have recently undergone internal reorganisation, including Sida (previously SIDA); FINNIDA, which is now the Department for Development Cooperation of the Ministry of Foreign Affairs; and DG VIII of the European Commission, which is in the process of being reorganised. The DAC Expert Group on Aid Evaluation has recently been renamed a Working Group. The Economic Development Institute of the World Bank is now called The World Bank Institute. In all these cases I have retained the old title as appropriate.

Part 1

A Brief History of
Aid Evaluation

Mr Jean Quesnel, Chairman of the DAC Expert Group on Aid Evaluation, 1993:

Experience reflected upon is the handmaiden of progress. Evaluation is an integral part of individual and institutional learning. By doing, evaluating and doing again we learn to do better. The pursuit of applied knowledge is a long-term endeavour through which we all strive to foster more efficient and effective international development.

Evaluation: A Systematic Approach, Rossi and Freeman:

Evaluation research is a purposeful activity, undertaken to affect policy development, to shape the design and implementation of social interventions, and to improve the management of social programs. In the broadest sense of politics, evaluation is a political activity. Evaluations are a real-world activity. In the end, what counts is the critical acclaim with which an evaluation is judged by peers in the field and the extent to which it leads to modified policies, programs and practices—ones that, in the short or long term, improve the conditions of human life.

1

A Brief History of Aid Evaluation

'Evaluation is an evolving work of art, a process in which accumulating experience is steadily allowing the boundaries of analysis to be pushed forward and the policy conclusions to become increasingly substantial'.

(Does Aid Work? Cassen)

'One has to admit that development is rather a learning process in which mistakes are unavoidable despite all efforts not to make them. This situation, in my view, warrants a flexible approach, allowing all involved parties to learn from mistakes and to adjust projects and plans accordingly'.

(H.E. the Ambassador of the Netherlands to Pakistan, opening a conference on evaluation, November, 1989)

'Experience isn't interesting until it begins to repeat itself—in fact, until it does that, it hardly is experience'.

(Elizabeth Bowen)

'You know more of a road by having travelled it than by all the conjectures and descriptions in the world'.

(William Hazlitt)

The evaluation of aid is still a relatively new subject, as indeed is evaluation in general. In fact, aid evaluation, in the UK at any rate, was well established some years before it came into use in other sectors. The reason for this is not hard to find—it is because the aid funds were being spent in other parts of the world, often thousands of miles away, by governments whose professional skills were spread all too thinly, and where the risks of failure were considerably higher than would be the case with public sector investments within the UK. Because of the obvious need to carefully monitor and evaluate what was happening to the aid funds, the ODA, and donor agencies in other countries, set up their own evaluation units, and their own staff had a major involvement in the evaluations that were carried out. In other UK government departments, it was more usual to commission evaluations to be carried out by university staff or by consultants. From the start, therefore, aid evaluation had a strong pragmatic character, with the emphasis on the practical usefulness of the results in improving aid operations, and the need to improve project planning and implementation so as to ensure more effective projects. This was in contrast to the situation in other sectors where there was a stronger theoretical component in the way evaluation work evolved, with a particular emphasis on concepts and methodologies: these academic evaluators were often not very concerned about the way in which the agencies that had commissioned them actually operated. Aid evaluators have much to contribute in the area of feedback and project management, but they also have much to learn in terms of theoretical approaches to evaluation and in terms of methodological diversity. It is only in recent years that aid evaluators have become more fully integrated into the wider world of evaluation debate and this cross-fertilisation has been a great benefit all round.

The Four Phases

In an article I wrote in 1988 (Cracknell, 1988a), I traced three distinct phases in the development of aid evaluation:

- Phase One (from the late 1960s to 1979): Early developments
- Phase Two (from 1979 to 1984): Explosion of interest
- Phase Three (from 1984 to present): Coming of age.

Since I wrote that article, Rebien has published his book (Rebien, 1996) in which he suggests that a fourth phase should be added to the three I suggested, namely, 'Aid evaluation at the crossroads' (ibid.: 51). He suggests that this should start from 1998 and that it continues to the present. He points out, quite correctly, that the last 10 years or so have been characterised by a growing unease about some of the features of aid evaluation that have become widely adopted in the past but which do not seem to be consistent with many of today's concerns. In particular, he refers to the rigidities of the logical framework approach, and the problems of reconciling it with the far more flexible 'process-approach' techniques, and participatory methods, that have come increasingly into use (these concepts are discussed in Chapters 5 and 6 of this book). He also refers to the complications caused by the trend from project aid towards more programme and sector support, and also to what he calls the 'embryonic academic interest in the evaluation field at a meta level, that is, how theory, methodology and methods for aid evaluation may be improved'. I agree entirely with Rebien, and indeed the whole of my book is concerned with the dilemmas that face the aid evaluation community regarding such issues as these. Aid evaluation is indeed 'at the crossroads' and one of my main purposes in writing this book has been to put up a few signposts as to the directions in which our profession might move. But we have jumped ahead of ourselves. It is time now to review each of the four phases of development.

Phase One: Early Developments (Late 1960s to 1979)

The first aid evaluation report to catch the imagination of the public (although aid evaluation work had been going on for some time) was Albert Hirschman's *Development Projects Observed*, published in 1967 (Hirschman, 1967). His thesis, of the effectiveness of the 'hiding hand' in helping to counteract initial errors, was rather startling, and could even have been taken as implying that evaluation work was not all that necessary. His book could even have killed off the subject at birth! However, in practice his ideas had rather little impact at the time. Most evaluators felt it was unwise, to say the least, to rely on such 'automatic' correction of errors, and they considered that good project design, and careful monitoring and evaluation, were essential. Hirschman's study, the result of a 12-month sabbatical, remained for years a fascinating but isolated oddity.

But now that the subject has 'come of age' and has gained some maturity, people have been more ready to go back to Hirschman, and they have found that his ideas were remarkably prescient and full of wisdom. In 1994, a volume of essays entitled *Provoked by the Work of Albert O. Hirschman* was published (see Rodwin and Schon, 1994: see also J. Winpenny, 1984), and these acknowledged the important contribution that he made.

At this time in the USA, and in a few of the larger United Nations (UN) organisations, evaluation was beginning to be established as a key part of the project cycle: but not only, or even mainly, as the last stage of the cycle. Rather, the emphasis was on getting the initial design right, and then establishing criteria for success against which project performance could be measured. For this purpose a very effective tool called the 'logical framework' was developed. A great promoter of this technique was Herb Turner who trained many evaluators (both in the USA and elsewhere) in its use during the 1970s. I had just been appointed as Head of the Evaluation Unit in the ODA at that time and I found myself attending one of Turner's one-week courses in Washington in 1974. I had expected the course to be all about what happens at the ex post evaluation stage (i.e., how one finds out what went right or wrong) but was astonished to find that it was all about what happens in the project preparation stage. Of course it makes a lot of sense to get things right at the appraisal stage rather than simply finding out what went wrong afterwards! The logical framework became an integral part of the project management system in USAID, but it was not until a decade later that it was incorporated into the project management systems in the UK and in most of Europe. The logical framework, its advantages and its limitations, are discussed in Chapter 5.

In the USA, evaluation had already become almost a professionalism in its own right during the 1960s and 1970s, as a result of the mandatory evaluation procedures built into the many federal and state-funded welfare and educational/training schemes. However, rather surprisingly, very little of this 'domestic' experience seems to have spilled over into the evaluation of aid programmes or projects. One searches in vain for any contribution from the people working at that time in the field of aid evaluation in the voluminous writings on evaluation in America. However, because of the high reputation of the Americans in the evaluation field, two of their leading evaluators, Rossi and Freeman, were invited by the Organisation for Economic Cooperation and Development (OECD) to act as consultants helping to produce a guidance manual on the evaluation of social projects (Freeman et al., 1979). I was a member of the reviewing panel, and my abiding memory is the realisation that neither of the authors appeared to have any first hand experience of aid evaluation and all their case studies related to social welfare programmes in the USA, so that great caution was needed in attempting to transfer this experience and these skills to the totally different situation in the developing countries. The OECD also produced another useful guidance manual at about the same time (Imboden, 1978). There is a massive volume of academic literature, and several internationally known textbooks, on the evaluation of social projects in the USA, but until recently it had little impact on the development of aid evaluation elsewhere in the world. In one way, however, this may have been fortunate because it meant that we in Europe were spared the bitter 'paradigm wars' between the so-called positivists and constructivists that caused so much dissension in the ranks of evaluators in America till quite recently (see Chapter 21).

Outside the USA, and a few UN agencies, evaluation in the late 1970s remained largely unexplored territory. Few donors had as yet established evaluation units and there was very little expertise available, and virtually no resources being devoted to the subject. The only glimmer of light at the end of the tunnel were the two reports produced by OECD, already mentioned, and their earlier report on technical assistance (OECD, 1969) which proved to be years ahead of its time. Together with the two conferences on evaluation that OECD organised during this period, the OECD involvement represented a tiny, but important, core around which experience could grow, as a pearl grows in an oyster. With hindsight, the European evaluation community owes a considerable debt to the OECD for the role it played in getting things moving on the evaluation front in those early days.

However, the evaluation situation was still pretty parlous everywhere else in Europe. Staff were very thin on the ground, and resources often virtually non-existent. In the ODA, during the early 1970s, I was forced to use students to carry out evaluations because there were no funds for engaging proper consultants. However, we did manage to commission one large study at that time by making use of research funds. This was carried out by the Overseas Development Group at the University of East Anglia. It was a study of the east–west highway in Nepal (Overseas Development Group, 1977). Academically this was an excellent study, which threw up some very important results, especially in terms of unintended effects (e.g., many thousands of head porters being put out of work). However, the report did not take sufficient account of the sensitive political situation in that country and a few critical comments in the text caused something of a political furore quite out of proportion to their real significance in terms of the findings as a whole. It was this experience, along with a few others like it, that led the ODA to conclude that evaluations should be conducted by joint teams comprising both ODA staff and outsiders, rather than by academics or consultants working alone.

In those early days there was some uncertainty as to whether evaluations should be confined to specific projects, or whether they could relate to a donor's total aid programme to a country. So a number of studies were commissioned from the Overseas Development Institute to throw light on this. Two books resulted, one on Kenya (Holtham and Hazlewood, 1976) and the other on Malawi (Morton, 1975), and there was also an article on Botswana, Lesotho and Swaziland (Jones, 1977). Eventually it was realised that this topic was something of a cul-de-sac because there were very few countries where one donor's aid was sufficiently dominant to justify evaluating the impact of the aid programme as a whole.

During this period, when resources were so scarce, the opportunity was taken to get other associated agencies interested in evaluation work so that the limited resources could be spread further. Examples are a tracer study that was carried out by the Asian Institute of Technology (Asian Institute of Technology, 1978) with a little trigger money from the ODA; an evaluation of textbooks in Tunisia which was carried out mainly by the British Council (ODA, 1979b); and a joint evaluation with Indian universities (the first joint evaluation with a developing country) of the Indian Institute of Technology in Delhi and the British Universities Research Collaboration (ODA, 1982).

Another innovation at this time was the carrying out of the first baseline studies, that is, in-depth studies of the situation on the ground before the first contractors' vehicles arrive. The largest of these was the baseline study of the Songea-Makambako Road in Tanzania carried out by Halcrows (ODA, 1980).

During Phase One, evaluation took very much a second place to economic project appraisal, which was seen as a crucial component of good project selection and formulation. The ODA's flagship was the manual *A Guide to the Economic Appraisal of Projects in Developing Countries* (1975), of which thousands of copies were sold throughout the world. It is interesting to recall (because it is hardly ever mentioned today as an important product of evaluation work) that one of the mainsprings for evaluation work in the ODA was the desire on the part of the economists to get some feedback as to whether their shadow pricing and other social cost-benefit analysis techniques were proving to be satisfactory in the real world. In practice, however, the evaluations seldom addressed themselves specifically to these aspects, so there was not a great deal of feedback of this kind. Apart from this aspect, the only other 'theoretical' aspect of evaluation work that emerged at this time was the growing appreciation of the need to focus on the 'with-and-without' situation rather than on the 'before-and-after' situation (discussed later in Chapter 6), and in due course guidelines on this were included in the ODA's *Guide to the ODA Evaluation System* (ODA, 1994).

Phase Two: Explosion of Interest (1979–84)

I have chosen 1979 as the divide between Phase One and Phase Two because it was in that year that an ill wind blew that did evaluation a lot of good. I am referring to the severe cuts that hit the evaluation programme in the UK, and also elsewhere, at that time. The cut in funds for new aid projects meant that for the first time in years staff were no longer working flat out just disbursing the funds and now the emphasis switched to searching for ways of optimising the benefit of the limited amount of aid money available. Suddenly evaluation became popular. In the ODA, the aid budget was increased by a factor of three and the staff of the evaluation department was doubled. The result was a rapid increase in the number and quality of evaluation reports. One consequence was that it now became possible to carry out syntheses covering several evaluations in the same sector and these were far more valuable for policy purposes than the previous one-off project evaluations had been. Examples of such syntheses were those for rural roads (Hill, 1982), and rural development (ODA, 1985).

The rural roads synthesis was one of the first fruits of a renewed interest in evaluation work on the part of the OECD. The Development Assistance Committee of the OECD called together an informal group of evaluators and this soon evolved into the DAC Expert Group on Aid Evaluation. Chapter 17 describes these events in greater detail. The new group first organised a series of synthesis studies and then they produced a compendium of donor practices in aid evaluation (OECD, 1986). I summarised the Group's activities in a paper to the European Association of Development and Training Institutes (Cracknell, 1986a).

This explosion of interest in aid evaluation led the ODA in 1983 to call a two-day international conference on the subject at the Institute for

Development Studies at the University of Sussex, the proceedings of which I wrote up as a book (Cracknell, 1984b). It is rather unusual for government departments to arrange conferences of this kind, and I am grateful that my senior colleagues at the time accepted the importance of making the subject as transparent as possible and of tapping the ideas and expertise of as many people as we could—especially in academia and in other donor agencies. One outcome of the publicity associated with this conference was a fresh interest in ODA's internal evaluation procedures, and this led in turn to the publication of two articles in *Public Administration and Development*, one of them by the Deputy Secretary who was responsible for evaluation in ODA and the other by myself (Browning, 1984, and Cracknell, 1984a). These three publications were the beginning of a public debate in the UK about the objectives, methods and achievements of aid evaluation.

In parallel with these developments there was also a new surge of interest in the subject from the academics, one of whom was Professor Paul Mosley who profited from a sabbatical period in the ODA to write an influential report on the evaluation of the effectiveness of ODA's poverty-focused aid (Mosley, 1981). He also made effective use of it in his later book on overseas aid in general (Mosley, 1986). Other academics were also finding interesting work as consultants doing evaluation work not only with the ODA (Feachem et al., 1978: Williams, 1985), but also for the European Community (Hewitt, 1986; ODI, 1979).

It was during this period that the fashion for setting up monitoring and evaluation units in the developing countries reached its peak. The arch-exponents of this approach were Casley and Lury (1982) of the World Bank, whose ideas led to the formation of many elaborate and expensive monitoring and evaluation units throughout the Third World. Chapter 8 goes into this in greater detail and describes how Casley later on had a change of heart and wrote another very important report (this time with another colleague, Kumar) in which he declared that this policy had been a bad mistake (Casley and Kumar, 1986).

Another development at this time was the beginning of multi-donor coordination of evaluation activities. An example was the European Community's coordinated evaluation of livestock projects in Africa, to which the UK's contribution was an evaluation of assistance for the prevention of animal diseases (ODA, 1983). It is an indication of the rapidly growing self-confidence of European aid evaluators that they were able to launch a coordinated large-scale evaluation of this kind only a few years after most of them had been established.

The World Bank has already been mentioned several times. From the early stages onwards it was an important leader in the aid evaluation field, devoting far more resources to it than most other donor agencies were able to do. Its internal operating guidelines (IBRD, 1979) were used as a model by many other agencies. It was so well-endowed with funds for evaluation that it was able to mount research-type evaluations that were far beyond the scope of other donors. For example, it was able to mount a major multi-year evaluation of the Muda Irrigation Project in north-west Malaysia to research into the question: 'Who are the beneficiaries, and how far upstream and downstream do the benefits of projects spread?' This very scholarly piece of evaluation research (IBRD, 1982) has had an important impact on evaluation thinking because it demonstrated that the second-round and third-round effects of aid can be very substantial. It was found, in fact, that the landless workers enjoyed at least as much benefit as the farmers themselves because of the latter's high leisure threshold (see Chapter 13 of this book for a more detailed discussion of this issue). The World Bank also took the lead in trying to stimulate the development of evaluation work in the developing countries. The Director of Operations Evaluation Department at the time, Mervyn Weiner, toured the developing world trying to drum up more interest in evaluation work—a far-seeing initiative which gave an important lead to the DAC Expert Group on Aid Evaluation to do likewise.

The development banks (e.g., Asian Development Bank, 1981) and other aid agencies (Food and Agriculture Organisation, 1984; International Fund for Agricultural Development, n.d.) were all developing evaluation systems of their own, and in some cases were pioneering such new fields as project benefit monitoring (Asian Development Bank, 1981). Also important has been the work of the Joint Inspection Unit of the UN (1979) in clarifying the terminology of the subject and in striving for more effective evaluation systems in the UN family.

Phase Three: Coming of Age (1985–88)

The year 1985 marks the coming of age of aid evaluation (so far as Europe is concerned) because it was at that time that two very influential reports appeared which really put the subject on the map and signalled that it had grown to adulthood. It was in 1985 that Professor Robert

Cassen and his team of helpers was commissioned to carry out a major study on the theme 'Does Aid Work?' (Cassen and associates, 1986). The report, a monumental effort involving many researchers, concluded that by and large the objectives of development aid had been achieved, although there were many weaknesses and failures that needed to be tackled. Although Cassen and his team made extensive use of evaluation reports, they reported that these were not altogether satisfactory as evidence of the effectiveness of aid as most of them had been designed with other objectives primarily in mind. It was this finding, together with others like it, that led the DAC Expert Group on Aid Evaluation to set about trying to improve the wider usefulness of evaluation activity. As if to underscore the coming of age of aid evaluation, another major investigation was carried out soon afterwards. This was the study by Roger Riddell of the Overseas Development Institute into the arguments for and against foreign aid which again made extensive and effective use of a large number of evaluation reports (Riddell, 1987). These two reports were significant milestones on the road to maturity for aid evaluation as a subject in its own right.

During this same period, the UK Treasury launched its financial management initiative, with its emphasis on target-setting, and it was this spur that led ODA to introduce the logical framework as a mandatory system of project management. A similar system, known as 'ZOPP', had already been in use for some years in Germany, and had been adopted by a number of other European aid donors. The new approach to project management represented a major advance on the rather disorganised and unsystematic methods that had been used previously. For the first time the objectives had to be clearly stated and criteria for measuring progress towards achieving them had to be identified. For a while the logical framework reigned supreme and its advantages were so great, compared with what had gone on before, that few people were inclined to be critical. However, its weaknesses gradually became more apparent. At the same time important sea changes were taking place in the way aid was being delivered, and even in the whole conception of aid as a donor-dominated relationship. The top–down methods of aid administration that had prevailed up to then began to be questioned, and a process of experimentation with new bottom—up approaches began. At first it was the NGOs and academics like Robert Chambers at the Institute of Development Studies (Chambers, 1988) who led the way, but soon others were recognising the importance of these new ideas and there began a ferment of experimentation and debate that has continued for almost a decade. Phase Four had begun.

Phase Four: Aid Evaluation at the Crossroads (1988 to the Present)

There is no obvious point at which one can say that the (short-lived) sense of maturity, and relative certainty about aid evaluation, that characterised Phase Three came to an end, but 1988, the year in which Robert Chambers' article 'Farmer First: A Practical Paradigm for Third World Agriculture' was published, will serve as well as any (Chambers 1988, see also Chambers et al., 1988). It was at about this time also (September 1989) that the path-breaking conference on the Evaluation of Social Development Projects was held at the University of Swansea (Marsden and Oakley, 1990). This conference, in which the ODA played a major role, signalled the beginning of a significant switch in emphasis of evaluation work from the previous emphasis on project management and the logical framework, towards a new emphasis on stakeholder analysis and a willingness to experiment with participatory approaches. At the same time, the group of social development advisers in the ODA was greatly increased in size (today there are around 70) and the initiative in evaluation work seemed to change from ODA's Evaluation Department more towards the Social Development Advisory Group. These developments are discussed in Chapters 18, 19 and 20 of this book.

The whole aid business is changing in significant ways: there are fewer discrete projects now and more emphasis on sectors and programmes and on types of aid that are intrinsically difficult to evaluate such as good governance, community empowerment, poverty alleviation, human rights, etc. The old donor-dominated aid relationship is rapidly giving way to a new conception of a partnership, with the donor working alongside those developing countries that are committed to pursuing sensible development policies. There is a growing realisation of the need to enhance the evaluation capabilities of the developing country partners, so that they can assume far more direct responsibility for the evaluation process. All these changes make evaluation a far more difficult operation than it once was. The old certainties are fast disappearing, and we are now clearly 'at the crossroads'. There are compelling arguments for moving further and faster down the road of participatory evaluation methods, but there are also important arguments counselling caution, mainly on the grounds of accountability. I discuss these arguments in the final chapter of the book. It seems to me that we have to move cautiously towards a more participatory approach, while at the same time not giving up altogether the ground that has been so hard-won over recent decades (especially the proven advantages of the logical framework approach). If this looks like trying to go down both roads at the same time, so be it. One can only guess at what an appropriate title for Phase Five will be, but it may be something like: 'The Emergence of Methodological Pluralism' and 'Horses for Courses'!

Part 2

Basic Issues:
Purposes, Techniques
and Methods

Mr George Foulkes, Parliamentary Under Secretary of State, Department for International Development, in a speech to the Annual Conference of the UK Evaluation Society, December, 1997:

We need to compress the timescale over which lessons are learned, and diversify the sources from which we learn them. This is already leading us in the direction of more formative evaluation than has been our practice in the past, to an organization where lesson learning is a more general part of the culture. We have always monitored and reported on our projects. What is new is the detailed attention we are now giving to investigating progress against each project's "logical framework" or logframe. The regular use of logframe matrices, with their requirement for specific indicators and means of verification, has not just brought clarity to project design, it has greatly extended our capacity for monitoring and evaluation. We now have to define in advance not just what we are seeking to do, but how we shall know whether, and when, we have achieved our goal.

2

A Basic Issue: Why Evaluate? For Accountability or for Lesson-Learning?

'I'd like to know
What this whole show
Is all about
Before it's out'

(Peter Hein, quoted in USAID Evaluation Handbook, *1976)*

'Vether it's worth goin' through so much, to learn so little, as the charity-boy said ven he got to the end of the alphabet, is a matter o' taste'

(Mr Weller, in Pickwick Papers, *Charles Dickens)*

The Accountability/Lesson-Learning Dichotomy

Ever since the evaluation of development aid first began in the early 1960s in the USA, there has been a tension between the two competing objectives of evaluation, namely, accountability on the one hand,[1] and lesson-learning on the other. According to the former, the main purpose of evaluation is to answer such questions as 'does aid work?', and 'how effective is development aid?' According to the latter, the key objective is to study selected successes and failures with a view to learning why some actions were successful and others not, and to ensure that the relevant lessons are learned and acted upon.

One of the principal stakeholders is the donor agency itself, and it generally prefers to emphasise the lesson-learning objective of development evaluation rather than the accountability objective since it is naturally anxious to improve the efficiency and effectiveness of its own operations. It looks to evaluations to throw up useful lessons for improving future performance. However, the accountability objective obviously predominates in the case of those stakeholders who might be called the 'paymasters', that is, those who represent the taxpayers who provide the funds for official aid. Their main preoccupation is to assess whether aid is successful or not. They are less interested in knowing **why** aid has succeeded or failed than they are in simply knowing **whether** it has succeeded or not. The accountability objective is crucially important for such stakeholders as the national treasuries (who are always comparing the effectiveness of resources directed to one purpose as compared with another); parliaments (representing the tax-payer and voter in general); pressure groups like the Real Aid Group in the UK, and other non-official organisations interested in aid issues, which often have strong views regarding the type and distribution of aid, and which depend on evaluation findings to provide evidence relating to whatever issue they choose to focus on; and the media.

The tension between these two basic objectives always has a major influence on how evaluation is organised in most aid agencies. The underlying difficulty is that it is not really possible to kill the two birds with one stone, and difficult choices have to be made. Figure 2.1 shows that the two objectives are generally incompatible.

The difficulties of trying to satisfy both objectives at the same time were highlighted over a decade ago when the Task Force on Concessional Flows of the Joint World Bank–IMF Development Committee commissioned Robert Cassen and a team of researchers to carry out the study (already referred to in Chapter 1) *Does Aid Work?* (Cassen et al., 1985). They studied a large number of evaluation reports produced by the main donors, but eventually had to conclude that this substantial volume of evaluation activity in fact contributed only rather little towards answering the question. This was because nearly all these evaluations had been geared primarily towards lesson-learning rather than accountability. Many of them concentrated on aid delivery aspects rather than on the impact of the aid on the intended beneficiaries. It soon became clear

Figure 2.1 Characteristics of Accountability and Lesson-Learning as
Objectives of Evaluation Activity

	Accountability as the Objective	*Lesson-Learning as the Objective*
Basic aim is:	Finding out about the past	Improving future performance
Emphasis is on:	Degree of success or failure	Reasons for success or failure
Favoured by:	Parliament, Treasury, media, pressure groups.	Aid agencies, research institutions, consultants, developing countries
Selection of topics:	Based on random samples	Projects selected for their potential lessons
Status of evaluation:	Evaluation is an end product	Evaluation is a part of the project cycle
Status of evaluators:	Should be impartial, and independent	Usually include members of the aid agency staff
Importance of data from evaluations:	Data itself relatively unimportant	Data valued for the planning and appraising of new projects
Importance of feedback:	Relatively unimportant	Vitally important

to Cassen and his team that these evaluations in no way comprised a representative sample. In the end they came to the conclusion, so far as the evaluation reports themselves were concerned, that evaluations aimed at lesson-learning could not safely be used as evidence for accountability purposes, although they certainly yielded useful lessons about many other aspects of development aid. A similar conclusion was reached by Roger Riddell in another major study of the effectiveness of aid (Riddell, 1987), and also by the DAC Expert Group on Aid Evaluation (OECD, 1986). The latter proposed greater coordination between the evaluation units of different aid agencies, and harmonisation of terms of reference for evaluations, in an effort to ensure greater comparability of the results. During my time as Chairman of the Group our main efforts were directed towards this objective.

This issue, of the relative weight to be attached to accountability versus lesson-learning, is vitally important because it determines the way evaluation work will develop in an agency. To a great extent the relative weight will be influenced by the degree to which the donor agency is dependent for its funding on other bodies. Thus for example, the World Bank attempted for many years to evaluate all its projects at the project completion stage not because it found the results of particular significance in improving its own internal performance, but because it felt it had a duty to the member states to demonstrate that all the Bank's expenditure was being systematically evaluated, that is, the evaluation programme was accountability-driven. By contrast, the bilateral aid donors generally have not felt themselves to be under the same degree of pressure from their national treasuries and parliaments, or from the media, and their evaluation programmes are geared more towards lesson-learning. In this connection it is significant that Professor Mosley (a member of the Real Aid Group in the UK), in his comparison between the evaluation systems of ODA and the World Bank (Mosley, 1983), criticised the former on the grounds that only a small proportion of projects were being evaluated and this made it difficult to draw conclusions regarding the effectiveness of British aid. Concerning the European Commission one might expect that accountability would take precedence because of the need to satisfy the member states, but when I was invited (with a Belgian colleague) to review the evaluation practices in the various Directorates General in 1991, I found that in fact the staff regarded lesson-learning as the main objective. Most staff said that the primary objective was to improve their performance. In other words, 'internal utility' is considered to be more important than 'external utility' (Sensi and Cracknell, 1991).

Non-governmental Organisations, now increasingly important as aid donors, too are torn between accountability and lesson-learning. But, in their case, the deciding factor is usually the small scale and large number of projects they handle, which means that they really have little option but to settle for some form of self-evaluation, like field staff evaluating their own activities, according to some agreed procedure. This certainly does not meet the impartiality criterion so important for accountability, but hitherto the NGOs seem to have escaped public criticism on this score. This is probably because they are considered to be far more successful in reaching the poorest people than government-to-government aid is, and therefore the people who make their contributions have hitherto not laid much stress on accountability. This issue is discussed at greater depth in Chapter 16.

Evaluation as it Affects Stakeholders on the Donor Side

The recent emphasis on the role of the stakeholders is not, or should not be, merely a matter of words. It represents an important change in perceptions about the aid process. Formerly stakeholders other than the donor agency had a very peripheral role. They stood on the outside looking in, being fed tidbits of information, such as evaluation reports, from time to time, but having no direct role (other than as suppliers of information) in what was going on, nor even (in many cases) any formal opportunity to comment. But with the stakeholder approach that is changing. Now these other organisations are seen as partners in the aid evaluation process, and more and more attempts are being made to integrate them more fully. There was a good example of how this works some years ago when the ODA decided that henceforth all project appraisals would have to include a logical framework matrix. ODA realised that consultant firms might not know how to prepare such a matrix, so they arranged for a series of training courses to be held so that consultants could be trained in these techniques. About 70 representatives of consultant firms, and research institutes engaged in consultancy, attended these courses. ODA is also working closely with NGOs engaged in aid activities, especially in ensuring that they understand ODA's aid objectives, and are aware of the methodologies that are available. What was once a distant relationship is fast becoming a real partnership.

In other countries, this process of involving other stakeholders on the donor side has gone even further than in the UK. For instance, in Italy there were until quite recently two formal committees, the Comitato Direzionale, and the Comitato Consultativo, which enabled a close relationship to be maintained between the Ministry of Foreign Affairs and other interested parties such as the Treasury, Department of Foreign Trade, trade unions, universities, industry and the NGOs. The Comitato Consultativo in particular, acted as a valuable forum for exchange of information and ideas on development. It had 34 members and met about four times a year. For some strange reason this system, which seemed to have so much to commend it, was abandoned in 1993. In Denmark, there is both a Development Board, which has been chaired by a leading Parliamentarian of many years standing, and a Development Council, which together act as a bridge between the aid agency and the other Danish stakeholders. Nothing like these exists in the UK and it is a decided weakness. Instead there are informal arrangements, as described next.

Parliament

Parliament in the UK is a stakeholder that has had a significant influence on the development of evaluation. The most important of the parliamentary bodies in this context is the House of Commons Committee of Public Accounts. It was this Committee which, back in 1981, recommended that

> First, ODA should examine the scope and balance of their evaluation programme in order to ensure that it covers a sufficiently comprehensive sample of bilateral aid projects and methods to provide all the assurance of effectiveness which is necessary, and second they should review their priorities for drawing both broad and detailed conclusions from evaluation results and initiating appropriate action (House of Commons, 1981).

The reference to the need for a 'comprehensive sample' indicates their concern with accountability. However, the Committee's report on the whole shows a fine balancing of the accountability objective with the lesson-learning one. It was as a direct result of the pressure exerted by Parliament at this time that the personnel in the ODA's Evaluation Department were almost doubled in numbers (at a time when staff numbers elsewhere in ODA were being cut) and the annual budget significantly increased. One cannot say to what extent Parliament would have favoured the accountability objective above the lesson-learning one, but in fact the ODA's overriding interest in lesson-learning has meant that the Department's evaluation work has developed more along that path than along the accountability one. Other arms of Parliament that have been influential are the Select Committee on Aid and the House of Commons Foreign Affairs Committee. These have pressed for certain aid policies, such as more help for the poorest, and they have made effective use of evaluation reports in the process. They have on occasion urged that more resources should be devoted to the evaluation of specific topics (House of Commons, 1987).

In other countries too, parliaments have had a major influence on the scale and direction of aid evaluation activity. In the Netherlands, the unit for 'external' evaluation (called rather unfortunately an 'Inspection Unit') was actually established by the then Minister of Development Cooperation (Mr Jan Pronk) who felt the need for his own personal investigative arm to check that aid policies were effective. The Minister reports directly to Parliament on the evaluation studies carried out by this unit. In Denmark too Parliament takes a keen interest, so much so that it actually carries out some evaluations with its own resources, as an independent check. The importance of parliament as a stakeholder in evaluation should certainly not be underestimated.

Treasuries

National treasuries are also important stakeholders. In the UK, the Treasury has been a leader in the development of evaluation activities in the Civil Service for many years. It took a leading part in the introduction of many new management techniques, such as management by objectives, network analysis, systems analysis, critical path analysis, decision trees, and programme analysis and review (PAR). Thousands of civil servants were trained in these methods at the Civil Service College, where for a number of years the 'Coverdale' system of project management was taught. I remember attending a senior management course at the College in the mid-1970s. The whole of the first week was devoted to the Coverdale system which involved working in small groups and undertaking simple tasks like building a column of child's bricks as high as we could. We had first to decide what our objectives were, what the risks were, and how we would measure success. At the time it all seemed rather puerile, but later on I came to realise that all this was in fact exactly what we are now doing with the logical framework system of project planning (discussed in Chapter 5) which is now in almost universal use in aid agencies.

In the early 1980s, the Treasury took a very important step when it introduced the financial management initiative (FMI), with all the authority of the then Prime Minister, Mrs Thatcher, behind it. This again focused on the same two criteria: clear objectives and indicators of success. In 1985, the Government established a Joint Management Unit (JMU) to 'familiarise project managers with the principles of evaluation, develop good methods, and ensure that evaluation was "built in" as an integral component of policy work' (Treasury, 1985). However, an FMI report to the Treasury in that year noted that 'the pressures of day to day business are not conducive to adopting a systematic approach to performance measurement', and it went on to stress that if they were serious about performance measurement, top management would have to make it clear that they accorded such an approach high priority (Treasury, 1985). This was followed in 1988 by the publication of the Treasury's *Policy Evaluation: A Guide for Managers* (Treasury, 1988). Since then evaluation has become firmly established in all the departments of the Civil Service, as was amply demonstrated when the Treasury organised a service-wide conference on evaluation in 1994. A decade previously, ODA had been one of only two or three Civil Service departments that had an evaluation unit, but by 1994 most ministries had one. As part of their watchdog role, the UK Treasury has continued to take a keen interest in the development of DFID's evaluation activities, and has strongly supported the introduction of the logical framework system of project management, which, in fact, it has recommended for use in all government departments.

Auditors

Another group of stakeholders who have a role to play in evaluation are the auditors, both internal, and external. However, it is only fairly recently that they have come to be regarded as stakeholders in the development process. Auditors have traditionally been mainly concerned with matters of financial probity and checking that proper procedures have been adhered to, but gradually they have been widening their scope to cover what they term 'value for money' audit (or sometimes 'performance audit', or 'comprehensive audit'). They now tend to place even more emphasis on the latter than on the former. On the face of it this brings the audit department (whether internal audit—located within the aid agency—or external audit—located outside it) on a collision course with the evaluation department. Undoubtedly the two need to work in close harmony, and it is even sometimes appropriate for evaluations to be conducted on a joint basis. It is indicative of this close link that the recently appointed head of the evaluation unit in Sida was previously head of the audit unit, whilst in the Finnish aid agency FINNIDA, for example, the evaluation unit has been formally combined with the internal audit in the same department. However, most evaluators would consider that it is preferable to keep the two functions administratively separate, because they serve different purposes, and because in the developing countries there has been an unfortunate tendency to regard the two functions as being identical and this has seriously impeded the development of an evaluation capability in those countries (see Chapter 18).

Despite this drawing together, the significant differences that still remain between the two will probably ensure that they will continue to pursue mainly independent, if often parallel, paths. Auditing generally takes the objectives of a project or programme as given, and concentrates on how the project/programme was implemented, whereas evaluation looks at the objectives and also considers alternative ways of achieving them. A practical difference is that the audit department uses only its own staff who have been trained in audit work (which still has a strong emphasis on financial probity and adherence to established administrative and financial procedures), and sometimes carry out their audits without the help of outside experts. This means that their grasp of the more technical details of whatever activity it is that they are investigating is generally limited, whereas evaluators are often selected from outside the agency precisely because of their particular knowledge of the kind of project being evaluated. Furthermore in the case of the external auditors, like the UK's National Audit Office, they are completely independent of the aid agency itself and therefore are not so well placed as are the staff of the evaluation unit to make specific recommendations of an operational nature. This is not to rule out their doing this if they feel they have a good case, and I recall that the National Audit Office's audit of ODA aid to India (which took a full year to carry out) led to some important recommendations of an operational nature which ODA subsequently implemented. But it remains true that external auditors are generally less well placed than an agency's own evaluators to translate broad evaluation findings into specific action-oriented recommendations. It is also still the case that auditors have to focus on financial and procedural matters, and they cannot therefore apply themselves in the same way as evaluators to the question of the ultimate impact of projects on the target population or to issues of sustainability.

Auditors themselves recognise these differences and are not claiming too much for their role as stakeholders. It is significant that no less an authority than Eleanor Chelimsky, one-time Assistant Comptroller General of the US General Accounting Office, has commented that 'Auditors are coming to recognise more and more that an evaluation is not at all the same thing as an audit' (Chelimsky, 1994). Nevertheless, evaluators and auditors need to work in close liaison and to share both their methodological experiences in the carrying out of evaluations/audits as well as the actual findings themselves. When I was Head of the Evaluation Department in the ODA, I instigated regular meetings with Internal Audit to discuss respective activities, and even to plan a few joint evaluations where appropriate, and this close liaison still continues.

One important aspect of audit work is that the audit reports are always published, and because they are frequently rather critical and hit the media headlines, and because senior aid officials generally are obliged to make a formal public response to the audit reports, they tend to have a relatively greater public impact than do the agency's own evaluation reports. When I was conducting a review of evaluation procedures in the Danish aid agency (DANIDA) I found that the evaluators were some-what mortified by the fact that the senior staff took far more notice of the auditors' reports than of the evaluation reports produced by their own evaluation unit. This is equally true of the reports of the European Commission's Court of Auditors in Luxembourg. Their reports always cause a stir in the press and seem to be taken even more seriously (if generally rather negatively) by senior staff than their own evaluation reports.

Pressure Groups and other Unofficial Bodies

In most donor countries there are also various privately organised pressure groups, representing the churches or charities, or special interests (e.g., the environment), and these are also important stakeholders because of the influence they can bring to bear on public opinion. In the UK, the Independent Group on British Aid (IGBA), sometimes called the Real Aid Group, has produced a succession of reports on various aspects of British aid, and these have had a considerable impact on aid policy. Ministers and Members of Parliament take them seriously, and in turn bring pressure to bear on the aid ministry officials. For the writing of these reports, the Group has depended quite heavily in the past on the evaluations produced by the ODA. To quote just one example of how the Group has used ODA evaluation reports to criticise an aspect of Britain's aid policy, Professor Paul Mosley (who has already been quoted earlier) in his evidence to the House of Commons Foreign Affairs Committee in 1986, said, 'The main failing in ODA's evaluation procedures is that out of three hundred reports or so, which is what the Evaluation Unit has produced, there is not a single one which attempts to assess the impact of British aid projects on low income groups. We find this scandalous and really surprising' (House of Commons, 1987). The ODA decided to evaluate the poverty impact of projects more rigorously as a result of this kind of criticism. Another group in the UK that both uses evaluation reports, and exercises considerable influence on the scope and nature of the ODA's evaluation programme, is the Overseas Development Institute. It was a staff member of this Institute who produced in 1987 the monumental review of foreign aid and its effectiveness referred to earlier (Riddell, 1987), which made extensive use of ODA evaluation reports, as indeed did Professor Cassen when he and his team were writing the report mentioned earlier. These bodies, and others like them, are significant stakeholders in the evaluation process.

Non-Government Organisations

There are a number of non-government organisations that have a special interest in aid issues, and which often work on a collaborative basis with DFID. Most of them see their role as including advocacy for aid issues in general, and for the poor people in the developing countries in particular. For example, Action Aid has organised a number of important seminars, where such issues as poverty-focused aid (Action Aid, 1987), and evaluation of aid for training (Action Aid, 1990) have been discussed, and where considerable use has been made of the evaluation reports. These agencies have a strong rapport with the public at large, and so it is important that they get good feedback from evaluation activities about the effectiveness of British aid. They are increasingly seen as important stakeholders, especially as they are often regarded as being better equipped to ensure that aid gets to the poorest people than are government agencies.

Universities, other Teaching or Training Institutions, and Consultants

These combine the two roles of users of evaluation reports, and suppliers of evaluators, and so have a double interest as stakeholders. Universities and institutes use the evaluation reports for their own purposes and also help to disseminate them, but that is not the case with commercial consultants who, once they have delivered their reports, tend to keep what they have learned to themselves—they regard this information as part of their stock in trade. Evaluation researchers have an important role to play in helping methodologies evolve (see the examples in Chapter 19 of how university staff have researched into the application of the latest ideas on stakeholder analysis), and also in teaching those methodologies to others, especially those from developing countries.

The Media

Finally there is the media, and they are also stakeholders because they have a role in representing the general taxpayer and voter. They seldom use the full evaluation reports, which are often too detailed for their needs, but they can use short summaries, and these are now an important form of feedback to the media.

It was in recognition of the responsibility that the donor agency has towards the needs of all the stakeholders mentioned earlier that the ODA organised a two-day seminar on evaluation at the Institute of Development Studies, University of Brighton, in 1983 (Cracknell, 1984b). Other donors now increasingly recognise the need to involve all the stakeholders in the evaluation process, but above all, of course, the beneficiaries themselves.

Evaluation as it Affects Stakeholders on the Beneficiary Side: Implications of the Participatory Approach

It is a curious irony that until recently, the most important stakeholders of all, the beneficiaries themselves, had very little role either in the design and implementation of projects or in their monitoring and evaluation. The recipient governments of course were heavily involved in project implementation, but even so the major decisions were often taken by the donors. Other local stakeholders (e.g., NGOs, consultant firms, academics, and researchers) were given only a very small part to play. This obviously could not go on indefinitely, and over the last few years energetic steps have been taken to involve the local stakeholders, and especially the direct beneficiaries, more closely in the development process and in monitoring and evaluation. This topic will be discussed more fully in Chapters 18, 19 and 20, but from the point of view of the present issue of accountability versus lesson-learning it is worth pointing out that the switch in emphasis from donor-oriented evaluation to an increasing use of participatory methods means that the dilemma between these two objectives is heightened. This is because with the participatory approach the evaluator no longer retains full control of the evaluation: he/she is merely part of the team that is participating in an on-going manner in the process of monitoring and evaluation. The donor commissioning the evaluation cannot decide in isolation what is to be evaluated, or the methods to be used, so the problem of accountability becomes even more acute than it has been up to now. All one need say at this point is that the participatory process is more likely to lead to successful projects, and meaningful evaluations, and that this is ultimately as much in the interests of the stakeholders on the donor side as it is of the stakeholders on the recipient side. But parliaments and treasuries may need some persuading to accept this! I come back to this crucial issue later on.

Note

1. The use of the term 'accountability' in this context relates to the developmental results and impact of development assistance as distinct from the kind of accountability which is concerned with the use of public funds in an accounting and legal sense (which is the province of audit).

———————————— 3 ————————————

A Taxonomy of Aid Evaluation

'The red plague rid you,
For learning me your language'
(Caliban, The Tempest, Shakespeare)

'Be not the slave of words'
*(*Sartor Resartus, *Thomas Carlyle)*

So much confusion has been caused in the past as a result of misunder-standings over terminology, that it seems important to clarify, at the beginning, the terms and concepts being used in this book. The reader who is already familiar with this subject may wish to go directly to Chapter 4.

What to Evaluate

Evaluation can cover any, and every, activity that an aid agency engages in. It can even cover other evaluations (i.e., 'meta-evaluation'). Although project evaluations are generally the most common, there are other types of evaluation, and the tendency in recent years is for these to become more numerous, especially evaluations of non-project aid such as structural adjustment financing and sector/programme aid (discussed more fully in Chapter 16).

The DAC Expert Group on Aid Evaluation has recommended that the following classification of evaluations, by type, be used:

EV 1: Sectoral evaluations
EV 2: Instrumental and thematic evaluations
EV 3: Global evaluations per country or region
EV 4: 'One-off' evaluations
EV 5: Guides, manuals, and basic principles
EV 6: Mid-term reviews, inter-phase and end-of-project evaluations
EV 7: Others.

When to Evaluate

Evaluation can take place at any stage of a development activity once it has started. During the 1970s, when aid evaluation began to take off in Europe, great confusion was caused by the fact that the word 'evaluation' was widely being used as if it were synonymous with 'appraisal'. Thus one never knew whether a report entitled say 'Evaluation of a Power Project in X' meant an ex ante appraisal, or an evaluation of an on-going or completed project. Because of this, the members of the DAC Expert Group on Aid Evaluation agreed not to use the term 'evaluation' to cover appraisals, and henceforth it would be used only for assessing an activity that had already started or had been completed, not one that was planned for the future. It is therefore rather confusing that some aid agencies, such as the World Bank, the United Nations Industrial Development Organisation (UNIDO), and some of the Directorates General of the European Commission, continue to use the term 'ex ante evaluation' to refer to the process of assessing a situation in depth before a commitment is made to a project.[1] For example, a so-called ex ante evaluation is often carried out of the situation in proposed beneficiary countries before substantial sums are allocated under the European Commission's Structural Funds Programme. This kind of prior investigation is certainly often necessary, and as they take place before specific projects have been identified it is not appropriate to call them 'appraisals'. Nor are they the same as baseline studies, which take place after a project has been approved (although the information will be very useful for evaluation later on). So there is a need for a suitable term, and provided these exercises are always called 'ex ante evaluations', and not just 'evaluations', there should be little risk of confusion. Even so, it seems to me that it would be more desirable to call them something like 'pre-investment reviews' because it is the element of retrospection that chiefly distinguishes evaluations from feasibility studies, appraisals and other 'prospective' studies.

To repeat, an evaluation can take place at any time after an activity has actually commenced, and many different types of evaluation have come into being, representing different stages in a project's life. For the sake of ensuring clear understanding of the terms used, the rest of this chapter comprises a taxonomy covering these various types of evaluations. Baseline studies have been included because, although they are not in themselves evaluations, they provide basic data needed for eventual evaluations, and therefore represent a key preparatory stage.

Baseline Studies

Baseline studies often comprise the first phase of what will eventually become an evaluation. As Box 3.1 shows (Freudenthal and Narrowe, 1992), a baseline study involves carrying out a detailed review of the situation immediately before a development activity starts. It often has to be carried out urgently, that is, before the first of the contractors' machines arrive on site, and it will always involve a field survey of some kind. For instance, I arranged for a major baseline study of the ODA-funded Songea-Makambako Road Project in Tanzania to be carried out, which involved surveys of villages and households along the line of the road to find out what kinds of journeys they had been making in the past; collecting data on the existing traffic flows along the rough track that linked the two towns; and studying other potential sources of traffic generation in the region (ODA, 1980). When the road was built all this information was available for the eventual (interim) evaluation study (ODA, 1989). The baseline study had to be done in a hurry because the contractor was due to start work within a month or two (which is one reason why a commercial consultant had to be used). Without such a baseline study it would have been very difficult, if not almost impossible, to measure the

Box 3.1   Baseline Studies

The Swedish International Development Authority (SIDA) in 1992 produced a baseline study handbook which is a very useful introduction to the subject. The following are some key points:
Baseline studies:

- Provide benchmarks (the situation 'then'), and suggest suitable indicators (the situation 'now').
- Provide valuable information for project planning, and help to specify and concretize objectives, e.g., for logical framework purposes (involving local participation).
- Should take place as close to project start as possible, because high expectations may be aroused, and a long subsequent gap should be avoided.
- Should be carried out as a matter of course, unless there are very cogent reasons why they are not required.

The steps in carrying out a baseline study are:

1. Decide if one is necessary (usual answer will be yes).
2. Draw up terms of reference. These should include:
   - Background information
   - Objectives of the study
   - Scope and focus of the study
   - Who will conduct the study
   - Methodology—generally a combination of methods will be appropriate, including interviews, public meetings workshops, surveys, ranking techniques, and participatory rural appraisal
   - Time plan
   - Reporting procedure
3. Choose the team.
4. Decide when to conduct the study.
5. Review the final report—check it covers terms of reference.
6. Disseminate and utilize the baseline information.

Coming to the core of the task, the information collected will of course depend on the nature of the project, but it will normally include the following:

A. Socio-economic information, i.e., demographic: information about the community, its social and economic organization and infrastructure; and information about households.
B. Sector-specific information, i.e., information related to specific sectors such as natural resources, health, education, environment etc.
C. Issues of local concern, i.e., issues that local people feel strongly about. Such information can only be obtained by participatory research methods, and it should also cover suggested solutions from the 'grass roots'.

Source: SIDA (1992).

full impact of the road on the local economy and on the people living there. Baseline studies are expensive because they involve field work and often have to be carried out with very tight time schedules, but they are increasingly coming to be seen as vitally important for impact evaluation. Of course they are not necessary for every project. Often the data collected in the ordinary course of preparing the project appraisal will be adequate. However, they are crucially important for all people-centred projects where project managers need to be well informed about the base situation and about the aspirations of the people being served by the project, and where on-going monitoring of social impact is a vital source of information for project managers.

Baseline studies, in addition to providing useful benchmarks, also serve to fine-tune the project design and strategy, particularly if there is a good balance between qualitative and quantitative data.

A particular problem associated with baseline studies is whether it is acceptable for whoever carried out the baseline study to also be involved in subsequent monitoring and evaluation. If it were a feasibility study there would be no question of the same consultant being used, because there would be too much of a temptation to present the feasibility study in as positive a light as possible. But in the case of a baseline study this consideration does not seem to apply as the decision to proceed with the project has already been taken. It would therefore seem to make sense for the agency that carried out the baseline study to participate in the subsequent evaluation, as it will be thoroughly familiar with the project, and could profit (in terms of the methodology for future baseline studies) from being able to learn how adequate the baseline information was for the eventual evaluation. However, some agencies take the opposite view and will not allow the same organisation to be used.

On-going Evaluation

Once a project is up and running the issue that arises is how should it be monitored or evaluated. This is such an important topic in its own right that a separate chapter is devoted to it (Chapter 8). Suffice to say at this stage that the idea that evaluation refers only to projects that have been completed (which was at one time quite widely held) cannot be right.[2] Projects may well run into serious problems during implementation, and these require a fresh look to be taken at the original objectives and at the whole problem that the project was intended to address. For this fresh viewpoint it is necessary to call in outsiders, and such an exercise is often called 'mid-term review', 'on-going evaluation', 'interim evaluation', or 'formative evaluation' (as opposed to 'summative evaluation', see p. 74). These mid-term reviews can serve a valuable purpose where there are unavoidable risks attached to the project, in that they provide for a thorough review to take place when the risks can be reassessed. On-going evaluation also serves another important purpose: it is increasingly coming to be recognised that it will only be practical to carry out an impact evaluation in due course if in fact there has been some kind of impact monitoring of the project during implementation—especially of the impact on the beneficiaries as the project unfolds. Thus monitoring and evaluation should not be seen as completely separate operations but as being in many respects complementary to each other (however, see the caveat in Chapter 8).

Inter-phase Evaluation

Some donors, like the Danish aid agency DANIDA, tend to fund programmes that stretch over many years, so that in any one year few of the agency's programmes will have been completed. Such agencies devote nearly all their evaluation resources to on-going evaluation. Other agencies prefer to split programmes, comprising a number of projects which may be spread over many years, into a series of phases. They stipulate that a new phase cannot be financed unless an evaluation has been carried out of the preceding phase and the results were satisfactory. This kind of activity is called 'inter-phase evaluation' and it is typical of such agencies as the World Bank and the European Commission. The main bilateral aid donors, however, tend to commit themselves only to projects lasting say 2 or 3 years, so that their evaluations are usually carried out fairly soon after the project completion stage or some years later.

Built-in Evaluation

Some aid agencies adopt a policy of planning ahead for evaluation as an integral part of project cycle planning. Thus a monitoring and evaluation plan will be prepared at the same time as the appraisal, and this will detail the type of information needed for these purposes during project implementation. This has the advantage that those responsible for implementing the project are forewarned of what is expected of them. It is also far more likely, with such a system, that if there is a need for a baseline study this will become apparent at an early stage (i.e., whilst there is still time to carry it out before the project implementation starts). However, some argue that drawing up an evaluation plan right at the beginning of the project cycle could be a waste of time because no-one can possibly foretell what will happen in the future since development is a dynamic process. Projects of a social nature, may require some kind of regular surveys to be carried out as a form of built-in project monitoring. In general, however, precise and over-specific monitoring and evaluation plans are best avoided, although the broad strategy for future monitoring and evaluation of the project should be established at the beginning. The adoption of the logical framework in recent years (see Chapter 5) has given a further impetus to built-in evaluation.

Self-Evaluation

Another type of evaluation, which is found particularly among the aid NGOs, and also some UN agencies dealing with large numbers of small projects (e.g., United Nations Development Programme—UNDP), is self-evaluation. Basically this implies that the operational staff evaluate their own activities. The risks, in terms of objectivity, of people being judge and jury in their own case are obvious, and this kind of evaluation breaks the general principle that evaluators should not have had any previous involvement in the activities they are evaluating. However, there may be little real alternative where the average size of project is small, because the cost of organising outside evaluations for such projects could well be as much as, or even more than, the projects themselves cost. Some of these agencies also have central evaluation units that help with methodology, and will possibly carry out a few selective evaluations of projects or programmes chosen as representative of the others, but basically the agency has to rely on the staff conscientiously evaluating their own work.

Self-evaluation methods can include the following:

- reflective practice;
- quality assurance, embedded in the organization's internal processes;
- self-evaluation that is undertaken for an NGO's own staff;
- locally determined evaluation undertaken with the help of outside expertise;
- locally delivered evaluation which addresses the agenda of the sponsoring agency (Sommerland, 1995).

Self-evaluation is generally used to cover effectiveness and efficiency aspects, rather than impact, for which outside evaluators are more often used.

Ex Post Evaluation

This term originated from a need to distinguish the process of looking retrospectively at projects from the process of assessing the feasibility of proposed new projects (i.e., appraisal). As indicated earlier, these two processes were often confused with each other, and it was to prevent this happening that the term 'ex post' came into use. Unfortunately this itself became a source of misunderstanding, because evaluation does not have to take place only 'ex post', that is, after the implementation phase has been completed. It can take place at any time once an activity has commenced. In other words, evaluation is not to be distinguished from appraisal because it takes place at a different time (although it generally does), but because it serves a different function. These days the term 'ex post evaluation' is generally taken to refer to evaluations that actually take place after implementation has been completed. Other terms for this are 'in-operation evaluation' or 'maturity evaluation': it is also called summative evaluation.

Impact Evaluation

In the early days of evaluation activity the emphasis was heavily on learning lessons about aid delivery, and the evaluations were usually carried out as soon as the aid had been completed, even though the project itself may hardly have started to operate. However, as monitoring procedures were improved, lessons about aid delivery began to lose ground as an objective of evaluation. At the same time, the donors were becoming uncomfortably aware that a large number of projects that appeared to have been successfully implemented (from the donor's point of view) were running into serious problems once they had been operating for a short time. The importance of this was brought home to the world aid evaluation community in 1985 when the World Bank published a report giving the results of 25 agricultural projects that had been revisited five to 15 years after project completion. All 25 projects had been deemed to be successful on the basis of the project completion reports, but 5 to 15 years later the story was very different. Only 12 could still be called successful: the rest had yielded very disappointing results with an average achieved rate of return of only 2.7 per cent. (World Bank, 1985). As a result of this realisation, the emphasis switched more towards evaluations carried out some years after project implementation, that is, impact evaluation. Impact evaluation is now so important that a separate chapter has been devoted to it (Chapter 13).

Internal and External Evaluation

These terms are sometimes used, but they tend to cause confusion. Internal evaluation is generally taken to mean evaluation by the staff of the aid agency itself, whether it be the same officers who implemented the project or those who planned it but were not directly involved in its implementation; or it can sometimes be taken to include members of the evaluation unit who are staff of the agency, but have had no previous connection with the project. Internal evaluation (in its more restrictive sense as given here) and built-in evaluation, are closely related. External evaluation, on the other hand, usually implies someone coming in from outside the agency, although the situation can become very confusing when some donors, like The Netherlands, use the term to refer to the activities of the Evaluation Unit as distinct from the 'internal' evaluations that are carried out at the operational level. Because of the potentiality for misunderstanding, and because of the general tendency for evaluations to be carried out by mixed teams (i.e., people from inside the agency and also people from outside it), it is preferable not to use these terms at all.

Other Types of Evaluation

Although project evaluations are generally the most common, there are other types of evaluation, and the tendency in recent years is for these to increase in importance, especially evaluations of non-project aid such as structural adjustment financing and sector/programme aid (discussed more fully in Chapter 16). Among the other types of evaluation are the following: thematic evaluations, which is related to selected themes such as the role of women, environment, etc; procedural evaluations, such as the selection of candidates for training programmes, or the appointment of experts to serve overseas; and country evaluations, that is, evaluating the totality of an aid agency's operations in a specific country. The last named are now rather rare because there are few developing countries where one donor is so dominant that there is a reasonable chance of attributing macro-economic changes to that donor's involvement.

Relationship between Evaluation and Monitoring

This topic is discussed more fully later (Chapter 8), but the discussion here has amply demonstrated that certain types of evaluation, particularly on-going evaluation, built-in evaluation, self-evaluation, mid-term reviews, and inter-phase evaluation, are all very similar to monitoring, whilst it is increasingly coming to be recognised that for certain types of people-centred projects ex post evaluation and impact evaluation are likely to be difficult to carry out unless monitoring has already collected the basic data required. Thus there is a close connection between the two, and when designing an evaluation programme this has to be recognised.

The decision regarding the relative allocation of resources to evaluation compared with monitoring is not likely to be a once-for-all one. It will be affected by changes in emphasis taking place from year to year within the agency, and also its response to outside pressures. Thus, as stated earlier, it was mainly due to pressure from the Committee of Public Accounts of the House of Commons in 1980/1 that the ODA decided to increase the resources allocated to evaluation (Cracknell, 1991). Later on, there was a period when aid funds were severely curtailed and few new projects were being started, and it was then that fresh efforts were made to step up the monitoring procedures, to utilise staff resources that had become available. The decision to increase the evaluation budget of Directorates General VIII of the European Commission, mentioned in the Introduction, was the result of sustained pressure from the British and Dutch governments, who were mainly concerned with accountability. The pressure in recent years to switch from aid-delivery aspects of evaluation (on-going and ex post) towards impact evaluation (with a special orientation towards environmental, gender and poverty issues) has come largely from outside pressure groups that have criticised the fact that aid projects and programmes have often failed to meet their ultimate objectives. All these factors have had an impact on how evaluation and monitoring activities are planned and implemented.

Although in the past there was little interlinkage between the resources allocated to evaluation and those to monitoring, in recent years this situation has changed, and now it is increasingly acknowledged that there is a close linkage. The more resources are allocated to monitoring, the less resources are needed to do the old type of aid-delivery evaluation, and the more emphasis can be placed on impact studies. Similarly, as improvements are made in project cycle management methods, including of course monitoring, the task of the evaluator is eased, as vital information about progress towards achievement of objectives, and the data required for indicators of success, will be routinely collected. The relationship is also a two-way one. Evaluation can feed into monitoring in the sense that baseline studies provide invaluable foundation information for monitoring and project management, as well as for eventual evaluation. Finally, the emphasis given to self-evaluation in some agencies is itself a reflection of the resource allocation problem, since, as stated earlier, it would be difficult to use evaluation methods involving outside consultants when each project costs only a few thousand pounds.

Considering the close inter-relationship between the two functions it is fortunate that evaluators are now generally closely involved in the design of monitoring systems, and in some agencies, such as the European Commission DG VIII, they have actually taken the lead in that direction, and there is now a fruitful two-way exchange of information and methodology.

Notes

1. Some agencies, such as the US General Accounting Office, carry out an extensive review of published research findings relevant to a proposed new

project before a decision is taken to proceed, and they call this activity 'ex ante evaluation' or sometimes 'prospective evaluation'.

2. ODA used to view evaluation as being only ex post, but was strongly criticised for this at the Conference organised in 1983 (Cracknell, 1984b). DFID no longer holds that view.

4

Organisation of Evaluation Activity

'Men are generally incredulous, never really trusting new things unless they have tested them by experience'

(The Prince, *Machiavelli*)

'Find out the cause of this effect, or rather say, the cause of this defect, for this effect defective comes by cause'

(Hamlet, *Shakespeare*)

'The knowledge of the world is only to be acquired in the world and not in a closet'

(Lord Chesterfield)

Chapter 2 was mainly concerned with some of the basic problems that have to be resolved in the carrying out of evaluations. But before an evaluation programme can even be set in motion there are some practical issues that have to be addressed. These include such topics as: where the evaluation unit should be located in the organisation; what resources can be reasonably devoted to evaluation in the face of many competing demands; who should do the evaluations and how such people should be selected; how one decides what is to be evaluated; and who should be responsible for ensuring that action is eventually taken on the findings.

These are all very down-to-earth practical issues, but the role and impact of evaluation in the organisation will largely be determined by how such issues are decided, so they are very important.

Location of an Evaluation Unit

Where in an organisation, whether it be development oriented or not, should an evaluation unit be located? Different organisations have adopted different solutions. Some have placed the evaluation unit as close as possible to the minister, board of directors or top-level management, so that it is removed from line management, and can have an influence on major decisions at the policy level (e.g., the World Bank), whilst others have located it (as an independent unit) nearer to the operational level (e.g., NORAD), whilst still reporting at a senior level. Others have opted for two evaluation units, one at the senior management (i.e., policy) level, and the other at the operational (i.e., project) level (e.g., CIDA). Some, like SIDA (before it was reorganised in 1997), have both an internal evaluation unit within the agency and also utilise an outside evaluation agency to ensure greater impartiality (Samset et al., 1994). In Norway (and this applies also in Denmark) the evaluation unit is combined with research 'in order to facilitate the use of commissioned research as a supplement to evaluation' (Stokke, 1991a). Other donor agencies, too, are finding that the more is expected of evaluation missions, especially in terms of the impact of aid, the less satisfactory are the short 2 to 3 week missions typically conducted by donor evaluation units. Increasingly research institutions, which have more time and staff resources, are being called in to carry out such in-depth studies.

The decision where to locate the evaluation function is influenced by a number of criteria, some of them mutually incompatible. It is generally accepted that the evaluation unit should be completely independent of the process concerned with policy making or the delivery and management of development assistance: this indeed was one of the 'principles for evaluation of development assistance' issued by the DAC Expert Group on Aid Evaluation in 1991 (OECD, 1991a). Staff should not have any direct involvement in other aspects of the agency's work whilst they are actually engaged on evaluation activity (Stokke, 1991c). A classic case of this is the World Bank where the Director General, Operations Evaluation Division (OED), is told on appointment that he/she will not qualify for further promotion in the Bank.[1] This is to ensure that the OED can be critical of the work of close colleagues without fear of the repercussions in terms of future promotion prospects. The OED reports directly to the Bank's Board of Executive Directors, rather than to the senior management within the Bank. Commenting on the establishment of the OED, Mr Rex Browning, who was the Alternate UK Director on the Board at the time, has written:

> The evaluation system at the World Bank is designed to help the Board, but in the minds of some of the directors when the system was introduced, the intention was that the evaluation system would act very much as a check on senior management, or even more than a check. There was a definite desire to separate the management of the programme from the overseeing of the evaluation process (Browning, 1984).

However, independence is not the only criterion. Another important criterion of a successful evaluation is that it should yield findings of direct relevance for the way the agency operates, both at the lower (project) level, and at the higher (policy) level. If the evaluators are totally divorced from the way the agency operates they are unlikely to be in a position to translate their general findings into practical recommendations for action. To quote a report of a Dutch Workshop held in Pakistan in 1989: 'Monitoring and evaluation studies are often undertaken by academicians without inside knowledge of the project, programme, its environment, or Pakistan. Evidently this cannot but result in incomplete, or sometimes even unreliable, research outcomes, which in turn may lead to wrong decision-making and policy formulation' (Frerks et al., 1989). A solution often found is for evaluations to be carried out by mixed teams of evaluators, consisting of one or two members from the agency's own evaluation unit, together with selected outside evaluators.[2] This ensures that the reports are geared closely to the agency's operational needs, whilst providing scope for a fresh and impartial approach. As the one-time Chairman of ODA's Projects and Evaluation Committee has commented: 'We need to be told how we as an aid agency can do things better, not how things can be done better in some cosmic sense' (Browning, 1984). One agency (The Netherlands) generally commissions outside evaluators to undertake the field work for its evaluations, and to prepare the first rough drafts of the report, but then a member of the evaluation unit joins the team and plays a key role in the writing of the final report. This ensures operational relevance.

The factors to be taken into account in deciding on the most appropriate mix between in-house evaluators and those appointed from outside the agency are listed in Figure 4.1. In some agencies the staff of the

Figure 4.1 Factors Influencing the Choice between In-house and Outside Evaluators

In-house evaluators	*Evaluators appointed from outside*
• Have a better grasp of the aid/development context and of how the agency works	• As they are less aware of the sensitivities of the aid relationship, or administrative problems, they may come up with fresh ideas and be more ready to employ lateral thinking
• Are well placed to foster instant feedback in an effective way	• Are not likely to be directly concerned with feedback, except in academic circles
• The experience gained remains inside the aid agency	• The experience gained is lost to the aid agency
• May lack specific technical skills or experience	• Are usually selected precisely because they are experts in their field
• Relatively inexpensive	• Tend to be expensive, especially if consultant firms are used

evaluation unit do not themselves participate in any evaluations at all, but are simply responsible for commissioning the studies and receiving the reports (this is largely the case with the evaluation units in the European Commission). If staff resources are limited, such a system may be unavoidable, but the problem is that unless the evaluation unit staff have some first hand involvement in the carrying out of evaluation studies they are not in a good position to advise on the methodology to be used, or to draw up the terms of reference, or to help in other ways. Moreover the learning process involved in the actual carrying out of the evaluations is totally lost to the aid agency itself, and remains with the consultants (who, as suggested earlier, tend, for commercial reasons, not to be very interested in sharing that experience with others). For these reasons, the tendency has been for most members of evaluation units to participate in at least some evaluation studies themselves. They generally find this a very stimulating experience, and enjoy the opportunity of taking time off from their normal, perhaps more routine, duties. Furthermore when they return to other 'mainstream' duties they are more likely to take with them a positive attitude towards evaluation work, and this helps the evaluation function to become firmly established in the agency.

An unfortunate consequence of the donor emphasis on objectivity in evaluation work (some would say 'over emphasis') is that insufficient encouragement is given to the recipient institutions to establish their own in-house evaluation capacities. Such a capacity, within a recipient organisation, can do a lot to enhance the effectiveness of project management. This issue is discussed at greater length in Chapter 18.

In view of the growing convergence between the functions of monitoring and evaluation (discussed in Chapter 8), it may be worth emphasising at this point that there is still general agreement on the principle that (self-evaluation apart) evaluators should be independent of the activities they are evaluating. This was restated in strong terms at the Dutch Workshop mentioned earlier: 'The Workshop fully endorses the well documented requirement that impact evaluation can only be meaningful when it is undertaken in an independent manner. This implies that foreign and Pakistan agencies that implement projects cannot themselves be responsible for evaluating their own performance' (Frerks et al., 1989). By way of illustrating the dangers of disregarding this principle, they quote the case of a chief technical adviser who not only drew up the terms of reference for the evaluation himself but furnished information to his self-appointed evaluation team in such a biased manner that the team later referred to their work as a 'blindfolded evaluation'.

One locational factor that has a significant effect on the efficiency of monitoring and evaluation activity in general is the extent to which the aid agency has field representation. If there are agency staff permanently stationed in the field they are far better equipped to ensure that effective monitoring is taking place, while they can also provide invaluable support to evaluation missions. The European Union is extremely well placed in this regard, with well-staffed offices in every country receiving significant aid. DFID and some other donors occupy an intermediate position, with field representation covering a number of countries, whereas some other agencies have no such field offices and have to rely heavily on their embassies.

Some of the various solutions that have been found to the problem of where to locate the Evaluation Unit are illustrated in Figure 4.2.

Staffing of an Evaluation Unit, and the Skills Required

There is no general consensus as to the extent to which an evaluation unit should be staffed by specialist evaluators who will spend all or most of

Figure 4.2 The Place of the Evaluation Function in Different Aid Organisations

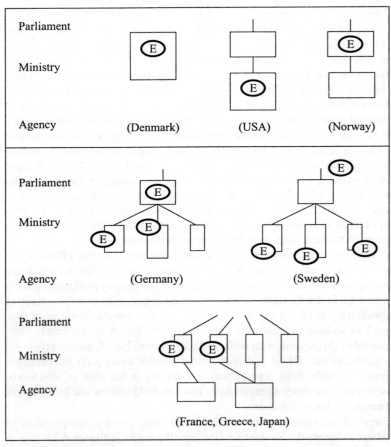

Source: Samset et al. (1994).

their careers doing evaluation work (and if so what kind of basic skills they should have), or whether it should be staffed mainly by members of the aid agency who are posted to it for say two or three years and then return to general duties. Sometimes a compromise solution is adopted, whereby the head of the unit tends to be someone who has specialised in evaluation work for some considerable time, but most of the other members of the unit serve in it for only a limited period. This has the advantage of enabling a degree of specialist expertise to develop, whilst spreading the experience of actually doing evaluations more widely round the organisation. However, as the discipline of evaluation continues to evolve as a professionalism in its own right, this approach is likely to be increasingly questioned, and the tendency in the future may be for rather more members of the evaluation unit to become specialists in evaluation.

This raises the associated issue of what skills are most appropriate for evaluation work. It is generally accepted that economists make good evaluators because their training requires them to have an analytical approach—seeking all the time for optimum solutions and carefully weighing alternatives. But at the same time they are generalists in the sense that economic criteria can be applied to all projects in whatever sector, while the economist's techniques (e.g., calculating realised rates of return or assessing cost-effectiveness) are relevant for nearly all evaluations even if they may not often be the dominant criteria. The experience of the last twenty years has shown that strictly economic factors are seldom the most critical ones influencing the success or failure of projects, and that socio-cultural ones are often at least as important, especially so far as people-centred projects are concerned. This explains why sociologists are now playing an increasingly important role in evaluation activities. Moreover, with the growing emphasis on such aspects as the environment, gender, poverty eradication and good governance, specialist skills in these areas are often essential.

Participatory Rural Appraisal Techniques in Evaluation

New techniques have been devised over the last decade or so to facilitate the more effective gathering of sociological information at the grassroots level—notably rapid rural appraisal (RRA), which later evolved into participatory rural appraisal (PRA) and has finally become participatory reflection and action (Blackburn with Holland, 1998). These new approaches were first developed by Professor Robert Chambers at the Institute of Development Studies, and they are now gradually being adopted not only for appraisal (which was the original context) but also for monitoring and evaluation. They involve working closely with the beneficiaries in the villages, in the fields, at the work bench, and in their homes, finding out from them what their aspirations were, and what their views are on the projects that are being, or have been, implemented. This is a very different kind of evaluation from economic cost-benefit analysis and calls for an altogether different approach and different skills. It requires patience, tact, an interest in people, and a lot of humility. It involves a multiplicity of methods (with most of which most economists are totally unfamiliar), including: time lines and ethno-histories, trend diagnosis, seasonal calendars, institutional diagrams, social and resource maps, flow diagrams, preference ranking, wealth and wellbeing ranking, matrix ranking, and transects. It is unlikely that economists or other professional staff will necessarily be the best people to carry out this kind of evaluation. In my experience some of the best practitioners of the art of PRA have been employees of aid charities like OXFAM or Christian Aid—often locally employed staff (i.e., from within the developing countries) who were trained in these techniques in Britain, and who can use them effectively because they know the local language and the local culture (Neefjes, 1993). One locally-engaged OXFAM project manager in Ethiopia who assisted me in 1993 in the evaluation of a rural development project near Dire Dawa in the eastern part of the country, was not only practising PRA methods very effectively but had integrated these with the logical framework matrix and was using this integrated system for monitoring and evaluation. Fortunately there has been a great increase in the training of people in PRA methods, and this should lead eventually to it being used more often in evaluations.

Some agencies, in particular the World Bank, where it is called 'beneficiary assessment', use some of the techniques of participatory rural appraisal, such as participant observation (this is the term that anthropologists use) and qualitative interviewing, to ensure that the views of the beneficiaries are taken fully into account in evaluations. The characteristics of 'Beneficiary Assessment' are:

- Listening to the local people; talking to them in their own language; living amongst them for a period of from several weeks to several months.
- Working closely with the decision-takers to ensure that the information being collected in the field addresses their concerns.
- Ensuring that the results are credible to development planners, e.g. by using representative sampling, and by quantifying, as much as possible.

- incorporating the values of the beneficiaries, i.e. to maximise sustainability (Salmen, 1995).

Admirable as they are, these beneficiary assessments still fall well short of the full participatory procedures involved in PRA. Beneficiary assessments constitute more a 'snapshot' at one point in time, rather than a continuous process of impact monitoring, whilst they contain little of the element of 'empowerment' which is so characteristic of the PRA approach.

Leaving aside the projects where PRA techniques are most appropriate (usually in the rural development and human resources fields) there will always be the more technically-oriented projects that call for evaluators with specific professional or technical skills. For example, a medical project will require a doctor or some other kind of medical expert on the team; a school project will require an educationist; a bridge an engineer; and so on. Should evaluation units aim to include staff with a full range of such technical skills? In nearly every case the answer has to be No. The number of evaluations in any one sector is very seldom sufficient to justify having such a specialist working full time in the evaluation unit, and in any case he/she might not have the particular kind of technical knowledge or experience required for the evaluation: a doctor for instance might not have the specialised knowledge to be able to evaluate a birth control project. It is usually much more satisfactory to borrow someone from another part of the agency (the Commonwealth Secretariat, for example, has established a panel of potential evaluators comprising a dozen or so members of staff with a range of appropriate skills, and some basic evaluation training), or to hire in from outside the agency the particular skills and experience needed. Whatever particular solution is adopted, the aim should be to achieve what the DAC Expert Group on Aid Evaluation has called 'a critical mass of professional evaluation staff' (OECD, 1991a), to ensure credibility of the process.

Resources to be Allocated to Evaluation Work

Every development organisation has to decide for itself what proportion of its available resources, in staff and finance etc, should be allocated to evaluation work. Practice varies greatly. Rules of thumb are not very helpful because a great deal depends on the nature of the aid programme itself. To evaluate a technical assistance project costing only say £100,000 may require almost the same resources as the evaluation of a £50 million construction project. Thus development organisations, like the British Council, which concentrate on technical assistance projects will usually have to spend a much greater proportion of their available resources on evaluation than agencies concentrating mainly on capital aid. The federal health programmes in the USA for instance have 1 per cent to 3 per cent built into budgets for evaluation (Patton, 1997). After an extensive study of the evaluation literature Rebien concluded that: 'Compared to overall aid budgets, the funds allocated...do not correspond to the importance and emphasis that agencies assign to evaluation at a rhetorical level' (Rebien, 1996). The American aid agency, USAID, reviewed its evaluation work a decade ago and found that it was spending only a very small proportion of its aid expenditure (0.2 per cent) on evaluation, compared with 1 per cent or more allocated to it in several other federal institutions (USAID, 1990). In NORAD the proportion is about the same (0.2 per cent). In DFID the percentage is approximately 0.05 per cent, although it has to be taken into account that a substantial part of the aid budget is passed on to the multilateral and other agencies, and also that if the work of the British Council in evaluating training and some aspects of technical assistance were included the percentage would be quite a lot higher (perhaps nearer 0.075 per cent). In Sida the proportion is about 0.1 per cent (Forss and Carlsson, 1997). In the World Bank the proportion is about the same as that of DFID, namely, 0.05 per cent. In the International Development Research Centre (IDRC), Ottawa, the budget for evaluation work averages around 1.5 per cent (IDRC, 1996). Most evaluation units are given an annual budget to be spent on commissioned studies: in the case of the DFID this is currently (1998) around £1 million. The European Union's budget for commissioned studies is of the order of ECU 5 million, which represents around 0.05 per cent of the total European Union aid budget. Some authorities recommend proportions substantially higher than the figures quoted above. For instance the Islamabad Workshop, already referred to, concluded: 'Although it is difficult to set a standard for appropriate evaluation cost ratios, the cost should bear some proportional relationship (e.g., 5 to 10 per cent) to the overall project budget' (Frerks et al., 1989). Most of the above figures are rather rough estimates, but they give some idea of the proportions in the various agencies.

In addition to the budget for commissioned studies, one has to take into account the internal resources of the Evaluation Unit itself, for example, staff costs, travel and subsistence etc. In the case of the DFID these would add approximately another £300,000 per annum. It is important to take into account both kinds of resource use when considering the effort allocated to evaluation work. Quite a number of aid agencies allocate a small proportion of the original project funding to be reserved for the eventual evaluation, in which case this is an additional cash resource as the funding comes from another budget. Where inter-phase evaluation is common, the resources required will often be incorporated into the original project funding.

Factors Influencing the Shape that the Evaluation Programme Should Take

Another crucially important decision that has to be taken relates to how the organisation decides which projects or programmes should be evaluated. This issue is of course closely linked to the accountability *vs* lesson-learning dichotomy discussed earlier. If accountability is the main objective, the need for selection criteria is less because the aim will be to evaluate all projects, if resources are available, or to select a representative sample if they are not. But if lesson-learning is the main objective, the organisation will have to decide what its selection criteria should be as the aim is to evaluate those projects that seem most likely to yield useful results. DFID is probably fairly typical in this regard, and it uses the following criteria (not listed in any special order of importance):

- Projects which are typical of others already in the aid pipeline or likely to enter it soon, that is, they are likely to be replicated.
- Projects which contain some innovative or unusual features on which feedback is sought as soon as possible.
- Projects which may be running into severe problems, and a decision may need to be taken whether to terminate or not; or if already completed, it is important to learn what went wrong and to avoid such mistakes in the future.
- Projects which seem likely to yield particularly useful impact information.

- Projects which may throw light on new or up-coming policy initiatives.

The World Bank uses similar criteria. Thus in selecting projects for performance audits, OED gives preference to those that are innovative, large or complex, those for which executive directors have requested audits, and those that, individually or as part of a cluster, are likely to generate important lessons (World Bank, 1994).

In addition to using selection criteria of this kind, most evaluation units take the view that some consideration also needs to be given to the accountability factor, when drawing up the evaluation programme. So they will try to ensure that the selection of projects is broadly representative of the organisation's total field of activity, that is, at least to make sure that whole sectors are not omitted, and that there is a broadly representative geographical coverage. In recent years there has been a further important selection criterion, namely the need to choose projects that fit into priority sectors for eventual synthesis analysis. The overall aim is to design an evaluation programme that will provide optimum feedback of useful lessons whilst at the same time being not too unrepresentative of the organisation's overall activities.

However, the question that still remains is how does an evaluation unit know what the most pressing evaluation feedback needs of the organisation are? In other words, what are the key issues that colleagues hope that evaluation will throw light on? It should be a cardinal principle of evaluation work (at least from the lesson-learning point of view) that it should be 'client-oriented', otherwise the results are unlikely to have much impact on how people in the organisation are behaving. This is discussed in more detail later (Chapter 10), but one obvious way of achieving client orientation is to ask key members of staff representing all the main activities what they think should be evaluated. DFID, for example, regularly circularises all departments inviting them to nominate projects or programmes (or indeed any topic) for evaluation, indicating the reasons for their choice, and showing how they relate to the agency's own selection criteria.

Concurrently, the evaluation unit will be holding meetings with specialist advisers and geographical desk officers, trying to establish some priorities for evaluation. However, there are dangers in relying too heavily on colleagues nominating projects for evaluation. They may choose projects that they know have been successful for fear that if they were to nominate unsuccessful ones their own careers might be adversely affected.[3] Therefore, the evaluation unit itself should retain the right, and indeed have a formal responsibility, to nominate projects for evaluation as it deems fit, and it will be influenced in its choice, to some extent at least, by the accountability considerations referred to earlier. In addition, there is a further source of suggestions for projects to evaluate. Ideally, as will be discussed later, there should always be a top-level policy committee in the organisation that not only receives the evaluation reports when they are ready but also feeds back to the evaluation unit its own thoughts on what should be evaluated—often geared to policy issues.

Considering that the typical annual evaluation budget will usually only be sufficient for say 15 to 20 projects to be evaluated, it will clearly be difficult to ensure that all the selection criteria listed above will be adequately represented. On the other hand, this reinforces the importance, bearing in mind how limited the resources are, of making the selection in the most effective way. The selection criteria are all designed to ensure that the organisation's annual evaluation programme is client-oriented, and that the eventual evaluation reports will be read because the recipients are really interested in what is contained in them.

Deciding Who Should be Responsible for Seeing that Action is Taken on Evaluation Reports

The whole topic of feedback is so important that three chapters are devoted to it later on. Sufficient to say, at this stage, that if the organisational structure for evaluation activity within the organisation does not include specific provision for ensuring that feedback takes place, then it is unlikely to take place effectively of its own accord. The same committee of senior staff referred to earlier, which approves the annual evaluation programme, should also receive the evaluation reports as they become ready and should decide what appropriate action should be taken. In many respects this is the most crucial decision that has to be taken if evaluation is to actually bring about improvements in agency performance, yet it is still the least satisfactory aspect of the way evaluation is organised in most agencies.

Notes

1. The World Bank's 1979 evaluation manual *Operations Evaluation: World Bank Standards and Procedures*, describes the procedure thus: 'Appointees to this post would hold rank equivalent to that of a vice-president, hold office for renewable terms of 5 years, be removable by the executive directors, and be ineligible for subsequent appointment or re-appointment to the staff of the World Bank, except in unusual circumstances' (World Bank, 1979).
2. The belief that outside evaluators are likely to take an independent and impartial viewpoint, is often questioned on the grounds that outside evaluators also have their own biases, and in particular they usually have a vested interest in getting further consultancy work and this may well influence the way they report their findings. Experience has shown that outside evaluators are often less willing to be critical than are in-house evaluators who have had no previous involvement in the project.
3. It can be argued, however, that this bias in favour of successful projects is counterbalanced by the opposite tendency, that is, for projects to be selected because they are running into difficulties.

---------------------- **5** ----------------------

Project Cycle Management: A Basis for Effective Monitoring and Evaluation

'If you don't know where you are going, any road will get you there'
(Old saying)

'Happy is he who has been able to learn the courses of things'
(Georgies, Virgil)

'Man is a tool-using animal.... Without tools he is nothing, with tools he is all'
(Sartor Resartus, *Thomas Carlyle*)

'Thomas said to Jesus, "Lord, we don't know where you are going, so how can we know the way?"'
(St John's Gospel, *The Bible*)

Why this Emphasis on Project Cycle Management?

The reader may be wondering why I have chosen to introduce a chapter on project cycle management even before the subject of monitoring and evaluation has been fully addressed. The reason is simple. Evaluation experience has shown, time and again, that unless a project has been well conceived in the first place, with clear objectives and criteria of success and some assessment of the likely risks involved, it is likely to run into problems during implementation, and will certainly be difficult to evaluate. When aid evaluation started, some 35 years ago, the project objectives were seldom clearly specified and it was never clear what they were intended to achieve in the first place except in very general terms. Trying to evaluate in these circumstances was like trying to ride a bicycle with loose handlebars! As the old adage says, 'if you don't know where you're going any road will get you there'. Maybe Figure 5.1 exaggerates a little, but really there can be no doubt that good project cycle management, with objectives clearly specified, is a vital ingredient for project success and for effective monitoring and evaluation.

Figure 5.1   It Helps If You Know Where You Are Going

Source: Development Forum (July–August 1991).

It is no accident that it has been the evaluators in most aid agencies who have been the most enthusiastic exponents of improved project cycle management techniques, and they continue to take a keen interest in the subject. It was the evaluators who first promoted the logical framework technique of project management in the 1960s, and I myself spent a week in Washington learning these techniques in 1974. However, it was not until a decade later (when the then Prime Minister, Mrs Thatcher, insisted that the Civil Service should adopt objectives-oriented systems of management) that the time was right for myself and a colleague to have the opportunity of promoting them in the ODA (Cracknell and Rednall, 1986). In the European Commission, the Head of the Evaluation Unit in DG VIII vigorously promoted the idea of the integrated approach to project cycle management and has had the gratification of seeing it incorporated into all on-going activities. In the World Bank, where the logical framework technique is currently being introduced, it is the evaluators who are taking an important role in this, and in trying to adapt and improve the system to meet the Bank's needs. In the light of past experience I would go so far as to say that one cannot be a good aid evaluator without having a thorough grasp of project cycle management techniques.

The Project Cycle

The concept of the project cycle was first developed by Baum, an economist in the World Bank (Baum, 1970). It was a very simple, but useful, concept based on the fact that every project passes through a sequence of stages, like project identification, project preparation, project appraisal, and supervision (or implementation). Eight years later Baum added evaluation to the sequence, so that it then looked like Figure 5.2 (Baum, 1978).

Figure 5.2   A Simple Version of the Project Cycle

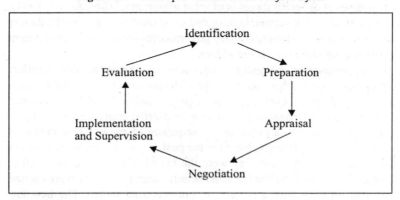

Source: Baum (1978).

Since 1978 there have been many other versions of the project cycle, but the one which captures most comprehensively all the many stages and interlinkages between the initial project identification and the eventual ex post evaluation, is the 'Project Sequence' developed by MacArthur and used for training purposes by the Development and Project Planning Centre (DPPC) at the University of Bradford. This is shown at Figure 5.3, and is described more fully in MacArthur (1994).

The DPPC version of the project cycle (or 'sequence') is slightly unusual compared with other versions in that it runs anti-clockwise, and it is divided into three phases: Pre-investment; Investment; and Operations. It will be noted that the sequence includes three evaluation stages, that is, 'on-going evaluation' (box 13), 'ex post evaluation' (box 18), and 'in operation evaluation' (box 19). The latter includes impact evaluation and sustainability monitoring. The one omission is that no provision is made for a baseline study to be carried out between project preparation and project implementation. Otherwise it is a very comprehensive description of the project cycle. The lessons learned from each project evaluation are fed back to the next project of a similar kind, so that there is a continuous cyclic process over time.

The project cycle was originally developed, and used, by donor agencies to help them in the management of their aid-funded projects. However, MacArthur is at pains to point out that his version of the project cycle 'differs from other published versions by looking at the situation from the viewpoint of the project itself. This view differs from the more familiar but selective donor viewpoint illustrated in procedures manuals and other places by financing institutions, to whom the organization of procedures at different stages is of great importance' (MacArthur, 1994). In other words, his version is designed to be used not only by the donors but also by the developing country governments for their own investment decisions, and by other stakeholders.

In the meantime, the donors themselves have begun to adopt a different attitude to the rather rigid concept of the project cycle depicted above. This kind of project cycle seems to be predicated on the idea that one can identify a project, more or less as a cut-and-dried entity, and then implement it according to a pre-arranged sequence of events. That indeed is how things were often conducted in the past, but all too often the projects failed, precisely because they were the brainchild of the donor (rather than being 'owned' by the intended beneficiaries), and they were carried out, like an engineering project, in pre-ordained stages. The new approach recognises that in real life people-centred projects are unlikely to

Figure 5.3   A Composite Diagram of the Project Sequence

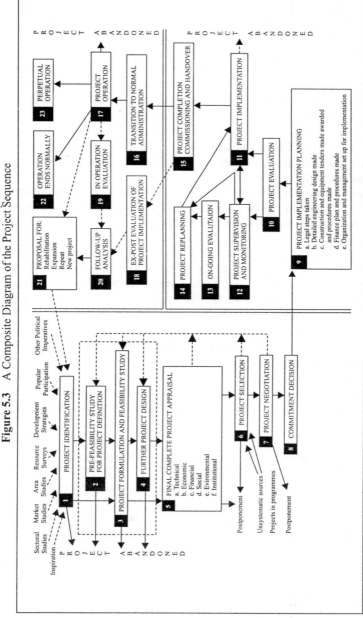

Source: J.D. MacArthur, 'The Project Sequence: A Composite View of the Project Cycle', in MacArthur and Weiss (1994), Avebury.

be successfully implemented like that. Now that there is widespread acceptance of participatory methods, it is recognised that projects can no longer be imposed on the beneficiaries, but have to emerge from a process of participatory discussion with them, so that they own the projects. There is also a new recognition of the need to assess adequately the risks involved, and to think more in terms of carrying out some trial runs on the ground so that the risks can be reduced, before projects are replicated on a broader scale. This new approach to the project cycle has been described by Picciotto, Director General, Operations Evaluation Department in the World Bank, and a colleague. They identify four stages in preparing and implementing projects. The first is a listening stage, where one listens to all the stakeholders to find out what best meets their needs. The second is a piloting stage when various alternatives are explored on a small scale to learn lessons and to reduce the risks that are associated with moving into the unknown. The third stage is a demonstration phase, when one further develops project concepts and tests out the various components of the proposed package, looking for a consensus in the light of the previous discussions and pilot projects. The final stage is devoted to the adoption, on a large scale (called 'mainstreaming'), of the package of project proposals that best fits the needs of the beneficiaries, often using NGOs or private sector institutions as agents for implementation. To quote the two authors, 'The new project cycle encourages early collaboration and resulting commitment to the goals agreed on. Its explicit focus on experimentation, organisational learning, and risk assessment, encourages more realistic project design and phasing. Most important, it makes the benefits from development operations more likely to be sustained' (R. Picciotto and R. Weaving, 1994). Figure 5.4 illustrates the new project cycle.

Figure 5.4 A New Concept of the Project Cycle

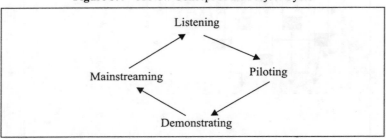

Source: Picciotto and Weaving (1994).

Whether this new approach to the project cycle, based on the use of participatory methods and flexible project implementation, is compatible with the accountability objective of evaluation is a hotly debated issue. Some writers (e.g., Smith, 1998) take the view that the two objectives cannot be achieved in the same evaluation and that a choice has therefore to be made, but others believe that it is possible to combine them. My own view is that although combining them will always be messy and unsatisfactory, the fact is that resources for evaluation are always limited and so evaluation units will generally be left with little alternative.

Analysing the Problem before Formulating the Project: The Problem Tree Approach

The discussion so far has assumed that a project has been identified, and the project cycle can therefore begin. But before a project can be identified a lot of work has to be done to identify the problem and to narrow down a range of possible alternative solutions to the one that seems to have most chance of success (or which is favoured for other reasons) (see the 8 activities listed above box 1 in Figure 5.3). Logically speaking, one would have thought that aid donors would have focused on these aspects as a priority, but in practice that did not happen, and techniques for managing projects came into use long before the techniques for improving project selection and formulation were widely adopted. The main reason for this is that most aid donors are not party to the kind of internal debate, and consideration of alternative solutions to problems, that takes place within the developing countries before they settle on a project and look around for a suitable donor. In short, most donors are asked to fund specific projects, not to advise on what might be the best solutions to problems. The latter tends to be a sensitive area, and to involve political objectives, and most developing countries would consider that it might infringe their sovereignty if they were to bring in the donors at that stage.

However, when it comes to small projects in the field of technical assistance these considerations do not apply to the same extent, and that is probably the reason why Deutsche Gesellschaft fur Technische Zusammenarbeit (GTZ), the German specialist agency for technical assistance, has been a pioneer in the problem tree approach (the Germans call this whole process 'ZOPP') to analysing problems before projects are identified. For some years they were almost alone in using this approach, but in recent years other donors have begun to adopt it too. One possible reason for this is the change that has taken place in the shape of most donors' aid programmes, from a major emphasis on project aid towards participation in developing countries' structural adjustment programmes aimed at improving their macro economic management. Thus project aid has been replaced, to a considerable extent, by sector aid, where the assistance is given to a whole sector rather than to selected projects. This in turn means that the donors are willy nilly having to get involved in discussions about macro economic policies with the recipients. There is, therefore, more scope today for the application of the problem tree approach (i.e., at the sector or sub-sector level) than there once was, and such important donor agencies as Japan and the European Commission, as well as NORAD, have now adopted it.

The basic rationale behind the problem tree approach is that one should first analyse the nature of the problem before deciding on the project(s) (FASID, 1993). Once the project has been identified it acquires a life of its own, and the convenient assumption has been made hitherto by the donors that the prior process of studying the problem and choosing optimum solutions has been systematically followed by the developing countries. But in practice it may well be that no such process took place and that the projects were chosen simply because they best fitted certain vested interests, or for political rather than economic or social reasons, or simply because a powerful figure espoused them.

The objective of the problem tree approach is to ensure that a systematic examination of the problem takes place, and that all the interested parties are involved at this stage, including the intended beneficiaries. Figure 5.5 uses a hypothetical example to illustrate what this process involves. The first step is to identify the 'focal problem' that is, the main one that needs to be tackled: this represents the trunk of the problem tree. The next step is to identify the root causes, as shown in Figure 5.5, and the final step is to identify the effects.

Figure 5.6 shows a problem tree analysis of a soil conservation programme in Kenya. Here the effects include first the immediate effects and then the development effects (i.e., the long term ones).

Once the causes and effects of the problem have been identified, one can begin to think of what the desirable outcome would be. This leads on to the objectives analysis (see Figure 5.7).

The next step is to consider the various possible ways of dealing with the problem (the alternatives analysis). Only when the most promising of

Figure 5.5　Problem Tree for a (Hypothetical) Rural Development Project

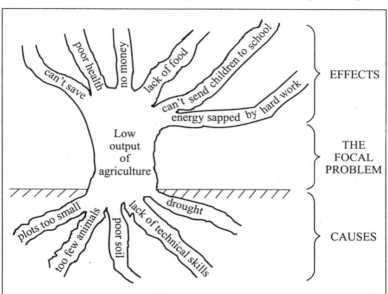

these has been selected (bearing in mind likely costs and benefits, risks, and any other relevant factors e.g., institutional, social, or environmental) does one have the makings of a project, and at that stage the logical framework comes into its own.

The Logical Framework

It was the evaluators in USAID who, around 1970, first introduced the system of project cycle management known as the logical framework. Soon afterwards the logical framework approach (or 'logframe' as it is often known) was adopted by the Canadian aid agency, CIDA, and indeed is now used for all public sector investment decisions in Canada, whether in the field of overseas development or not. It was also adopted by the German technical assistance agency GTZ, and they have been one of the main centres for training and research in the logical framework for the last two decades or more. In 1985, the ODA adopted the logical

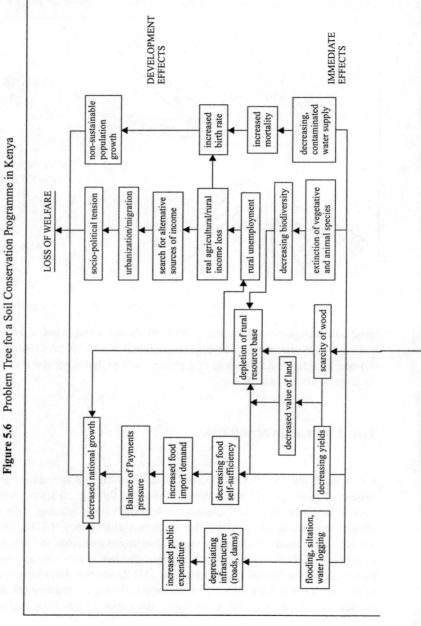

Figure 5.6 Problem Tree for a Soil Conservation Programme in Kenya

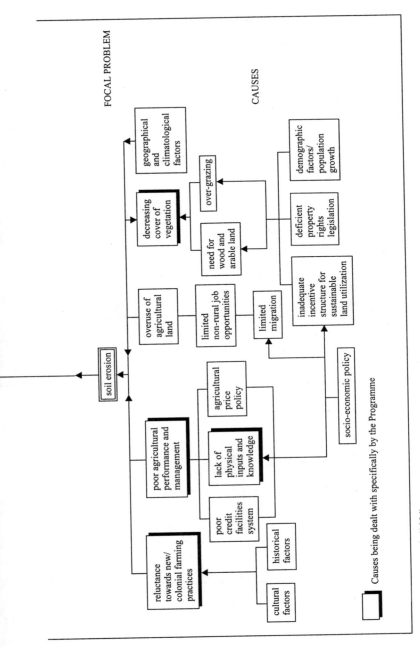

FOCAL PROBLEM

CAUSES

soil erosion

geographical and climatological factors

decreasing cover of vegetation

over-grazing

need for wood and arable land

demographic factors/ population growth

deficient property rights legislation

overuse of agricultural land

limited non-rural job opportunities

limited migration

inadequate incentive structure for sustainable land utilization

poor agricultural performance and management

agricultural price policy

lack of physical inputs and knowledge

socio-economic policy

reluctance towards new/ colonial farming practices

poor credit facilities system

historical factors

cultural factors

Causes being dealt with specifically by the Programme

Source: Carlsson et al. (1994).

Figure 5.7 Objectives Tree for a Soil Conservation Programme in Kenya

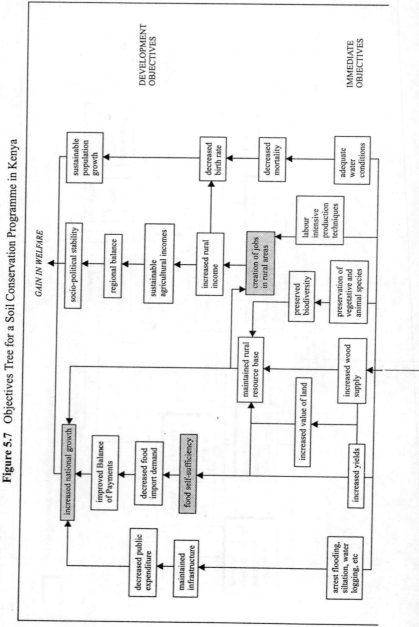

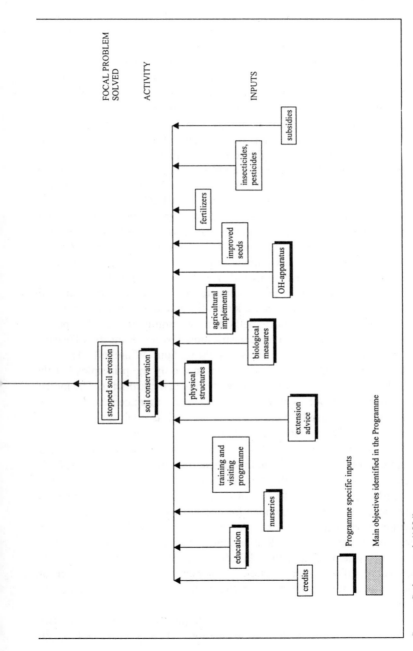

FOCAL PROBLEM SOLVED

ACTIVITY

INPUTS

stopped soil erosion

soil conservation

physical structures

biological measures

agricultural implements

OH-apparatus

improved seeds

fertilizers

insecticides, pesticides

subsidies

extension advice

training and visiting programme

nurseries

education

credits

Programme specific inputs

Main objectives identified in the Programme

Source: Carlsson et al. (1994).

framework system for all projects above a minimum size (currently £250,000), and more recently DG VIII of the European Commission has adopted it, and has completed a ECU 600,000 training programme so that all project staff have now been trained in the technique. Japan has now adopted it and has borrowed heavily from the procedures established by GTZ, modified a few years ago by experts from NORAD.

The latest aid agencies to adopt the system are the World Bank and Sida (which has recently launched a logical framework training programme for all its staff). In addition, many other UN agencies, development banks (like the African Development Bank), and non-government organisations (including Save the Children Fund and the Agency for Co-operation and Research in Development—ACCORD), have also adopted the system. In the UK, I had the good fortune to be able to play a part in getting the logical framework system adopted by the ODA (Cracknell and Rednall, 1986), and since then I have helped to introduce it in other aid agencies and non-government organisations, and have run many training courses and written several articles on it. I still believe it to have been a major advance in aid administration but, as later chapters will show, there is now a question mark over the extent to which it can be reconciled with the participatory methods now coming into use. The principles underlying the system have been adopted by Her Majesty's Treasury as a guide to new policy decisions throughout Whitehall (Treasury, 1988). In Canada, as mentioned earlier, not only the principles but the actual matrix are mandatory for all government departments. The logical framework approach is now the project cycle management technique most commonly used by aid agencies, as well as many public sectors, throughout the world, and it is vitally important for evaluators.

Considering the impact it has had worldwide, it is very surprising that so little had been written about the logical framework, at least until fairly recently—especially by the Americans who first developed it. Most of the early references to it were in documents (sometimes described as 'grey material') mainly intended for internal use, such as the report (following visits to aid agencies in America and Europe that were using it) prepared by my colleague Rednall and I, recommending that the ODA adopt the system (Cracknell and Rednall, 1986). However, following the publication of Coleman's article (Coleman, 1987) there has been an encouraging stream of further articles exploring different aspects of the subject (see especially Gasper, 1997, 1998).

So what is this logical framework technique, and how is it being used to strengthen monitoring and evaluation? It was described by its originators as a 'set of interlocking concepts which must be used together in a dynamic fashion to permit the elaboration of a well designed, objectively described and evaluable project' (Practical Concepts Incorporated, 1979). There are now many versions, and considerable variation in terminology, but basically the logical framework comprises a simple 4 × 4 matrix which breaks down a project into its component parts, namely, inputs resulting in activities, outputs, immediate objectives (or project purpose) and wider objectives (or project goal), together with the risks and assumptions involved, and indicators of progress towards the achievement of objectives. A typical example is the one currently being used by DFID (see Figure 5.8).

Figure 5.8   Project (Logical) Framework Matrix Used by DFID

Project Framework

Project Name ....
Country...
Date of Preparation ....
Design Team ....
Latest Date of Revision ....

Narrative Summary	OVIs		MoV	Assumptions
Goal:				
Purpose:	EoPs:			
Outputs: 1 2 3 4 5				
Activities: 1 2 3 4 5	Inputs:	£000s		
	Total			

Key: OVIs = Objectively verifiable indicators
  MoV = Means of verification
  EoPs = End of project status

Source: DFID (1998).

The column on the left hand side of Figure 5.8 contains the 'structure' of the project, namely the goal or wider objectives of the project, (those that are beyond the immediate scope of the project but towards the achievement of which the project should make a contribution); the project purpose or immediate objectives, (i.e., those which are generally within the scope of the project itself to achieve); outputs (i.e., practical results consequent upon certain inputs being put into place); and the activities needed to turn inputs into outputs.[1] Across the top, the second column contains the indicators of progress, and the third shows how these will be quantified or assessed (this column is to ensure that indicators are not used that do not lend themselves to assessment, for example, '20 per cent reduction in the incidence of poverty'—but how is poverty to be measured?). The last column is for the assumptions (and risks) involved in moving from one level to the next one above, in turning activities into outputs, or outputs into immediate objectives. Another variation quite often encountered is to interpose a level for 'intermediate objectives' between immediate objectives and wider objectives. This copes with the difficulty that some projects comprise several phases, and some intermediate objectives need to be achieved before the main ones become possible (but see also the reference to 'nested hierarchies' later in this chapter). The underlying logic of the logical framework is that if certain activities are undertaken (and inputs provided), given certain assumptions, a set of outputs will result: and this set of outputs, again given certain assumptions, will make a contribution, towards the achievement of certain wider objectives. This is called the 'means-ends relationship' or the vertical logic.

The Three Main Functions of the Logical Framework

It Ensures a Clear Statement of Objectives

The first main function of the logical framework is to ensure that the objectives of a project are clearly stated at the outset, and to make absolutely sure that the difference between outputs and objectives is clearly understood. For example, building a new road is not in itself an objective but rather an output. The project purpose might be something like opening up a remote region, providing access to a mineral resource, enabling heavy lorries to convey bulk commodities to a factory, etc. The project goal may relate to such aspects as improving foreign exchange earnings, integrating a remote region into the rest of the political and economic structure, and so on. All this may seem pretty straightforward, but, after having run a hundred or so workshops on the logical framework, I can vouch for the fact that it is not always simple in practice to decide what is an output and what is an objective. In former days, before the logical framework was introduced, it was commonly assumed that erecting a building, such as a school or a hospital, or running a training course etc, were objectives, but they are not. They are outputs. The great merit of the logical framework, above all its many other advantages, is that it helps the project analyst to be clear about what the objectives of any activity are. And of course this makes it so much easier, in due course, to monitor and evaluate the extent to which the objectives were achieved.

Despite all this, however, one constantly comes across cases where even those instructing others in how to use the logical framework get this basic distinction wrong. To quote Dr Eggers, who helped to introduce the logical framework into the European Commission (DG VIII): 'The Logical Framework has consistently failed to avoid confusing project "outputs" with project "purpose". It is a tragi-comical feature of the Logical Framework method that its protagonists and instructors have constantly warned against such confusion, while with the inexorability of fate succumbing themselves to this error over and over again' (Eggers, 1992).

It Introduces Indicators

The second main function of the logical framework is that it ensures that attention is given, right from the start, to the question of how progress towards the achievement of objectives will be measured. In the past (i.e., before it was introduced) indicators of performance were sometimes used, but nearly always only at the outputs level. Thus a firm of contractors building a road would be required, as a matter of course, to report regularly on the physical and financial progress in terms of yards of macadam laid, and percentage of project budget expended. But they were not required to report on progress towards meeting the project objectives.

For example, the market for the products to be hauled on the new road may have collapsed, but it was never part of the contractors' remit to pay attention to such aspects. For them building the road was the objective, and so it was also for many of the donor agencies themselves. Performance indicators linked to the achievement of project objectives are relatively new. As time goes by, the donor agencies are acquiring more experience in how to devise suitable indicators (often called 'objectively verifiable indicators'). Some agencies, like GTZ and USAID, have produced 'indicator banks', that is, comprehensive lists of indicators that have been, or might be, used for projects in various sectors (GTZ, 1989). However, there are dangers attached to this approach, and the GTZ indicator banks even contain a 'health warning' in the Preface advising users to regard the indicators simply as illustrations of what can be done, rather that searching through them for an indicator that meets their particular need. The World Bank is currently devoting a great deal of effort to devising suitable indicators, sector by sector. It is important that the person preparing the logical framework matrix thinks through, case by case, what are the most appropriate indicators, and to be as innovative as possible.

The indicators are a particularly important part of the matrix, and in my experience one can usually judge whether the person(s) completing the matrix have done a good job or not by first looking at the indicators. If they cover, in an imaginative way, the real objectives of the project, that usually means that the whole matrix will have been well completed. But if they are just superficial, often related to outputs or inputs rather than to objectives, that will usually mean that the whole matrix has been done in a hurry and without proper thought. Indicators need to be verifiable, reliable, relevant, sensitive, specific, cost-effective, and timely. There should be no biases, for example, towards males, or assuming that everything has to be done by the public sector. Sometimes it will be possible to use quantified indicators, and where this can be done in a meaningful way, and cost-effectively, so much the better. But often this will be impossible, and even undesirable if the effect of quantification is to put the spotlight on what may be in fact relatively unimportant aspects, for example, the number of people trained on a course rather than the quality of the training, or the receptiveness of the trainees.[2] This has been called the 'irony of measurement', that is all too often we measure the relatively important things because the really important ones cannot be measured. Rather than straining for quantification, it is often better to use qualitative indicators which may be mainly descriptive, or which may depend upon an opinion given by someone well qualified to judge.

A particularly troublesome problem regarding indicators is whether they should contain a motivation element or not. For instance, if it is known that veterinarians in a beneficiary country tend to prefer working from an office in the town rather than in remote rural areas, should one base an indicator on this knowledge, or should one build in at least some 'motivation' factor? Obviously the indicator has to be realistic and attainable, and it should be decided through a process of consultation with the project manager. If this procedure is followed it is likely that an achievable motivation element can be included (Cracknell, 1989).

Indicators should not be selected in a 'top–down' fashion, but in close consultation with the programme manager in the field—even if this means deferring a final decision on them until the project has been launched and some experience has been gained on the spot.

In USAID, a new kind of 'macro' indicator, 'performance measurement system' (PMS), was developed in the 1980s. It is based on quantitative indicators that can measure the collective performance of several projects in a sector or sub-sector. This system, which is now a requirement in all US federal agencies, is being used to measure the progress of sectoral programmes—particularly in the field of agricultural and rural development programmes (Kumar, 1995). Experience has shown, however, that the system is only effective with regard to the monitoring of inputs and outputs, and short-term or intermediate effects. It is unable to cope with higher-order objectives, nor can it be used to re-examine the basic rationale of programmes. A weakness of the system is that it measures only what can be quantified, and ignores what cannot be quantified.

Finally, indicators can involve costly data collection, and therefore it is essential to be very selective and only choose those that are likely to throw real light on project progress. When my colleague and I recommended the logical framework for use in the ODA in 1985, we made a particular point of advising that care should be exercised in case the introduction of the indicators were to be used as a justification for costly statistical surveys, and we recommended that rapid rural appraisal techniques should be used as much as possible (Cracknell and Rednall, 1986). The World Bank's attitude is similar, namely that 'any list of indicators must be parsimonious…yet even a parsimonious list will most likely have budgetary and staff time implications for both the borrower and the donor' (Carvalho, 1995).

It Focuses Attention on the Assumptions

The third main function of the logical framework is that it focuses attention on the key assumptions that have been made, and by implication the risks involved, in moving from one level of the matrix to the next. These risks are wholly or partly outside the control of the project manager, yet they are sufficiently important to threaten the ultimate success of the project (relatively unimportant risks should be ignored). All too often in the past the assumptions and risks were either played down, or even ignored altogether. Naturally those involved in preparing projects for funding, often against tight timetables, are not too anxious to highlight the risks involved in case those who are responsible for approving or rejecting the project take fright and turn it down, or ask for fresh work that could cause long delays. There is no escaping this and it will always be a factor, but at least the logical framework should give a hint of what the main risks are. The persons completing the matrix have to bear in mind that if it becomes evident later on that known risks were not mentioned in the matrix they could be held responsible. As mentioned above, some of these risks will be wholly outside the control of the project management, while some will be at least in part subject to its influence. A useful suggestion that has been made is that some means should be found (such as the use of italics) of separating out the latter, as a reminder to management that there may be something they can do to reduce the risk element (Wiggins and Shields, 1995). But others argue that only those risks that are beyond the scope of the project management to control should be included on the grounds that the project should be designed to cope with controllable risks. It is indeed a valuable by-product of the assumptions/risks column that the very act of listing the risks should lead the project analyst to consider whether or not there may be ways of reducing the risks through a partial redesign of the project. In fact, Wiggins and Shields have gone so far as to suggest that the bottom right hand corner of the matrix should be virtually empty by the time implementation starts. They point out that the two main risks are that (*a*) the resources will be inadequate, and that (*b*) management may not be up to the job. They add 'it is simply unprofessional folly to proceed with a project for which significant risks surround the availability of resources and the competence of the designated management. Specifying them in the Logical Framework makes no difference. Ensuring such preconditions is something project designers have to do, rather than writing that it should be done' (Wiggins and Shields, 1995).

Use of the Logical Framework for Monitoring and Evaluation

At first the logical framework system was used mainly at the project appraisal stage: it helped busy decision-takers decide 'thumbs up' or 'thumbs down' on proposed new projects. Certainly the synoptic view that it provided, especially the identification of risks and assumptions, was greatly appreciated by the senior officials in aid agencies who had to approve or reject the project proposals. It is still greatly valued for this purpose, but over the years the emphasis has shifted and the logical framework has come to be integrated more fully into the whole process of project cycle management. The obvious subsequent use of the matrix, after the project appraisal stage, was in project implementation and monitoring. It was clearly important to ensure that the monitoring process was geared as closely as possible to the logical framework, especially of course the indicators. The matrix provides almost readymade terms of reference for monitoring missions, and similarly when the time comes to evaluate the project ex post. These uses of the logical framework will be discussed more fully in the following chapter, which deals with monitoring, and there the importance of using the logical framework as a dynamic tool, being revised again and again as the project is implemented, is stressed. It is important to note that the logical framework is not a tool of economic management, and that cost-benefit analysis, and cost-effectiveness analysis, are just as important for appraisal and evaluation as they were before the logical framework was introduced.

Difficulties in the Use of the Logical Framework

First, as with every useful tool, the logical framework can be misused. The very existence of the matrix, leading to what can all too easily become a routine process of 'filling in the boxes', can tempt the busy project analyst to short-cut the effort of critical thought that should go into it. Fortunately, with a little experience, one can quite easily detect when this has happened, which is in itself a measure of the self-authenticating character of the logical framework matrix.

Second, it has to be admitted that there is a degree of unreality about the crude assumption 'if (a) then (b)' that constitutes the underlying logic of the system. Life is never that simple. There is seldom an automatic sequence of achievements outside a highly controlled scientific experiment. It may work for some mechanistic projects, but once people are involved the outcome of an intervention cannot be taken for granted. This caveat certainly has to be borne in mind, but it does not mean that the matrix is useless. All planning involves making basic assumptions that if you intervene in a certain fashion, certain results will follow. One can hardly make any progress without making some such assumption. So the warning should certainly be heeded, but the matrix still has a crucial role to play.

Third one cannot ignore what Professor Ingersoll has called 'a scientistic reliance on quantitative measures' (Ingersoll, 1988). How many of the important variables involved in the project are really amenable to quantification? Where people are concerned, the most vital success factors are linked in some way to interpersonal relationships, but no performance indicators can reflect these satisfactorily. One can only accept that this is a difficulty with the matrix, but then it is a basic problem with any attempt to monitor and evaluate projects involving human development. At least the use of performance indicators in the logical framework matrix helps to highlight the problem, and in due course some possible improvements in methods may be found.

Fourth, there is the problem, already mentioned, of a fairly complicated project having not one set of objectives (or rather two, the immediate ones and the wider ones), but a whole series of objectives at different levels, with some of them needing to be completed before those above them can be achieved. Thus a rural development project may contain a fertiliser supply component, and an ox-training component, both of which contribute towards the achievement of an increasing output of cereals, which in turn feeds into the objective of increasing farm incomes, and ultimately of reducing cereal imports. We are faced here with a hierarchy of objectives. How can one best cope with this situation while still using the logical framework approach? If the array of objectives is limited, the simplest solution is the one already proposed earlier, namely, the interposition of an extra line for 'intermediate objectives'. But if the situation is more complicated than this, that solution may not be adequate, and it may be necessary to fall back on what Wiggins has called the 'nested hierarchy' approach as depicted in Figure 5.9.

Figure 5.9 A Nested Hierarchy of Logical Frameworks

Smallholder Crop Development Programme
Agricultural Sector Programme

Perm. Sec, Min of Ag.	*Dep Sec, Min of Ag.*	*Dist Agric Officers*	(Primary projects)
		OX TRAINING PROJECT	FERTILIZER DELIVERY PROJECT
GOAL: Higher rural welfare Better balance of trade			
PURPOSE Higher farm incomes Fewer cereal imports	GOAL High farm incomes Fewer cereal imports		
RESULTS More cereals produced Etc	PURPOSE More cereals produced	GOAL More cereal produced	GOAL More cereals produced
ACTIVITIES Greater area cropped to cereals Cereal yields up. Etc	RESULTS Greater area cropped to cereals Cereal yields up. Etc	PURPOSE Greater area cropped to cereals	PURPOSE Cereal yields up
INPUTS Smallholder Crop Development Agro-processing Road improvement	ACTIVITIES More use of ox ploughing Increased fertilizer use	RESULTS More use of ox ploughing	RESULTS More fertizer applied by farmers to cereal crops
	INPUTS Ox training project Fertilizer delivery	ACTIVITIES Ox training Provision of ploughs Veterinary care	ACTIVITIES Fertilizer delivery Extension of fertilizer messages
		INPUTS Ox trainers Ploughs Animal health assistants Etc	INPUTS Fertilizer imports Trucks Drivers Extension agents. Etc

Source: Wiggins and Shields (1994).

Fifth, USAID's experience with the logical framework, and the PMS system mentioned earlier, has shown that, although it is excellent at the project level, it is less well adapted to tracking performance of programmes and policies at a higher level. This helps to explain why a new system has been evolved in USAID called PRISM (Programme Performance Information for Strategic Management). This system operates at the strategic level. It helps operating units to clarify their programme objectives, decide on appropriate performance measures, and then use them to improve decisions relating to the management of programmes and the allocation of funds. Unlike the logical framework, PRISM does not at present involve the recipient, and this has been a subject of criticism. Although the underlying logic of the logical framework and PRISM are very similar (i.e., clear specification of objectives, and use of performance measures), there has so far been little direct linkage between them because the two systems function at such different levels. (OECD/IDB, 1994).

Sixth, there is the difficulty of deciding where the accountability of management for project success or failure should lie, that is, at the level of outputs, or at the level of project purpose or immediate objectives. Most authorities, including the American consultants Team Technologies who have prepared software for a number of users in Europe and elsewhere, consider that project management can only be held responsible for the achievement of project outputs because only these are wholly within their scope as project managers. There are various extraneous influences that could influence the achievement of the project purpose. This may indeed be the case, but the basic objection to this argument is that it represents a return to the old discredited approach whereby project managers judged their success or failure in terms purely of physical progress in implementing the project, rather than in terms of whether the objectives were being achieved. In my opinion the project managers should be encouraged to regard the achievement of the project purpose as their primary task, regardless of the fact that they may not be in complete control of all the factors. It is up to the project manager to steer the project in that direction, and to make whatever adjustments are needed, if it seems that the extraneous factors are threatening the achievement of the project purpose.

Lastly there is the problem that the logical framework matrix makes no provision for unintended effects (often adverse, but not necessarily so) since it concentrates on the positive aspects of what the project is meant to achieve. This is such an important topic that it is discussed more fully in Chapter 7, but it needs to be emphasised here that these unintended effects, insofar as they can be foreseen at the appraisal stage, should be included in the logical framework matrix.

Neutrality of the Logical Framework vis-à-vis Development Criteria

In addition to the above problems associated with the application of the logical framework, there is a conceptual weakness that is rather more serious, and that is the fact that it is neutral with respect to whether the project is well conceived or not in development terms. As an experienced user of the technique has expressed it: "This (neutrality) can manifest itself in the production of a framework which displays flawless internal logic but addresses an inappropriate purpose" (Cordingley, 1995). To some extent the process of prior consultation with all the parties concerned, including the intended beneficiaries, during the preparation of the problem tree, can ensure that this doesn't happen, but it would be more satisfactory if some way could be found of achieving this by modifying the logical framework itself. A key test of a project's developmental appropriateness is its sustainability: if it survives after the aid funding comes to an end it must be meeting a felt need. Unfortunately, as at present conceived, the logical framework matrix does not make any specific provision for sustainability. It is possible, of course, to cover this to some extent in the instructions to staff on how the matrix should be completed, and DFID for example insists that certain aspects of sustainability, such as maintenance, environment and the role of women, should be specifically covered as part of the objectives of the project. The European Commission, with its integrated approach, described next, has adopted a rather similar solution by specifying that all seven factors of sustainability (discussed in Chapter 14) have to be systematically covered at all stages.

These devices apart, the issue remains, is it possible to incorporate sustainability more directly into the logical framework system itself? Some work on this has been done by a group of Scandinavian researchers, commissioned by NORAD, and they have demonstrated that the elements of sustainability can be interlinked both with the criteria of evaluation and with the logical framework matrix, as in Figure 5.10. The

Figure 5.10 Integrating Development Determinants and Evaluation Criteria into the Project Management Cycle

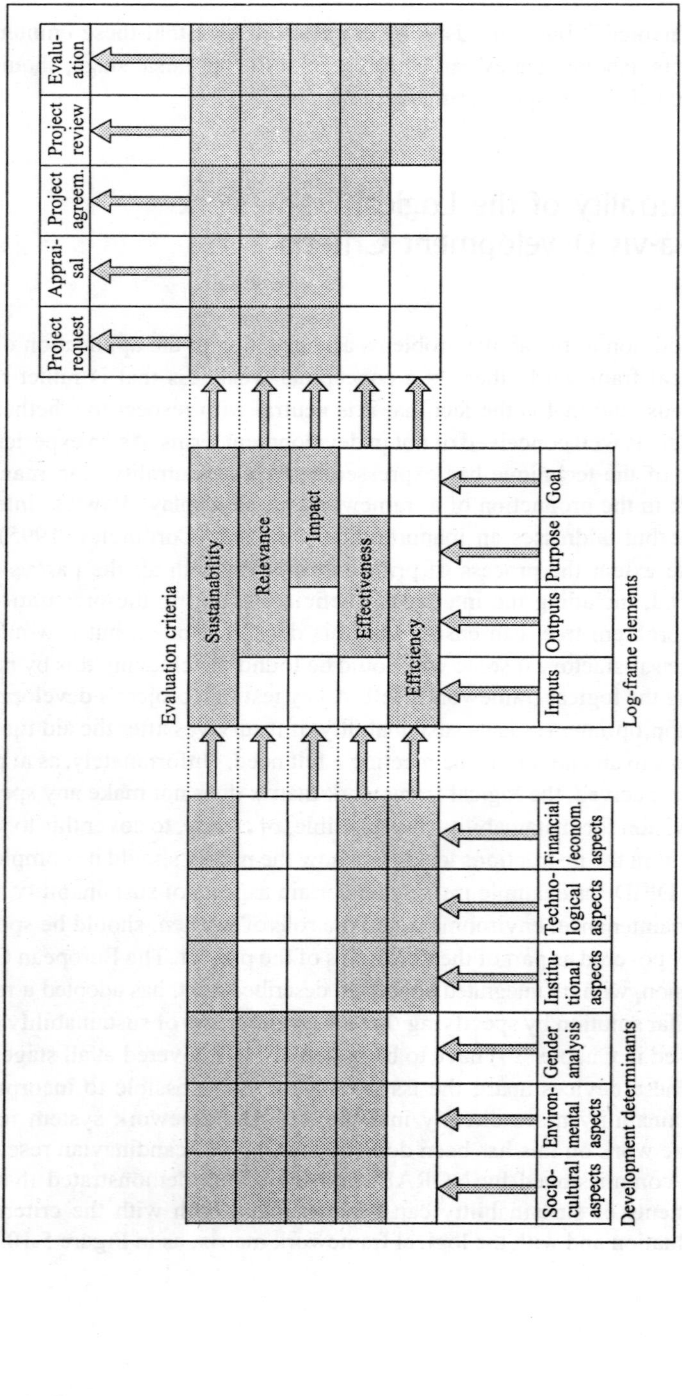

Source: Samset (1992).

search continues for possible ways of incorporating the sustainability factors as an integral part of the logical framework matrix, without overloading it or destroying its simplicity.

The Danger of Rigidity

An ever-present risk, with the logical framework, is that it may engender a rigid mentality in the minds of those who use it. A lot of work, often involving a process of painful confrontation, goes into the production of the matrix if it has been well done, and no one is anxious to have to go through that process again too soon. In fact, the matrix can easily seem to have become set in concrete. Yet all evaluation experience shows that, with regard to people-centred projects, flexibility in management is a key to success. It was this realisation that led to the development of the process approach discussed in the next chapter, which encourages the 'listening, piloting, demonstrating and mainstreaming' style of project management referred to earlier. The issue of how to reconcile the logical framework with the process approach is discussed in the next chapter. In theory at least it should be possible to get the best of both worlds, but there is no denying that the very logicality of the logical framework can at times be its worst enemy!

Strengths and Weaknesses of the Logical Framework

Gasper at the Institute of Social Studies in The Hague has made a particular study of the logical framework. He presented a well-reasoned critique of the method in a paper to the Development Studies Association at its annual conference in Bradford in September 1998. His general conclusion was that while the system has many advantages it also some significant disadvantages. It needs to be used in a careful and flexible manner (rather than slavishly), and in conjunction with other approaches rather than by itself. Much depends on who is using it and for what purposes. His paper included a very useful summary of the potential strengths and weaknesses of the logical framework as shown in Figure 5.11.

Figure 5.11 Strengths and Weaknesses of the Logical Framework Approach

Debates On LFA	Objectives and Potential Strengths	Common Problems	Potential Dangers
About vertical logic	1) A synoptic, integrated view—relatively thorough yet concise—of project objectives and activities and their links to environments 2) Distinguishes levels in temporal and value hierarchies 3) Encourages examination of interconnections and assumptions	a) In clarifying and gaining consensus on objectives; intellectual and political problems b) Interpreting and applying the terms for different levels c) To state objectives as a linear chain d) Over aggregation, esp. at high levels e) So many implied assumptions present f) Time-consuming	i) Oversimplification of objectives ii) Hides disagreements iii) Rigidification of objectives ("lock-frame") iv) Ignoring or downgrading of unintended effects v) Downgrading types of value not well reflected as end-points in a chain vi) Ritual claims to have faced uncertainties vii) Hopeful box-filling not based on problem analysis ("lack-frame")
About horizontal logic	1) To give measurable, operationalized, clear reference-points for use in appraisal, management, and evaluation 2) To deepen examination of meanings of objectives	a) To obtain practicable, valid, quantified indicators, especially for higher levels and for "social" types of project b) To separate out the influences of complementary factors	i) Downgrading of less quantifiable objectives ii) Invalid use of gross outcomes as indicators iii) Mishandling of co-determined effects iv) Disproportionate work might be required v) Rigidification of targets (and conflation with indicators) vi) Distorted incentives

Figure 5.11 continued

Figure 5.11 continued

| About format and application | 1) Visually accessible; relatively easy to understand 2) Shared focus for different parties 3) Matrix can (and should) be systematically linked to a situation analysis (eg as in Zopp) 4) Can be applied in a participatory way (eg in ZOPP and its derivatives) | a) Prepared too late b) Pressure to use a pre-set format, at risk of distortion of the case c) Assumptions analysis is marginalised d) High demands for training, judgement and motivation | i) Excessive simplification of cases, with a partial summary fetishised as whole truth ii) Can deaden thought and stifle adaptation iii) Can become a method for enforcement of one view, rather than for debate of several; mainly used for one-way accountability only iv) Can alienate staff v) Can become a fetish, rather than a help |

Source: Gasper (1998).

The Integrated Approach to Project Cycle Management

The European Commission (DG VIII) has taken the process of basing the project cycle management on the logical framework to its logical conclusion and has introduced what it calls the 'integrated approach to project cycle management'. Under this approach, the same criteria are used at every stage of the project cycle. The integrated approach is illustrated in Figure 5.12, and is described in detail by Dr Eggers, one-time Head of the Evaluation Unit in DG VIII of the European Commission, in an article in *Project Appraisal* (Eggers, 1992). GTZ has also followed a similar course. It called a temporary halt to its training programmes on the ZOPP system a few years ago, while it developed a new approach in which the ZOPP system is embedded in a comprehensive project cycle

Figure 5.12 The Integrated Approach to Project Cycle Management

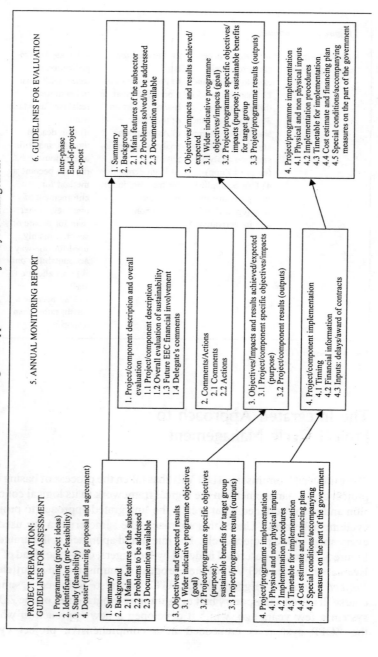

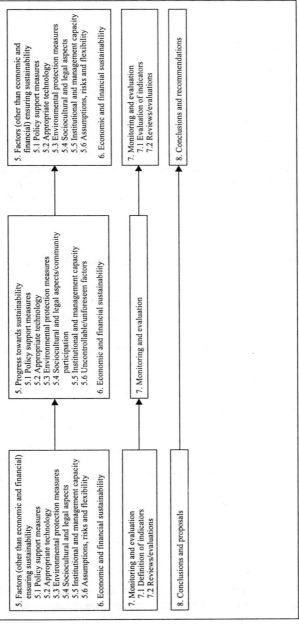

Source: Eggers (1992).

management concept, and is also made more flexible in its implementation (Blackburn with Holland, 1998).

The reader may wonder what is especially significant about such an obviously sensible procedure. It is surely self-evidently desirable that the same criteria should be used at each stage. However, in the past this did not happen, because responsibility for project appraisal, monitoring and evaluation were divided between different departments of the organisation, and there was no harmonisation. The result was very patchy. Some items that were considered to be important at appraisal were totally neglected subsequently, while aspects that may not have been considered at all in the appraisal (such as gender or the environment) figured prominently at the monitoring and evaluation stages. With the integrated approach there is complete harmonisation of approach throughout the project cycle.

Feeding Evaluation Results into the Project Cycle

As mentioned at the beginning of this chapter, the most important reason why evaluators have been at the forefront of these improvements in project cycle management in all the main donor agencies, is that they have a vested interest in ensuring that the objectives of a project are well understood, and clearly stated, right from the start. This will always be at the core of an evaluation unit's concern for project cycle management. But there is another important reason why evaluators take such a keen interest in project cycle management techniques, and that is because they are always searching for effective ways of ensuring that evaluation findings are fed into the project management process from the earliest moment in the life of a new project. It is at the time of preparing the logical framework matrix when the evaluators can most effectively bring to bear the distilled experience from evaluation findings. Just how this can be done is the subject matter of feedback, which is dealt with in Chapters 10, 11 and 12.

Notes

1. The original matrix showed only inputs and outputs (i.e., not activities), but as inputs need to be translated into outputs through various activities, and these in fact constitute the backbone of the project, it became the practice to list the

activities. The advantage is that this helps with project implementation, monitoring and eventual evaluation, but a possible disadvantage is that the activities relate to a 'process' whereas the other components of the matrix represent 'states', that is, means or ends.

2. Quantified indicators can actually have unfortunate consequences. I recall a case, relating to a forestry project, where the indicators used were the number of saplings planted per day, until it was discovered that the workers were digging a shallow hole and shoving in the saplings without proper care, just to reach the target. More sinisterly, I have heard it suggested that the massacre by American troops at Mylai in Vietnam happened because the Americans had introduced the concept of the 'body-count' as an indicator of military success.

Techniques and Methods of Aid Evaluation

Part One: The Counterfactual, Effectiveness and Efficiency

'To measure is the first step to improve'
(Sir William Petty)

'There is measure in all things'
(Horace)

'What is measured often is not important, and what is important often is not measured'
(Measuring the Performance of Agricultural and
Rural Development Programmes
K. Kumar)

Initial Review and Structured Interviews

Over the past three decades, evaluators have used, and gradually improved upon, an array of techniques for carrying out evaluations. The first task, with any evaluation, is to study carefully the files and documents relating to the project being evaluated. Generally speaking, the first such review is carried out by the staff of the evaluation unit (or by outsiders engaged for that purpose), as the basis for drawing up the terms of reference for the evaluation. As soon as they are appointed, the evaluation team will naturally want to make their own study of the main documents since it is important that they brief themselves thoroughly on the project beforehand. They will also wish to read any monitoring mission reports, or a project completion report if there is one, and they will also conduct a literature review to place the project in its broader context (some people regard the quality of the literature review as an acid test of the quality of the whole evaluation). The logical framework matrix, if one was prepared, would of course be a key document, but it may not be available for projects approved some time ago. Hopefully the matrix will have been used in a dynamic way during the life of the project, so that there will be a fresh version prepared whenever there has been a significant change in the way the project was implemented. The evaluators will take special note of the indicators, and the out-turn results.

Once the initial briefing is over, and the key documents have been studied, the evaluation team will usually move to the project location for a period generally lasting a few weeks. They will conduct interviews of key personnel, probably using the 'structured interview' technique whereby a list of key questions is drawn up before the interview and the interviewer tries to follow that sequence as the interview takes place. However, if the interviewees want to go down avenues of their own choosing they are encouraged to do so and the interviewer returns to the list of structured questions when that becomes possible. Usually the structured interview questionnaire will be piloted on a small sample in advance to make sure that it is comprehensible and covers the main points. In the interview itself, the usual practice is to start by using the list of questions, allowing deviations to occur naturally, and then trying to get back to the basic structure so that all the questions are eventually covered. Experience shows that it is important to use some structure such as this, partly so that the results can be written up in a systematic and structured way, but also to ensure that the ground is covered fully. On the other hand, flexibility is important because one cannot always foresee what will happen, and sometimes the unexpected can be very important. If the interview is conducted in too systematic a way, slavishly following the questionnaire, the interviewee will answer only the questions put to him or her, and one may never learn important things that he or she would have mentioned if there had been an opportunity to do so.

The main problem with structured interviews is that the results are difficult to quantify. Sometimes it is possible to categorise the answers retrospectively, but this is laborious and the results are seldom very reliable. So it is often desirable to supplement structured interviews with questionnaires that may be completed either by the interviewee, or by the interviewer immediately after the interview has been concluded. The questionnaires will usually include open-ended questions of the type: 'What are your views regarding "x"?', and also a number of pre-coded questions of the type: 'Would you say that "x" is important, fairly important, of little importance, or of no importance?' The latter lend themselves to tabulation, and this kind of quantification can be important in an evaluation report as it imparts an element of precision to what might otherwise seem too impressionistic. However, reports based almost entirely on this kind of quantified information can be rather colourless and lacking in depth, so it is necessary to supplement the quantified information with the more qualitative material which can be obtained from the open-ended questions.

The Counterfactual

Coming now to the techniques to be used for the actual evaluation, the first and most important issue to be faced is whether it is necessary, or possible, to employ the counterfactual technique. This is a technique for measuring change over time. The two main purposes of evaluation are: (a) to assess the outcomes and impacts of projects, and (b) to compare these with the objectives as set out originally, so that lessons can be learned to enable future project design and implementation to be improved (ODA, 1994). So far as (a) is concerned, this is relatively straightforward, at least in concept, if not in practice. However, (b) presents more difficulties. The obvious direct method is the 'before and after' approach, that is, simply comparing the situation at the time of the evaluation with what it was before the project started (ODA, 1994). This indeed is still how many evaluations are in fact carried out. It, however, suffers from a serious defect. If the project has spanned a period of several years, a number of changes will have taken place during the life of the project that would have happened in any case, even if there had been no project, and it would not be right to attribute them to the project. These are sometimes called 'pollutants' but that is a rather unfortunate term because many of these will be of positive value to the project.[1] For instance, if the project relates to a proposed improvement in agricultural production spread over a period of years, it is very likely that the farmers would take advantage of the improved farming practices, such as fertilisers, seeds, pesticides, extension advice, etc, that might have eventually become available to all farmers regardless of whether there was a special project or not. Therefore, such changes should, if possible, be excluded from the benefits attributed to the project as they would have happened in any case. To take another example, the improvement of a road may be necessary because the existing one has become overloaded. Looking only at the before-and-after situation would be to ignore the fact that without the road improvement, road traffic might have come almost to a standstill.

The alternative approach, which is to use the 'with and without' comparison, is rather inelegantly called the 'counterfactual' approach. It focuses on 'additionality', that is, what can safely be attributed to the project and not to other influences. A practical example illustrating the importance of the counterfactual is given in Box 6.1.

Although the counterfactual approach seems on the face of it to be very sensible, in practice it is rarely adopted in aid evaluations in any rigorous fashion. The reason is that it is inherently very difficult to assess what the 'without project' position would have been. One way would be to set up an experimental 'control', that is, to select a location as similar as possible to that of the project and to monitor development in this control area. I once tried very hard to set up such a control for a road project in Sierra Leone, but it was not successful. The difficulty is that it is well nigh impossible to find a location similar in all essential respects to that of the project. Moreover, it is expensive to duplicate the data collection process and it can also be quite embarrassing trying to explain to the participants in the control area why they have been selected, and damping down their expectations of some future donor involvement! Some very experienced evaluators are now doubtful whether it is ever possible, with people-centred projects, to establish causal linkages between development interventions and possible outcomes. Professor Robert Chambers, the arch exponent of participatory methods, has recently expressed his doubts on this score. In his experience, the beneficiaries themselves do not think in terms of the 'impact', that is, the specific effect of aid inputs: they are concerned simply with what is happening to them, not with the causes. Another experienced evaluator has commented on this issue as follows: 'To establish experimental conditions, e.g. using control groups or villages to analyse outcomes with and without activities, is very difficult in the context of a rural development project or an industrial urban

Box 6.1   An Example of the Importance of the
Counterfactual Approach

In the mid 1970's the Employment Guarantee Scheme was introduced in the Indian State of Maharashtra. It was designed to provide employment in small-scale public works projects, and anyone requesting a job would be given one, but at a very low wage. The Scheme appeared to be a success, with around 100 million person-days a year in employment being provided. However what would have happened without the project?

Three possible scenarios were identified as follows:

1. One could assume that in the absence of the scheme the poor would have earned nothing, i.e. the total wages paid represent the benefits to the workers.

2. Or one could assume that in the absence of the scheme the participants would have earned as much as those who did not have access to it. Research suggested that in this case the net benefit was about 50% of the wages paid.

3. Or alternatively one might study the socio-economic and demographic characteristics of the participants themselves and then predict what they might have earned if they had not participated in the scheme. A careful econometric investigation of two villages suggests that the incomes fore-gone by the participants as a result of their taking part in the scheme were in fact quite small (28% for men, and 10% for women).

This analysis demonstrates how important the counterfactual can be in assessing the results of a project over time.

Source: Squire (1995).

project, in particular since the number of possible causes of impact is very large, and to isolate the variables from each other seems nearly impossible' (Nielsen, 1990). If a control is not used, an alternative is to use published statistics and other available information about secular trends relating, if possible, to the region where the project is located, or failing that, to the country as a whole.

As the experience of most aid agencies is that controls seldom work satisfactorily, alternative approaches have been developed. For example, the evaluators of the Asian Development Bank, where project benefit monitoring is an integral part of their project lending procedures, have evolved alternative methods, such as non-equivalent group designs which seek to explore specific effects as they influence different sets of sub-jects, and the quasi-experimental analysis of time series relating to a beneficiary group. In the latter case, the researcher accepts the limita-tions of the 'before-and-after' comparisons, directing his attention to irregularities and quantum shifts that can be explained in terms of system processes and environmental shocks.

When comparing the situation of the project at the time of the evaluation with the 'before' position, it is difficult to escape the problems that arise from hindsight. Thus one is in a better position to forecast the future stream of benefits and costs at the time of the evaluation than was possible at the appraisal stage. Obviously the up-to-date information has to be used in assessing the project's present, and likely future, situation. However, in making judgements about the way in which the project was originally designed, one has to try to think back to the situation as it was, and to judge whether the best possible attempt was made to forecast the future, given the state of knowledge available at the time.

Effectiveness and Efficiency

The first main task of the evaluation team is to establish whether the objectives of the project were achieved. This is called the *effectiveness* criterion.

The second main task is to find out whether the objectives were achieved at the least cost, and this is called the *efficiency* criterion. A project can hardly be considered to have been successful if the objectives were achieved at exorbitant cost. So the two criteria have to be considered in tandem.

Unfortunately, these two terms tend to get confused with each other, and indeed the scope for confusion is considerable when one bears in mind that the term economists use for comparing alternative ways of achieving a given objective is 'cost-effectiveness', although this is clearly a measure of efficiency rather than effectiveness. Confusion is piled on confusion when one discovers that in French the two terms in fact have the same meaning. The existing confusion in terminology is unfortunate because the concepts themselves are of course of crucial importance: two of the principal tasks of any evaluation team are to assess whether the objectives were achieved, and whether they were achieved in an economically efficient way.

Cost-Effectiveness in Evaluation

The analysis of cost-effectiveness is more common in evaluations than full cost-benefit (discussed in Chapter 7). This is because it is a technique that avoids having to put a value on the benefits of the project, and when the latter are in the social sphere it is often impossible to quantify them satisfactorily. Instead, the emphasis is on the cost side, and the technique comprises a comparison between the costs of alternative ways of achieving the same objective. Sometimes the comparison is made for design choices that relate to only a part of the whole project. For example, the ODA carried out a cost-effectiveness evaluation of different ways of bagging fertilisers at a fertiliser factory in India, mainly to establish whether labour-intensive methods would have been more appropriate than mechanical methods (Turner et al., 1980). The problem with cost-effectiveness analysis in evaluation is that the necessary cost figures are readily available only for the particular technology that is chosen. Entirely fresh information, not only on costs but also on techniques, needs to be obtained if a comparison with an alternative technology is to be made, and this can be very time-consuming. In the ODA case mentioned earlier, the need for a cost-effectiveness evaluation became apparent as a result of the broader evaluation of the whole fertiliser plant, and it was then decided to fund a supplementary evaluation to look more closely into the question of alternative technologies. It is seldom possible, in the course of a two–three week evaluation mission, to collect sufficient data to enable an alternative technology to be thoroughly evaluated.

One of the problems in the use of the cost-effectiveness approach is that the output from different technologies or methods may not be exactly identical. For instance, if a comparison were being made between training someone from a developing country in Britain and training that person in his/her own country or in another developing country, one cannot assume that the benefits would be identical and that all one has to consider are the costs. That is clearly not the case. Training in Britain would expose the trainee to a different culture, and that would be part of the training experience (for good or ill!). Finally, it is necessary to decide what unit of cost is to be compared. If it is a water supply project aimed at improving health, is the appropriate unit the cost per water connection, or cost per household connected, cost per person, or cost per gallon of water supplied, cost per village, etc? However, as the stockpile of information on such unit costs grows in size, and improves in quality, it should become possible to make use of this kind of comparison more readily for the purposes of cost-effectiveness evaluation.

The results of a major study of how nine aid agencies used cost-benefit analysis and cost-effectiveness techniques in evaluation are given in Box 6.2. They illustrate the difficulties inherent in this approach, although the study recommended renewed efforts to overcome them if possible.

Box 6.2 Use of Cost-Benefit Analysis and Cost-Effectiveness
Techniques in Evaluation

In 1993 the Swedish Government called on SIDA to improve its evaluation methodology through better use of cost-benefit and cost-effectiveness analysis techniques. SIDA conducted a major study, including a review of what nine bilateral and multilateral agencies were doing in this field.

The SIDA team found that all the nine donors visited had experienced great difficulty in applying cost-benefit analysis techniques to "soft" projects, such as health, education, and human resources. The World Bank was doing its best, but often incurred criticism from other donors on the grounds that the results were unreliable. Where aid agencies were using cost-benefit analysis techniques it was generally in relation to project appraisals, and very rarely for the evaluation of on-going or completed projects.

There is a basic problem with the cost-effectiveness approach in that it cannot be used to assess economic efficiency. A project may be cost-effective without being economically efficient, if the benefits don't exceed the costs. Cost effectiveness is thus a necessary, but not a sufficient, condition for economic efficiency. Another problem is the sheer difficulty of getting hold of reliable data on costs for project inputs originating in the recipient country: the tendency is to ignore these if possible and to focus on the inputs supplied by the donor, but this may give a misleading picture of ultimate sustainability.

The SIDA team's recommendations were:

1. Despite the difficulties, SIDA should continue to use economic approaches at appraisal, and should try to ensure that data are generated during implementation to enable similar economic analyses to be made during monitoring and evaluation.
2. Evaluations should systematically follow up the economic analyses made at appraisal
3. Even if cost-effectiveness cannot be measured, it should still be possible to make some qualitative assessment of whether it is reasonable to believe that the outputs are efficiently producing the intended effects, and whether the relationship between outputs and costs is reasonable compared with SIDA's experience with similar projects.

Source: SIDA (1994b).

A survey of the attitudes of project officers in the same agency (SIDA) to economic assessment revealed that poor goal formulation was considered one of the main problems. Often project goals were stated in very general and vague terms, which could not form the basis for monitoring or evaluation, and, in fact, the first time the objectives were clearly stated in an operational way was often when the terms of reference had to be drawn up for an ex-post evaluation! Activities were confused with objectives, and monitoring often comprised simply the measurement of physical progress rather than the achievement of objectives. Moreover, target groups were frequently described in such a vague way (e.g., 'urban poor') that it was difficult to decide who the intended beneficiaries really were (Carlsson et al., 1994). It is no doubt as a result of these findings that SIDA (now Sida) has recently decided to adopt the logical framework system.

Significance (Relevance), and the Problem of Unclear, Conflicting or Changing Objectives

The cost-effectiveness approach looks at operational performance, but evaluation must be concerned with more than this. In logical framework terms that would be like saying that it is sufficient merely to look at inputs, outputs and the achievement of immediate objectives. Clearly that is not enough. One must also consider the contribution of the project towards the achievement of the wider objectives. This is sometimes called the 'significance' test. It does not follow that if the immediate objectives are realised, the wider objectives will also be achieved. In the World Bank the word 'relevance' is used to refer to the process of checking whether the objectives of the project were appropriate to deal with the problem. To quote Robert Picciotto, Director General of OED, 'To do things right is one thing: to do the right things is even more important' (Picciotto, 1995a). As stated in Chapter 2, this element of evaluation, that is, the reassessment of the objectives, is one of the factors that most distinguishes the evaluation function from auditing.

Whether one is looking at the wider objectives or at the immediate objectives, assessing whether, and how efficiently, objectives have been achieved is not always as straightforward as it may seem. Often project objectives are either not specified in any detail, or are described in a way that makes evaluation very difficult. Sometimes they may have been set out adequately at the appraisal, but have undergone change during implementation yet no one has thought to set out what the new objectives are. Sometimes the objectives are described in such abstract terms that it is impossible to monitor or evaluate progress towards achieving them. In this context the discipline involved in systems like the logical framework is very valuable in forcing those responsible for preparing projects to set out objectives for which indicators of achievement can be devised. Sometimes objectives relate to far distant targets, to the achievement of which the project can only be expected to make a minor contribution (but again the logical framework matrix is useful because it requires these wider objectives to be specified).

One of the most difficult problems is how to cope with mutually incompatible objectives. For example, the primary objective may be to establish a viable industry, whereas the secondary objective may be to enhance employment opportunities. Yet sometimes it may not be possible to achieve both together. For example, if an industry is over-manned it may be necessary to make some workers redundant if the industry is to be commercially viable. How does one cope with this problem? This is where the logical framework can be useful. It helps clarify what the primary objectives, and the secondary objectives are, and places the evaluator in a better position to weigh one against the other. Even so, it is most unlikely that anyone will take it upon themselves to give 'weights' to different objectives (normally this task should fall on the politicians but they are notoriously reluctant to say what they think such weights should be), so that it may be difficult even to establish which are the primary objectives and which the less important ones, and almost impossible to do any systematic 'weighting' of the results. When faced with conflicting objectives, the evaluator has to draw attention to this fact. However, evaluators are best advised not to attempt any system of 'weighting' on their own account but simply to report the results, positive and negative, and let the reader form a judgement as to how these relate to each other in the final analysis.

Sometimes this problem of conflicting objectives is tackled through a 'two-step' approach. The first step is for the evaluator to get the operational units of the agency to review the project's stated objectives and either reaffirm or deny them. The second step is to carry out the evaluation itself taking the objectives as they result from this re-examination process.

Another problem arises when the objectives of the project change during implementation—what some evaluators call the problem of 'moving goalposts' (Guerrero, 1995). If the changes have been documented in successive logical framework matrices there should be no difficulty. But if this has not been done (and in my experience the logical framework is not always being used in this dynamic way), the evaluator only gradually becomes aware that de facto the management have been pursuing objectives different from those laid down in the appraisal, and this can create serious problems. A change in objectives may be perfectly reasonable, and indeed it is often desirable when a process approach is being used (see p. 137), but clearly the evaluator has to establish what the new objectives are, and should also examine how and why they came to be changed. In this way he/she may be able to throw useful light on design changes that may be needed with future projects of a similar type.

Whose Welfare is Being Maximised?

Another difficult problem concerns the differing value systems in developing countries and among the donors. For example, the donor agency will nearly always take, as a critical criterion of project success, the economic rate of return. It will strive to ensure that the project achieves an acceptable level of economic return, even if, for instance, that might entail having a considerable input into the management of the project. But the recipient country may not regard the economic rate of return as the most important criterion of success. It might put a higher value on its own nationals being allowed to gain experience as managers, even though they may make mistakes, provided of course that they learn from them and do not repeat the mistakes next time. The issue of the different value systems of the donor and recipient is discussed fully in Chapter 18. Whose welfare is being maximised? Inevitably, with most evaluation teams being heavily dominated by evaluators from developed countries, it tends to be the donor's value system that is most strongly represented in evaluation reports. However, in recent years, donors have made a conscientious attempt to have the beneficiary's viewpoint reflected in their evaluations, and hopefully this will mean a more balanced approach to evaluation reports in the future.

Measurement of Success or Failure

A problem which has always taxed evaluators is that a project may turn out to be a success or failure because of factors which could not possibly have been foreseen at the time when the original appraisal, and decision to proceed, was made. For example, an ODA project which aimed at increasing the production of tobacco in Sumatra had been well designed and implemented, but then the world tobacco prices collapsed, and producers were forced to abandon it in favour of another crop (ODA, 1979a). Is such a project to be considered a success or a failure? The first comment one can make is that obviously the facts themselves are valuable, and the sponsors of the evaluation can make their own judgement if they are supplied with all the information. So an important task of the evaluation team is to describe what happened, and what the present state of the project is. This is purely factual and does not involve making any judgement. However, it is equally important to evaluate how well the project was planned and implemented, and whether any improvements can be made to these processes in the light of experience. It is necessary to make a distinction between factors related to the initial design (the 'design-dependent impact'), and factors related to the subsequent circumstances (the 'environmentally-determined impact'). In the case of the crop switch, cited earlier, a judgement had to be made about whether the market collapse could reasonably have been foreseen. Even if the answer had been No, there must surely have been the possibility of a market collapse, and the inference may be that to have concentrated so much on one crop was unwise, and some diversification may have been desirable. In logical framework terms, the risk of a market collapse should have been noted in the *Assumptions (Risks)* column, and this might well have alerted the person preparing the project to the possibility of reducing the risk by introducing an element of crop diversification.

Problem of How to Cope with Process Approach Projects

Some projects such as installing night flying equipment for an airfield, building a dam or a bridge, etc are technological in nature. Such projects lend themselves par excellence to what is called the 'blueprint approach'. They generally have to be implemented more or less exactly according to the original blueprint: one cannot, for example, change the design half way through building a bridge!

However, many projects are mainly concerned with people, and these are often called 'people-centred projects'. They are socially oriented projects, and typical examples would be: a birth control project; a school-feeding programme; or a job-creation scheme for the unemployed. Because people are the principal actors, and because no-one can be quite sure how people will respond to particular incentives and initiatives taken on their behalf until they are actually faced with them (even the people themselves may not be able to say beforehand how they would react), the blueprint approach is inappropriate. Instead, the aid donors have introduced a different concept called the 'process approach' (Conlin et al., 1985; Rondinelli, 1987 and USAID, 1986).[2] This is based on the realisation that implementing a people-centred project is a continuous learning process. The project manager tries a particular package of inputs that he/she hopes will prove to be what the people want, but as time goes by he/she finds that some components are very successful and others are not. As a good manager, he/she will change the product mix, reinforcing those components that are going well, and reducing the others. Of course this means that the project manager has to be given a great deal more autonomy to make decisions (within prearranged tolerances) than previously. It also means that the process approach projects are likely to finish up looking rather different from what had been originally envisaged.

The problem that now arises is how can one evaluate a process approach project? Obviously it is not adequate to simply take the original objectives and to compare the final outcome with them. A better approach is to look at the pattern of objectives as they have evolved over the life of the project (hopefully revised logical frameworks will have been produced at each change of tack: for example, the German aid agency GTZ's manual on the logical framework [or ZOPP] approach states that the matrix is likely to be revised at least four or five times during the project's life) and to assess success or failure in that context. Rapidity of change, in response to changing circumstances, could well be a measure of good project management in such a project. Measuring management responsiveness could be a vital element in the evaluation of a process approach project. But the problem is that the evaluation usually has to take place at one point in time, usually some years after the project was first launched, and it is very likely that the information available to the evaluator about the changes that took place during project implementation may be very limited. Moreover, a key objective of any evaluation of a people-centred project must be to assess the impact of the project on the intended beneficiaries, and this may be very difficult to do if the evaluation is deferred until the project has come to an end. It may well be necessary to set up some kind of continuous monitoring of impact on beneficiaries during the implementation of the project. As mentioned earlier, the Asian Development Bank has given a lead in trying to encourage its borrowers to develop this kind of 'project benefit monitoring' on a continuous basis for all the people-centred projects it finances. Other donors too have come to the conclusion that it is not sufficient to think in terms of evaluating people-centred projects at the end of their life, but that such evaluation needs to be built into the whole process of project management. The director general of operations evaluation in the World Bank has proposed two alternative solutions to this dilemma, which the Bank is currently exploring. They are as follows:

(*a*) To subordinate the evaluation of projects to the evaluation of the programmes they are part of (e.g., incorporating externalities into the evaluation process);

(*b*) To conceive of projects as flexible instruments with a built-in capacity to adapt to changed circumstances (Picciotto and Weaving, 1994), and to evaluate them not in relation to their initial goals (efficacy) which may be quite vague, or may no longer be appropriate, but simply in terms of their observed development impact (relevance and efficiency) (Picciotto, 1995b).

The process approach can be seen as a major step in the direction of participation, and the issue of whether, or to what extent, the logical framework can co-exist with participation was the topic of a 'ZOPP Marries PRA?' workshop called by GTZ in 1996. The chief spokesman for participation was Robert Chambers, and he and his PRA colleagues were pitted against the full might of GTZ (which was at that time in the process of revamping its ZOPP system). The question mark in the title proved to be very apposite. In fact, there was no unanimity that a marriage was possible, despite the goodwill towards it from both sides. It must to be said, however, that the GTZ/ZOPP side was more keen about this than the PRA side, whose spokesmen feared that it would introduce, 'a fixed, inflexible and often routine, relationship' (Forster, 1996). However, there was a good deal of common ground regarding the importance of the participatory approach, and GTZ has since taken a number of consequential measures externally to ensure that their stakeholders are given a voice, and internally to facilitate participation and to speed up the learning processes within the organisation. To quote the report on the workshop (written by a GTZ staff member), 'Thus the principles of participatory development ("sit down, listen, start where people are", "don't rush", etc) not only apply to our interaction with stakeholders in partner countries but would also shape the structure and corporate identity of our own organization' (Forster, 1996). So the marriage never took place, despite the attempts of the marriage brokers, and even today the PRA enthusiasts are deeply suspicious of what they see as top-down management systems.

Notes

1. Other terms for this are, 'confounding variables' (Pawson and Tilley, 1997), and 'extraneous confounding factors' (Rossi and Freeman, 1993).
2. The terms 'blueprint' and 'process approach' seem to be used mainly in relation to aid evaluation. Comparable terms used in other sectors are 'preordinate designs' and 'emergent designs' (Smith, 1998).

Techniques and Methods of Aid Evaluation

Part Two: Use of Cost-Benefit Analysis, Unintended Effects and Rating/Scoring Systems

'Count what is countable, measure what is measurable, And what is not measurable, make measurable'
(Galileo, 16th Century)

'What gets measured gets done'
(Old saying, quoted in Patton, 1997)

'If you can't measure it, you can't manage it'
(A New Zealand adage)

Use of Cost-Benefit Analysis Techniques in Evaluation

Although most of the standard terms of reference for evaluations stipulate that an attempt should be made to calculate the costs and benefits and the 'realised economic rate of return'[1] of a project, in actual practice this is often not done at all, or done only superficially. To quote one recent review of this topic: 'The knowledge we have on the economic impact of aid is at best ambiguous, or more commonly non-existent' (Carlsson et al. Kohlin and Ekbom, 1994). The main reason is probably that many aid projects have social objectives such as poverty alleviation or providing education; or objectives of a rather abstract kind, such as good governance, community empowerment or institutional building, none of which lend themselves readily to economic quantification. This, of course, is just as true for appraisals as it is for evaluations. Some attempts can and have been made, and examples in the technical cooperation sector are given in Chapter 15. But the problems are daunting and full cost-benefit analysis (CBA) is unlikely to ever be a dominant feature of most evaluations. Nevertheless more could be done than is currently being done, to systematically examine the economic impact of projects especially in the field of cost effectiveness (Parot, 1993).

Where the CBA approach comes into its own is with projects that have a readily quantifiable output. These are primarily manufacturing projects, where the product is sold, and public service industries, such as transport, water supplies, and electricity, where the output has a market price. It is usual for some attempt to be made to estimate the realised rate of return for such projects in evaluations, although often the concept of consumer surplus has to be introduced when it comes to evaluating service industries where the public tariff clearly fails to mirror the true cost or the real demand (e.g., often electricity and water tariffs are kept deliberately low as a result of government pressure).

Even for these projects, however, it is not often that the full apparatus of CBA, such as is used at the appraisal stage, is applied in the evaluation, including the use of border prices (Little and Mirrlees, 1974), and shadow wage rates for instance. Where these techniques have been used it is apparent that there are some difficult problems in applying them. It can be extremely time-consuming, as well as frustrating because of a basic lack of information, to try to obtain time series figures of border prices over a period of years, or to calculate shadow wage rates over the lifetime of a project. To quote Professor Paul Mosley, who has had more experience in this area than most, 'Estimates of the ex-post rate of return on projects frequently depend on guesstimates of a high order of magnitude. Most aid-financed development projects of which I have experience lack monitoring systems good enough to tell us accurately what increased outputs were caused by the project and what price they were sold at, let alone to give us useful measures of the shadow prices of inputs and outputs' (Mosley, 1986). During my 15 years in the evaluation field in the ODA, I was only aware of two evaluations where Little and Mirrlees' techniques were applied ex post with any real rigour. One of these was a minerals project in Jordan, and the reason why shadow pricing was used in the evaluation was that it soon became evident that no adequate economic assessment of the realised rate of return could be attempted without using a shadow wage rate for labour. The labour supply situation had changed dramatically over the lifetime of the project, from labour surplus at the beginning to labour shortage at the end (because of the growing demand from oil-rich states), and using a shadow wage rate had a dramatic effect on the realised economic rate of return. In the other evaluation, which involved a textile factory in Egypt, a conscientious attempt was made to calculate the ex-post economic rate of return, using Little and Mirlees' border pricing methods, but it was a very complicated and time-consuming operation. Because of these practical difficulties, evaluators may have tended to fall back on the argument that the economic rate of return is seldom likely to be the most critical component of an evaluation, and that those who sponsor the evaluations are now more interested in such aspects as the impact on target groups, impact on the environment, whether the technology was appropriate, and whether the project is likely to be sustainable (Renard and Berlage, 1990).

Even if the will is there, the problems of calculating an economic rate of return ex post will always be considerable. For instance, a key factor is the counterfactual (see Chapter 6), and clearly some attempt has to be made to assess this, but in the last analysis it can only be a matter of guesswork since nobody really knows what would have happened in the absence of the project. The concept of opportunity cost is of course basic to all economic analysis and it is the 'without project' situation that must concern the evaluator (for instance expenditures that had no value in an alternative use may be regarded as sunk costs). But the resources available are seldom sufficient to enable this approach to be adopted in any systematic fashion.

Another problem is that it will be necessary in many cases to make the same sort of forecasts, for working out the rate of return, as were required at the appraisal stage, since the economics of the project will depend on a long-range forecast of supply and demand. However, most evaluations are carried out only a few years after the project has been implemented so we never know how accurate the long-range forecasts were. To test this we would need to carry out some 're-evaluations' when the projects reach the end of their useful life. But by then things would have moved on and everyone would have forgotten the original circumstances. However, it might be desirable for a few 'termination of project' evaluations to be carried out, if only to check whether the evaluators are as prone to take an optimistic view of the future as appraisers do (see below). In the meantime, the results of evaluations carried out soon after project implementation should be treated with caution, and judgements about controversial projects should await the results of re-evaluations when the projects have reached the end of their economic life.

Regarding the problem of forecasting supply and demand, there is no reason to think that many of the assumptions that had to be made in the appraisal, such as people's future willingness to pay for goods and services, should be significantly more accurate at the evaluation stage than they were at the appraisal stage; while it is impossible really to test the quality of the forecasts made at appraisal because the circumstances will have changed. The economic analysis at the appraisal stage would have comprised some set of predictions, or a probability distribution of predictions, but how does one select an appropriate test ex post of ex ante probability assessments?

Important as these intellectual problems are, perhaps equally significant, in explaining why few economic calculations of realised rates of return are attempted by bilateral donors, is the fact that the volume of work involved in doing this kind of evaluation is daunting in the extreme. Generally speaking, far less money is devoted to evaluation than is spent on appraisal, and few evaluation units (except perhaps those of the development banks, where a typical project is much larger than is the case with most bilateral aid agencies) would be prepared to allocate the resources required for an in-depth ex-post cost-benefit analysis.

Even if, despite all the obstacles, the realised rate of return is calculated, and it turns out positive, it still does not follow that the project will necessarily benefit the country's macroeconomic development. Mosley has pointed out some reasons for this. Aid is 'fungible', that is, by supporting an economically worthwhile project that the recipient government would otherwise have had to finance, the donor is enabling the government to spend that money on other politically attractive, but possibly wasteful, projects. Sometimes the impact of aid tying may negate the assessed economic benefits. And third, the burdens and complications of aid administration may deter economic enterprise elsewhere, for example, by monopolising the energies and resources of ministries. (Mosley,

1986). In short, it may not be sufficient to look only at the economic rate of return for the project; one also has to look at the wider context.

In view of these difficulties, it is not surprising that when those arch exponents of the use of cost-benefit analysis, Little and Mirrlees, went back to the World Bank in 1990 to see, 'twenty years on', what had happened regarding how their ideas had been incorporated, they found that even in that august institution, which is so closely associated in people's minds with the conscientious application of economic analysis techniques, these had been 'diluted to the point of being virtually powerless as analytical tools' (Little and Mirrlees, 1990).

In a recent article, the director general, operations evaluation department, in the World Bank reported that only a third of the Bank's projects today are being justified on the basis of the cost-benefit analysis approach. The others are judged on the basis of a much wider set of criteria, including assessing projects as vehicles for policy reform and capacity building (Picciotto, 1995b). In a recent article in *Evaluation* entitled 'Towards an Economics of Evaluation', Picciotto discusses the steady decline in the use of economic criteria in evaluation work and comments: 'The decline of cost benefit analysis as a standard evaluation instrument emerges as a worrisome indicator of the gap which still divides evaluators from economists' (Picciotto, 1999). One can only agree with Picciotto that the pendulum has now swung too far against the use of economic methods in evaluation and it is time it began to swing back again.

The last word on this subject can perhaps be left to three Swedish researchers who carried out an exhaustive study of the role of cost-benefit analysis (CBA) in evaluation. They concluded that, 'the role of CBA can in some cases be useful, but its usefulness is generally overstated. The evaluation information provided by CBA is often subordinated to other criteria when decisions are taken on a project. However, if CBA is applied alongside other economic policy tools, the methodology can have a role to play' (Carlsson et al., 1994).

Use of Cost-Benefit Analysis by the Developing Countries

So far as the use of CBA in evaluations by the developing countries is concerned, the fact is that these techniques have not yet taken root, nor do they seem likely to, at least for a long time. This is partly because they are extremely complicated, and are not understood by the politicians and most decision-takers, and partly because they require complex data collection systems, and resources of skilled labour, that are simply not available. Some attempts have been made by donors to give training in CBA techniques for evaluation, but not on any sustained basis, and the results so far have been negligible.

Even more important than these practical problems is the fact that the typical public investment project has moved away from infrastructure and technologically oriented projects towards more socially oriented projects that do not lend themselves to CBA techniques. Qualitative indicators are now often seen as more appropriate. The more the donors, and recipients, move towards structural adjustment policies, social cost-benefit methods should become less necessary, in the sense that the most severe market distortions should gradually be ironed out, so that accounting prices and shadow wage rates do not make a great deal of difference. Furthermore the practice of channelling funds more directly to the private sector takes the pressure off the public sector authorities to use CBA methods (i.e., since it can reasonably be assumed that there will be competitive markets).

Evaluations as a Check on the Parameters Used at Appraisal

Where evaluation can be especially useful is in providing a check on the accuracy of some of the economic parameters used at appraisal. It is well known, for instance, that there is such a thing as 'appraisal optimism', that is, the unconscious (or indeed often conscious) bias that a project sponsor has in favour of believing in its success. Some authorities even habitually use a 2 per cent point premium on the test discount rate to allow for this factor. A review by the World Bank of their completed projects published in 1991 (World Bank, 1991) found that the realised rates of return were considerably lower than those estimated at appraisal, and it attributed this to a combination of overestimation of benefits, underestimation of project costs, and time overruns. There may be many small ways in which a project can go wrong, even after allowance has been made for the major ones that can be envisaged, but as these are so small they tend to be ignored even though cumulatively they can threaten the success of the project. Another kind of optimism bias that affects appraisals relates to the macroeconomic climate of the project: politicians are reluctant to accept realistic forecasts of economic growth, employment growth, etc, that may be at variance with the upbeat projections they are using. Then there is what Professor Sugden has called 'elasticity pessimism' (Sugden, 1987), that is, a prevailing tendency for economists to underestimate elasticities of supply and demand. Finally there is the optimism that springs from the pressure to disburse aid funds that exists in most aid agencies. The World Bank re-estimated the rates of return at completion for 1105 out of 2200 projects completed between 1974 and 1987, and they found that the mean estimated rate of return at appraisal had been 22 per cent while the mean re-estimated rate of return at completion was only 16 per cent (Pohl and Minaljek, 1994).

One of the key functions of evaluations is to provide some feedback on these aspects so that future appraisals are more realistic. They may also be able to suggest ways in which appraisal methodologies could be improved, in the light of hindsight. It is interesting to reflect, as mentioned earlier, that it was the economists in the ODA who were most enthusiastic about evaluation from the earliest days, and that one of the reasons for this was that they saw it as a means of checking some of the CBA techniques and parameters that were currently being promoted. This is still an important, if rather overlooked, function of evaluation work.

Unintended Effects

Experienced evaluators soon come to expect the unexpected, and often these prove to be among the most valuable of their findings—precisely because they were not foreseen. It is important that the terms of reference for evaluations are not drawn up so tightly that they do not leave much scope for the discovery of unintended effects. Scriven has warned that too much emphasis on goal achievement as the main criterion for evaluation could mean that unintended effects may be overlooked (Scriven, 1972, quoted in Patton, 1997). Often unintended effects may be peripheral to the main project, but crucially important for its success or failure. To quote just one example, the evaluation of ODA's involvement in a section of the East–West Highway through the Terai region of Nepal found that the construction of this road had adversely affected the liveli-hoods of thousands of head porters who travelled north–south between India and Nepal. This had not been adequately taken into account in the appraisal, but it represented an important negative component in the CBA (University of East Anglia, 1976). Often there are unintended nega-tive effects in such fields as environmental pollution or traffic conges-tion, while there can be windfall gains in such areas as technical skill spin-offs, or the stimulus given to innovations and new techniques as a result of capital investments. As mentioned earlier, one of the weak-nesses of the logical framework approach to project planning is that the matrix focuses exclusively on project objectives. Because it can never be an objective to harm anyone there is always a risk that by-product adverse effects may be omitted from the matrix. Even desirable side effects may also be omitted if they are incidental to the project purpose. DFID's instructions on completing the logical framework draw attention to these possibilities, and they emphasise that anticipated disbenefits need to be incorporated into the matrix in the same way as intended benefits. Wiggins and Shields have commented, 'The classical Logical Framework, with its Objectively Verifiable Indicators column, stresses verification (rather than falsification): it checks only that what is ex-pected to happen is happening, and ignores any unwelcome evidence of unexpected processes and events which threaten the underpinning of the project. This is a distinct weakness of the tool' (Wiggins and Shields, 1995).

An unfortunate disbenefit which is often a consequence of aid funded projects (and which tends to be overlooked in evaluations), is the ten-dency for the aid to go to medium and large enterprises (because they are in a better position to utilise it quickly), leading to the crowding out of the smaller enterprises, and putting them in an unfavourable position. Some-times the large enterprises are multinational in character and may not necessarily be working in the best interests of the recipient country.

Sometimes unintended effects are so all-embracing in their impact that they are very difficult for the evaluator to deal with. For example, Stephan Musto in his critique of Germany's evaluation policy and perfor-mance has drawn attention to what he calls an 'unresolved problem of aid', namely the fact that development aid may stifle initiatives for find-ing one's own solutions, create disincentives, and foster unjustified expectations. He comments, 'Awareness of being responsible for solving a given problem breeds motivation and often creativity. Awareness that others can be called to account for one's own problems allows motivation and initiative to perish' (Musto, 1988). It is difficult to cope with such negative effects in project evaluations because they are almost inseparable from the aid/recipient relationship itself, but the evaluator surely cannot just ignore them, and if it is found that local initiatives are being discouraged, they should be mentioned in the report.

Rating and Scoring Systems

Most aid agencies have now developed systems of rating the relative success or failure of completed projects. These are needed not only for accountability purposes but also for lesson-learning: i.e. one can cross-analyse projects classified according to their success rating, by size, type, location, sector, etc, and hopefully learn something about the reasons for success or failure.

A typical rating scheme is that used by DFID, whereby projects monitored and evaluated are classified according to whether they are deemed to have been 'highly successful' (rated A +), where *objectives were achieved completely (or exceeded targets)* with very significant overall benefits in relation to costs; 'successful' (rated A), where *objectives were largely achieved* with significant overall benefits in relation to costs; 'partially successful' (rated B), where *some objectives were achieved* with some significant overall benefits in relation to costs; 'largely unsuccessful' (rated C), where there was *very limited achievement of objectives* with few significant benefits in relation to costs; or 'unsuccessful' (rated D), where *objectives were unrealised* with no significant benefits in relation to costs and the project was abandoned.

These overall project ratings are the end product of a process of rating various performance objectives which fall into two categories. The first relates to the project's contribution to the achievement of DFID's priority objectives. The second relates to the project's contribution to the achievement of other performance objectives. Some of these objectives, like environmental impact, may not be relevant to the project being assessed, and no rating is appropriate, in which case the symbol '-' is used (see Figure 7.1). As to the rest, the degree of relevance can vary: if it is thought to be highly relevant it is classified as 'Principal', and if it is less relevant but still significant it is classified as 'Significant'. Where no specific objective was established at appraisal the assessment is shown in brackets. Each performance criterion is then awarded a rating based on the underlined sections of the five-point scale given earlier. DFID is currently reviewing this format, but the new version was not available at the time of writing. Figure 7.1 shows how this rating system worked in relation to an evaluation of a project in northern India.

Figure 7.1 Example Showing how DFID's Rating System Works
(The markings relate to an evaluation of a contraceptive social marketing
project in northern India)

(A dash indicates that the criterion was non-applicable)

Project Performance Criteria	Relative Importance	Success Rating
DFID's Priority Objectives:		
Economic Liberalisation	–	–
Enhancing Productive Capacity	–	–
Good Governance	–	–
Poverty Impact	–	–
Human Resources: Education	–	–
Human Resources: Health	–	–
Human Resources: Children by Choice	Principal	B
Environmental Impact	–	–
Impact upon Women	(Significant)	C
DFID's Other Objectives:		
Social Impact	Significant	C
Institutional Impact	Significant	B
Technical Success	Significant	C
Time Management within Schedule	–	–
Cost Management within Budget	(Significant)	A
Adherence to Project Conditions	–	–
Cost-Effectiveness	(Significant)	A
Financial Rate of Return	–	–
Economic Rate of Return	–	–
Financial Sustainability	(Significant)	C
Institutional Sustainability	(Significant)	B
Overall Sustainability	(Significant)	C
OVERALL SUCCESS RATING		B
Source: Crapper et al., (1997).		

These ratings are of course subjective, and there is also the problem that at project completion, or even some years later at ex post evaluation, it is still too early to make a final judgement. Nevertheless such a rating system can give advance warning of projects that look as though they may be running into problems, and which may well be candidates for eventual evaluation.

In 1990 the ODA carried out a synthesis review of its ratings over the previous decade (a four-point scale was then being used), and the results are given in Figure 7.2.

Figure 7.2   Ratings of ODA Projects/Programmes Evaluated During 1980–89

	Number	% of Total Number	% of Total Value
Highly Successful	3	3.8	4.4
Successful	40	50.6	51.8
Partially Successful	23	29.1	31.0
Unsuccessful	13	16.5	12.8
Total	79	100.0	100.0

Source: Higginbottom (1990).

It should be borne in mind that the selection of projects was not random, and the sample size was relatively small. Moreover, this analysis in itself, useful as it may be for accountability purposes, does not add much to the existing stock of knowledge regarding the factors influencing success or failure—this only emerges from any subsequent cross-classifications that may be carried out.

The aggregation of success ratings to arrive at the overall success rating in the ODA system is done purely subjectively. However, some rating systems use the various performance criteria ratings as weights, and they then combine the weights to produce a weighted average as the overall success rate. Thus various criteria of project performance are given a score say in the range 1–10. The resultant scores are then added together, and an overall score obtained (Wheatley et al., 1985). The rating system currently being used by the African Development Bank is of this type. A number of criteria of performance are identified, namely, the achievement of goals, objectives and outputs; sustainability of benefits; implementation at least, or forecast, cost; and implementation within planned deadlines and envisaged internal rates of return. A system of weighted marking is then followed and projects with 80 per cent or more are classified as 'satisfactory', those with 40 to 79 per cent are classified as 'partially satisfactory', and those below 40 per cent are classified as 'unsatisfactory'. The results for all the 116 projects or programmes evaluated between 1987 and 1993 show that 24 per cent were satisfactory, 62 per cent were partially satisfactory, and the remaining 14 per cent were unsatisfactory (ORU/DGIS/ODA, 1996).

Of course, the obvious problem, as mentioned earlier, is the subjectivity of the person doing the scoring. An attempt is sometimes made to cope with this problem by inviting other independent evaluators to allocate scores and then to compare them (Jennings, 1990).

Rating systems are sometimes used for accountability purposes (see for instance their use in the UNIFEM Knowledge Bank, Chapter 12), where the emphasis is on the overall success rating, but because of the subjectivity objection they are now more frequently used mainly as a way of researching the likely causes of project success or failure. The World Bank applies a scoring system to all the 200 or so evaluations it carries out annually. Five areas of project performance are identified: (*a*) economic impact (*b*) sustainability (*c*) impact on institutional development (*d*) financial performance of the Bank, and (*e*) financial performance of the borrower. There is also a four-level scoring system similar to that used by DFID. The scores are given by the project managers (i.e., this is a form of self evaluation) but nearly half are also independently scored by the Operations Evaluation Department as a check (Toulemonde et al., 1998).

The DAC Expert Group on Aid Evaluation has carried out a joint study of success rating systems. The first phase was an inventory of the various systems now in use (ORU/DGIS/ODA, 1996), and the second phase is an attempt to identify the core elements of such systems. The review of the first phase concluded that rating systems are generally considered to be worthwhile. The extra workload on staff was minimal, and compliance was easily obtained. The main reservations related to such aspects as the definition of criteria, or of rating scales, rather than to the use made of the ratings. Most systems are being refined and improved, and are becoming ever more complex. Some rating systems are integrated into day-to-day management practice and are being used routinely in decision-making. Visual evidence of this kind of feedback motivates the staff to make the systems work. As a result of the increasing emphasis on accountability, rating systems now have to serve various purposes for different users, as Figure 7.3 illustrates.

The DAC study found that some agencies were reluctant to introduce rating systems for fear that the results, if published, might adversely affect them, but agencies that had been using these systems for a number of years had not found this to be a problem. However, all agencies seemed

Figure 7.3 Rating Systems Serve Different Purposes at Different Management Levels

	Supervision	*Completion Reporting*	*Evaluation*
Supervisors/ Evaluators	Helps to formulate a well structured and comprehensive judgement on progress and short-term results	Helps to formulate a well structured and comprehensive judgement on achievements	Helps to formulate a well structured and comprehensive judgement on achievements, effectiveness, efficiency and sustainability
Middle Management	Provides an overview of the current status of the portfolio; signals problems during implementation; focuses management attention	Summarises achievements; permits learning of direct lessons	Helps to analyse the lessons learned from one or several projects; makes the results easily accessible; permits learning of more complex lessons for direct use in other projects
Senior Management	Signals problems during implementation; focuses management attention; input for on-going accountability reporting	Summarises achievements; permits learning of direct lessons; input for on-going accountability reporting	Helps to analyse the lessons learned from a number of projects; permits learning of strategic lessons as input in policy formulation

Source: ORU/DGIS/ODA (1996).

to be reluctant to involve the beneficiaries in rating systems in case this were to introduce an element of 'negotiation', a warning perhaps of the potential problems of pushing the participatory approach too hard.

Need for Credibility

Many different techniques of evaluation have been discussed in this chapter, but the key requirement, above all, is that the evaluators should establish their credibility in the eyes of the potential users. This means being transparent and honest about the methods used, and the extent to which they can be relied upon to give a true and accurate picture of the situation. A degree of self-criticism, that is, a willingness to discuss any weaknesses in the methods, or any unreliability in the results, may be a necessary part of establishing credibility. All too often, when evaluation findings are unpalatable to the decision-takers, they take refuge in criticising the methodology used. It is important to foresee this happening and to take steps to justify the methods used. Of course credibility in terms of methods is only half the equation: the other half is credibility in the way the results are presented. But that is the stuff of feedback which is discussed in Chapters 10, 11 and 12.

Cost-Effectiveness of Methodology

Some of the experimental and quasi-experimental methods of evaluation, using controls and requiring extensive field surveys, involve considerable expenditure and tie up scarce resources. It is therefore important to bear in mind, when choosing a methodology, the need to ensure that it is cost-effective. Here is an area where the best can easily become the enemy of the good. Similarly, despite the general consensus in favour of participatory methods, there is not much evidence on the cost-effectiveness of the various participatory methods now being used, although a recent study by the DAC Expert Group on Aid Evaluation did find evidence that the benefits of using participatory methods outweigh the costs (OECD, 1997a). An ODA synthesis study of NGO evaluations found that many NGOs were so firmly wedded to the concept of participatory methods that they were using them in a totally uncritical way and without any regard to their appropriateness or cost in relation to the benefits (Surr, 1995). More research is needed on these aspects before one method can be said to be generally more appropriate than another. It is not just a matter of cost-effectiveness—one also has to consider the potential benefit to be gained from the evaluation: it is worthwhile only if the benefit is likely to exceed the cost. Generally it is necessary to be selective. You cannot evaluate everything. In the Inter American Development Bank the philosophy is that, 'It is more important to report on 60% of the information necessary for decision making, than to try to report on everything possible at the cost of much time and resources' (Quesnel, 1995).

Triangulation

The term 'triangulation' is used by evaluators to represent the use of several different approaches at the same time when carrying out evaluation studies, for example, qualitative methods, quantitative analysis, cost-benefit analysis, etc. Despite the appearance of confusion that may sometimes result from this multiplicity of methods, evaluators see a positive merit in it. If one technique fails to hit the target, another may succeed. The targets are very different in kind, ranging from the impact on the macro economy, to the impact on an individual farm household, and no single technique is likely to work at all levels equally satisfactorily. Moreover different techniques complement each other. Thus statistical techniques have the advantage of yielding 'hard' quantified data, whereas participatory methods yield 'soft' data that may well get closer to the heart of the problem, even though it may be very difficult to aggregate. In the past a lot of energy was expended in trying to prove that one methodology was superior to another, but now the tendency is to welcome any approach that seems best fitted to address the problem. Maybe in time a consensus will develop as to the best methods for particular circumstances, but for the time being the main emphasis is on exploring all possible methods.

Notes

1. This is the DAC term. The World Bank refers to it as the 're-estimated economic rate of return'.
2. The DAC Expert Group on Aid Evaluation studied the available literature on the cost-effectiveness of participatory methods (OECD, 1997a), and found that, 'The costs, in terms of time and money spent, tend to be relatively higher for participatory projects in their early phases, but they pay off in terms of greater effectiveness and sustainability in later phases'. They carried out a statistical analysis of 121 rural water supply projects in Asia, Africa and Latin America which showed that beneficiary participation was the single most important factor in determining the overall quality of implementation.

Part 3

Monitoring, Learning and Feedback

Eleanor Chelimsky, in her memorable address to the Inaugural Conference of the European Evaluation Society at The Hague, December, 1994

('Where We Stand Today in the Practice of Evaluation: Some Reflections')

Perhaps evaluation's greatest accomplishment today is that it can no longer be said—as it used to be said in 1980—that our work is not used in policy making. On the contrary, credible evaluations are today conducted on a regular basis, their findings ARE typically incorporated into policy, and they're being done more and more as part of routine organizational practice. So as evaluation spreads internationally, and as political support for it develops, it may be that we will at last get the chance to see evaluation do what it was intended to do: help make institutions more effective, more responsive, more trusted, more accountable, and even—who knows?— better managed.

-- **8** --

The Links Between Monitoring and Evaluation

'Men must know that in this theatre of man's life, it is reserved only for God and angels to be lookers on'

(The Advancement of Learning, *Francis Bacon*)

'With a clear distinction being drawn between monitoring and evaluation, it has not proved useful, in describing the precise components involved in these functions, to use a phrase that embraces components of both. We have preferred therefore to label each component individually'

(Project Monitoring and Evaluation in Agriculture, *Casley and Kumar*)

'It is costly wisdom that is bought by experience'

(Robert Ascham)

There has always been a close link between monitoring and evaluation—at times too close for comfort, as will be shown later. In the nature of things it is inevitable that these two activities will be closely related, but just what the nature of that relationship should be (just friends, or cousins, brothers, or even Siamese twins?) is an issue which has been hotly debated over the years—and still is! This chapter assesses the crucial importance of monitoring as an important stage in the project cycle, and as a key source of data for evaluation, while at the same time emphasising that the two functions fulfil different purposes and cannot be treated almost as if they were synonymous.

The Role of Monitoring in Project Cycle Management

Partly as a result of the pressure from evaluators (who early on realised that more effective monitoring could prevent projects from ending up as failures), monitoring has become more and more important as part of project cycle management. Monitoring fulfils a function different from evaluation. It should normally be carried out by the staff responsible for the implementation of the project. Its main purpose is to enable project management to keep careful track of what is happening, and especially to check that progress is being made towards the achievement of the objectives. It differs from evaluation, which is carried out by staff from outside the project for the purpose of learning lessons primarily for application to any future projects of a similar kind (or of course for accountability). Figure 8.1 shows how monitoring can take place throughout the life of the project. Monitoring is needed even when the project has reached full development, and the donor has left (this is referred to as 'sustainability monitoring').

It is common these days for monitoring to be built into project planning in an integral way, with the necessary funds being allocated from the overall project budget, and with at least an outline plan from the outset of how the monitoring will be carried out, that is, by whom, how often, and using what kind of methodology. Usually the donor takes the lead in organising monitoring missions going out from the donor country. But if the donor has a field office in the country where the project is located the monitoring is more likely to be carried out from there. With large projects it is customary to make special provision for on-going monitoring to take place, usually as a joint operation with the beneficiary organisation (e.g., the monitoring of ODA's multi-annual Fertiliser Supply Project in India). Where special expertise is needed, the monitoring may be carried out, on behalf of the aid agency, by development research institutions (located in the donor country, in the beneficiary country, or jointly). Often standardised guidelines are developed, although these need to be adapted for each project. As described later, the logical framework provides a vital input into the drawing up of terms of reference for monitoring exercises.

Before the introduction of the logical framework, the techniques used for monitoring were somewhat rudimentary. Often they comprised merely

Figure 8.1 Cognitive Model of Monitoring and Evaluation

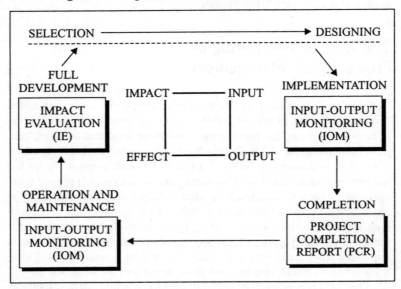

Source: ADB (1995).

a simple bar chart (sometimes called a Gantt chart or Implementation chart), which mapped the expected progress of the progress (in terms of time and money) and the out-turn. Sometimes a Network chart was also prepared, mapping the critical path analysis, and highlighting which activities had to be completed before subsequent ones could be undertaken. These were supplemented by regular monitoring reports which focused on activities completed. Conspicuous by its absence was any reference to whether the objectives of the project were being achieved or whether it seemed likely that they would be. Switching the focus of monitoring from the tracking of physical inputs and outputs, to the assessment of progress towards the achievement of objectives, has been one of the main achievements of the logical framework.

Distinction Between Monitoring and Evaluation

Monitoring should primarily serve the needs of the immediate project management, and only secondarily the needs of senior management at the headquarters or the needs of statistical data collection. Unfortunately, this has often not been the case in the past, mainly because monitoring was promoted by the donor agencies as a means of keeping a watch on what was happening to 'their' projects. So monitoring largely comprised data collection (often involving periods of several years, e.g., in collecting data on crop yields) with very little relationship to the on-going needs of management. Even when the reports were eventually made available to management they were often couched in technical language that was largely unintelligible to the layman. Inevitably monitoring came to be seen as a donor device to ensure some measure of accountability, and even to act as a check on what local management was doing. It is hardly surprising that local managers resented this intrusion, and found monitoring not only unhelpful in their day-to-day task of management, but frequently a constant irritant and a source of confusion and management weakness, since they had little control over the monitoring staff who felt that they were primarily responsible to the aid agency headquarters.

This unhappy situation was made even worse by the virtually universal practice of combining monitoring with evaluation in one organisation—the 'Monitoring and Evaluation Unit' (M & E Unit), almost as if the two functions were synonymous. It was the World Bank which was mainly responsible for the creation of these units in many developing countries during the 1970s and early 1980s: in fact, establishing an M & E Unit was often made a condition of World Bank funding. I recall visiting a major World Bank development project in Malawi where masses of data relating to crop yields had been collected over a period of years (at considerable cost), and had been computerised, but no-one was available to analyse the results. So, this data had had no effect on the management of the project. Backlogs in analysing the results of over-ambitious data collection exercises commonly meant that it was several years before the results were made available to managers, by which time they were of little practical use (Maddock, 1993). Eventually the World Bank realised that this 'M & E Unit' policy had been a mistake and it took steps to rectify the situation. An important World Bank report published in 1986 (Casley and Kumar, 1986) stressed that monitoring and evaluation were different functions and should be kept separate if possible: 'Are monitoring and evaluation such distinctly different functions, serving distinctly different users, that they should be considered independently of each other? The answer is Yes. Hence we disapprove of the universal acronym "M and E". Monitoring and evaluation are separated by their objectives, reference periods, requirements for comparative analysis, and primary users'.[1]

As stated already, monitoring should be linked directly to management on a day-to-day, or at any rate week-to-week basis, and management should have direct control of the monitoring function, which it should be able to depend upon as a provider of key information for management. A problem arises, however, where a project has local management assisted by managers and experts supplied by the donor agency. Here the lines of authority tend to become confused, as indeed does the role of monitoring. The fact that the monitoring process is still often set in motion by the donor agency implies that it may continue to have a 'checking' function, rather than being seen primarily as a small team of people available to serve the on-going needs of management—the management's right arm as it were. If the project management feels that certain components of the project are running into problems it should be able to use the monitoring team as trouble-shooters, carrying out highly focused, very short term, investigations, feeding in the results in time for management to make effective use of them.[2] Wherever possible maximum use should be made of qualitative, rather than quantitative, methods of collecting information, because these can be carried out quickly, and can home in on the sort of issues that are important to management, such as people's attitudes, and reactions to specific interventions. Often this kind of 'short feed-back loop' monitoring may not be compatible with the more routine, project-wide, flow of information that the donor agency is seeking, but if there is a conflict the former should prevail. After all, the donor's primary concern is that the project is a success, and that is more likely to be the case if management is the recipient of a constant flow of decision-oriented information. This should always be the primary task of monitoring.

Despite the now widespread recognition of the fact that monitoring and evaluation are different functions, one still frequently finds Monitoring and Evaluation Units in both developing and developed countries, and often the two terms are still treated as if they were virtually synonymous. One reason for this may be that in practice the two operations are carried out in similar ways and call for similar skills: they both make use of surveys, interviews, questionnaires, reports, etc. Monitoring and Evaluation Units still tend to be found in large projects or programmes because in such circumstances there is in any case a need for a substantial monitoring unit which is likely to become somewhat distanced from on-going management simply because of the sheer size of the project or programme, and it may therefore seem logical to locate the evaluation function there as well.

In recent years, the pendulum has tended to swing back towards a close link between the two functions, mainly because of the need to monitor the impact on project beneficiaries as a vital input to subsequent evaluation. Some people regard the attempt to keep the two functions separate as a mistake because it would impede their continued development, and because they see monitoring as contributing vital data inputs for evaluation (Cameron, 1993). But the more general view is still that they are best seen as fulfilling different, if complementary, functions.

Use of the Logical Framework in Monitoring

The effectiveness of the logical framework as a monitoring tool depends mainly on how well the indicators have been drawn up, and especially whether they accurately reflect the real objectives of the project, or just the activities being undertaken (i.e., inputs and outputs) as so often happens. There are many cases of the latter. For instance, the World Bank Staff Appraisal Report on an environmental project in Madagascar contained 12 pages of what were called 'major objectives', with literally hundreds of key indicators. But on examination only two of them were actually measures of the achievement of the objectives (which were 'to protect the area considered', and 'to promote eco-tourism'): the rest were all linked to project activities, inputs and outputs (Carlsson et al., 1994).

The traffic should of course be two-way. Monitoring is also vital for the success of the logical framework as a system of project cycle management. If the framework is not used in a dynamic way it will either be ineffective in management, or may become an obstacle. It is the flow-back of results from monitoring that provides the occasion for a formal review of the matrix, and if necessary a revised matrix should be constructed to meet the changing circumstances. The importance of keeping the logical framework up to date in this dynamic way (rather than it being merely a static tool for use at appraisal) may seem self-evident, but in practice it is often overlooked. In the case of process approach projects, this can be particularly unfortunate; yet as Kumar has pointed out, 'once a measurement system is established and indicators are selected, the system tends to take on a life of its own, irrespective of the changing direction of the programme' (Kumar, 1995). If the logical framework is to play its proper role in monitoring and evaluation, the risk of this happening must be guarded against as vigorously as possible.

The usefulness of the logical framework for monitoring is greatly enhanced if it is computerised and incorporated into the agency's on-going management information system. The main requirement is for the key data from the logical framework to be carried forward automatically to the project monitoring form and ultimately (together with the latter) to the Project Completion Report (PCR). Not only does this save having to copy the details again and again, but it also ensures consistency in that the same criteria used in the initial logical framework are also used subsequently throughout the project cycle. The way these information flows are organised will be taken up more fully in Chapter 12, but for the moment it is sufficient to say that quite a number of aid agencies (including the DFID) have adopted the logical framework software (called 'Team-up'), developed by an American firm called Team Technologies.[3] Not only does this enable the matrix to be made an integral part of the corporate memory, but it makes the drawing up of a sequence of trial matrices very easy (compared with the laborious task of typing them out), which encourages a flexible and dynamic use of the matrix as recommended earlier (Team Technologies Inc., 1990).

Usefulness of Monitoring to the Donor

In 1987 the Overseas Development Administration carried out an evaluation of its monitoring system (Scott et al., 1987). It concluded that the monitoring of aid delivery aspects was being effectively carried out (i.e., the ways in which aid funds were being disbursed and the provision of inputs and outputs), but that the monitoring of progress towards the achievement of project objectives needed to be much improved. Nor was the monitoring system giving adequate warning of projects that were ceasing to be viable. The evaluation also found that the monitoring system was not sufficiently dovetailed into the logical framework system of project cycle management. This finding led to a major review of the situation. A decision was taken to computerise the logical framework matrices and to link the monitoring process systematically to this computerised system (Vernon, 1992). For this purpose, the desk officer responsible for monitoring is now able to bring onto the computer screen the logical framework matrix and he/she can then incorporate the results of each monitoring mission, especially noting against each objective whether the progress is satisfactory or not, and the reasons for any problems that appear to be emerging. A decision was also taken to introduce the 'A to D' rating system, measuring the extent to which the project objectives were being achieved, as already described in Chapter 7.

Reference was made in Chapter 7 to the lack of attention in general to the cost-effectiveness of the various evaluation methodologies. This applies in particular to monitoring and evaluation systems (M & E). Maddock has been able to collect some information on this aspect. He writes, 'The cost of M & E for agricultural and rural development projects is generally between 2% and 3% of project base costs, although some intensive M & E operations can cost as much as 5% of base costs' (Maddock, 1993). He points out that it will always be very difficult to work out whether the benefits from monitoring and evaluation justify the costs, since it is well nigh impossible to assess what improvements in management (and therefore project outcomes) can be attributed to the feedback from M & E. However, he comments, 'The widespread acceptance and introduction of monitoring and evaluation suggests a perception that the returns from these activities exceed their costs' (Maddock, 1993).

Role of Project Completion Reports

Project completion reports (PCRs) are prepared when the donor's involvement in the project comes to an end. They therefore represent the end-stage of monitoring. Often of course this is when the project itself begins to operate (although in some cases the project will have come into operation, at least partially, before final completion), so it is often impossible for a PCR to give any indication of the impact of the project, or of its ultimate success or failure. However, even at this early stage there should be some signs of whether the project is likely to run into trouble or not, and some donors now insist that those preparing PCRs should be prepared to chance their arm and give at least some indication of whether they think the project will be sustainable or not.

Project completion reports should be prepared by the staff who were most closely associated with the project during its implementation. Donor agencies such as the World Bank sometimes commission outside consultants to prepare PCRs, but this is not a good practice. Outside consultants, because of their lack of involvement in the implementation process, tend to produce reports which are long on facts but short on useful comments regarding the lessons learnt during implementation. Such PCRs are mainly aimed at the accountability objective rather than the lesson-learning objective. However, project staff are usually under great pressure, and do not have the time to write lengthy PCRs. So it is essential to keep the reports as pithy and to-the-point as possible. Ideally they should focus simply on what went wrong, and why, and what went well, and why; but inevitably they also have to include a certain amount of factual information for reasons of accountability. The trick is to keep the latter to a minimum so that the former does not get squeezed out.

The Overseas Development Administration carried out an evaluation of PCRs in 1994 (Dyer and Bartholomew, 1994). This showed, on the positive side, that good monitoring of projects had had a major influence in identifying problems at an early stage. It also showed that where there had been good participation by recipients in design, appraisal and implementation, the projects had benefited greatly. On the negative side, the report reinforced the lessons on the positive side, namely that where inadequate attempts had been made to ensure recipient participation in and 'ownership' of the projects, they had tended to run into serious problems. In particular the report highlighted the need for more careful consultation with beneficiaries at the design stage, and for objectives and targets to be assessed more realistically. An earlier synthesis of PCRs, carried out by the ODA in 1990 (Higginbottom and Henderson, 1990), had revealed the disturbing finding that many of the staff who had completed PCRs did not regard them as being very important. They felt that the senior staff of the Ministry took little notice of them, and so the time spent in preparing them was largely wasted. The PCR format was revised in 1991, in the light of the comments received in that evaluation report, and it seems that the staff are now satisfied that the PCRs are useful. There have been fewer adverse comments, and a higher completion rate of PCRs since 1991. The 1994 report shows that PCRs were completed for 85 per cent of those projects for which they were due, and they covered about 90 per cent of total project expenditure.

In the light of its experience with the PCRs to date, and also of the 1994 evaluation, ODA produced a fresh version of the PCR format in September 1995. This contains a revised rating system. For instance, the respondent has to indicate whether the project outputs were: completely realised, largely realised, partially realised, or whether there was only very limited realisation of outputs, or whether outputs were completely unrealised and the project abandoned. Then the respondent is asked to rate, on a scale of 1 to 5, the activities undertaken during the implementation phase, according to various criteria (i.e., whether it was appropriate?, sufficient?, timely?, well co-ordinated?, or efficiently procured and delivered?). There is a section on the conditions attached to the financing, and the respondent has to complete various ratings to assess whether the conditions were met, and whether compliance (or not) had any significant effect on project success. Turning to the likelihood of the project's objectives being realised in the future, the respondent is asked to rate on a scale of 1 to 6 whether the immediate objectives, and the wider objectives, are likely to be achieved. The form also asks some important questions regarding likely future sustainability of the project. What is probably the most important part of the form is also the simplest—it merely asks what the main lessons to be learned from the implementation phase are, first the negative ones, and then the positive ones. Finally, the respondent is asked to indicate whether the project is suitable for further evaluation, and if so on what grounds.

The Project Completion Report as a Form of Self-Evaluation

The PCR is in effect a form of self-evaluation, and in some development agencies, such as the Commonwealth Secretariat, which have a large number of small projects, the PCR is the corner stone of their evaluation system. In such agencies evaluations can be carried out for only a small proportion of their projects and the PCRs therefore represent the main source of data for evaluation (CFTC, 1985), as well as being a valuable tool for programme managers. Unfortunately, the PCR format originally used by the Commonwealth Secretariat proved to be far too complicated and time-consuming with the result that not many were completed. The Secretariat asked me to review the situation in 1995, and it soon became clear to me that there were two main problems, namely, the PCR format was too all-embracing and took too long to complete, and there was a perception among the staff that the results had little impact on the Secretariat's performance. I recommended a drastically streamlined format and this has led to a substantial increase in the number of PCRs completed each year. Moreover, the Strategic Planning and Evaluation Unit of the Secretariat now widely distributes the results of its annual review of PCRs and the staff clearly appreciate this kind of feedback.

A clear lesson from evaluations of PCRs is that they should be used to improve future performance, and not simply filed away unread and unused. Generally this means that the evaluation unit will need to synthesise the lessons from PCRs so that they become available to senior management, and to all departments in the office. The great merit of the PCRs, compared with evaluations, is that they relate to events that are happening now rather than events that took place some years ago. Their weakness, from the lesson-learning point of view, is that they tend to be oriented towards aid-delivery lessons rather than impact (for obvious reasons), but aid-delivery lessons are not so valuable because most of them will have been picked up already through the on-going process of monitoring. On the other hand, PCRs are now coming to be seen as a vital input into the evaluation process, and evaluation units are only now getting round to exploring ways of utilising them more efficiently for this purpose.

It is indicative of the new approach to PCRs that the World Bank has recently abandoned its PCR format and has introduced a new 'Implementation Completion Report' (ICR). The ICR focuses more on the transition from the end-phase of aid delivery to the efficient operation of the project. Thus it stresses the extent to which the objectives have been achieved, and what the borrowers are doing to enhance the chances of a successful transition, especially vis-à-vis future sustainability (Choksi, 1995). Quite often these ICRs are prepared by the staff of the recipient institutions themselves.

The European Commission's Experience with Monitoring Systems

The Department for International Development's latest computerised monitoring/rating system represents a form of 'early warning system'. But the European Commission (DG VIII) carried this idea even further in the 1980s with its experimental 'traffic lights' system (EEC, 1988). This required the desk officer at regular intervals (once a year) to indicate, against each component of the logical framework matrix, whether progress was going according to plan (green) or whether there were problems which were: minor (amber) or serious (red) (See Box 8.1). It is noteworthy that under this system the desk officer had to indicate the situation, in terms of these 'traffic lights', for each of the seven factors of sustainability (see Chapter 14), and this was an advance on the early warning systems used by other donors at that time.

Box 8.1 An Experiment with an Early Warning
('Traffic Lights') System

In 1989, DG VIII of the European Commission introduced, on a trial basis, a new early warning system in an attempt to ensure that remedial action is taken as soon as it becomes apparent that a project is running into serious difficulties (or it may even have to be aborted). The system relied on the regular monitoring of projects within DG VIII. Previously monitoring had been related mainly to the physical achievement of project targets, and it seldom focused on difficulties until it was too late to do anything. The new system called for the officers reporting progress on projects to indicate whether the project was making good progress (green); having problems, but these problems were not too serious and were being dealt with (yellow); or having problems that were so serious that they needed urgent action, or even termination of the project (red). The assessment was made not only for the project overall but also for each of the seven categories of sustainability discussed in Chapter 14. Thus a project might be showing satisfactory progress overall, while the situation vis-à-vis the role of women in the project, for instance, might be unsatisfactory. The EC delegate was required to comment, and to say what action he was proposing to take, if in fact any was required.
The three key categories were as follows:

The project has grave viability problems and is in danger of failing.
Action is required to save, re-orientate or terminate the project: **RED**

The project has serious viability problems that can be overcome, but
assistance or corrective action is required: **YELLOW**

Project progress towards viability is satisfactory: **GREEN**

Sadly the system proved to be too burdensome and it was eventually replaced by another one that was far less time-consuming. However, it represented a brave attempt to give more bite to the routine process of monitoring and to gear it more closely to the logical framework and to sustainability.

Under the Commission's system, if a project as a whole was classified as 'red' it was up to the senior staff in Brussels to take some quick action. They were to either set in motion remedial measures, or, if nothing could be done to save the project, to abort it as quickly as possible, rather than letting it drag on. In the past it quite often happened that projects that were clearly going off the rails continued to be funded simply because of inertia, and because no-one had the specific responsibility for highlighting the fact that things were going wrong and that some action should be taken. Aborting a failing project is never easy (politically it can be a nightmare), but at least this early warning system puts a clear responsibility on those receiving the reports to take appropriate action. Unfortunately, the end of the tale is a sad one. The system proved to be too burdensome, and only a small proportion of monitoring forms were completed, so it had to be abandoned. In its place the Commission (DG VIII) has now introduced a project monitoring system which is rather similar to the British one. Under 16 specific headings the staff member completing the form has to indicate whether the project's performance to date has been 'poor', 'average-to-poor', 'average-to-good', or 'good', according to the following guidelines:

- Poor performance: The project has serious problems and is likely to fail.
- Average-to-poor performance: The project has serious problems which require corrective actions and/or assistance.
- Average-to-good performance: The project has problems which can be controlled by undertaking internal corrective actions.
- Good performance: The project is viable and is progressing satisfactorily.

Of special interest is the requirement to report progress regarding: 'the level of coverage of beneficiaries' needs', and 'the degree of achievement of the project purpose'. The fact that the latter comes under the heading 'beneficiaries' suggests that the emphasis is on whether the project is achieving the benefits intended for target groups. These are both very important aspects in any monitoring system, and it is good to see that the European Commission has given them this degree of importance.

Also noteworthy is the emphasis on the factors of sustainability. Sustainability refers to what happens after project completion, but at this stage the project still has not been completed. Yet it is by no means too early to start taking steps to ensure that the conditions are in place, so far as possible, to ensure that the project will survive when the aid stops. The overall appreciation of the project's performance is very useful in enabling the problem projects to be separated from the others. Such an exhaustive system of monitoring should go far to ensure that the failing projects are spotted early on, and remedial action is taken.

New Approaches to
Participatory Impact Monitoring

The distinction between monitoring and evaluation is more difficult to sustain in the case of people-centred projects, like rural development, than with most other projects, because the data requirements are almost identical. Experience has shown that one cannot wait until these projects are 'completed' before collecting information for evaluation. In fact, such projects are seldom 'completed' in the sense that a bridge is built or a power line installed—they tend to run on without any obvious end date. The information needed for the eventual evaluation has to be collected on a continuous basis as the project evolves, which is precisely what happens in monitoring. So the solution often employed is to adapt the monitoring system so that it is able to serve both purposes at the same time, namely, the on-going needs of management and the need to collect data for evaluation.

An excellent example of this new kind of monitoring-cum-evaluation of a rural development project is the Greater Noakhali Rural Development Project in Bangladesh, funded by the Danish aid agency DANIDA from 1978 onwards. It comprised a series of packages aimed at meeting the needs of the poorer people in particular, including packages for agriculture, extension, cooperatives, cottage industries, mass education, etc. The project had (in the late 1980s) a staff of 1000, and there was a Monitoring and Evaluation Unit comprising 12 professionals.

Although the monitoring and evaluation procedures had been originally planned along traditional lines, that is, monitoring of progress taking place on a continuous basis, with evaluations taking place at intervals of several years, as free-standing exercises, it soon became apparent that this pattern would not work. The key factor was that the information required for evaluation was in fact virtually identical to the data required for monitoring, and more importantly, it was data that could not be collected at widely spaced moments in time. It had to be collected on an on-going basis. To quote one of the project staff, 'To distinguish the functions of monitoring and evaluation, as suggested by Casley and Kumar, might be useful analytically, but in practical terms it is mainly the timing and depth of data collection which makes the difference, and not the objective, the reference periods, or the users' (Nielsen, 1989). They found that even when a baseline survey had been carried out, the subsequent movements of population were so great that it would have been useless to have waited up to ten years for an in-depth evaluation: 'If such population changes are not monitored closely in an on-going way the follow up of a baseline survey 10 years later will be extremely difficult in a community where no reliable population registration exists' (Nielsen, 1989).

Thus developed the idea of building an 'impact monitoring' system on a continuous basis, partly to provide instant monitoring feedback to management, and partly to collect the data needed for evaluation later on. This was the origin of the 'village-wise impact monitoring system' (VIMS) (later re-named 'village level monitoring system'). This comprised in part a randomly selected sample of households to be followed up on a continuous basis, and in part a survey of some villages (to capture changes in the population that might be missed by the household sample approach).

In an article summarising his experience with this new kind of participatory monitoring, Nielsen included the chart, reproduced at Figure 8.2, to illustrate how monitoring and evaluation, although still separate, are closely interrelated throughout the project cycle (Nielsen, 1990).[4]

Figure 8.2　How Participatory Monitoring and Evaluation are Inter-related throughout the Project Cycle

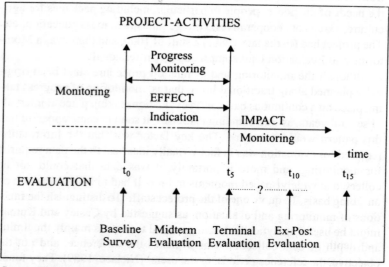

Source: Nielson (1990).

A key feature of the VIMS was the direct participation by the beneficiaries in the planning and implementation of the surveys. This necessitated using local staff, as they could speak the local language. It also involved training the local VIMS staff in certain basic techniques. A sample of villages was selected with a balance between those affected by the project and those not affected by it. Mature and reasonably well-educated residents of villages were chosen, one male and one female per village, and they were engaged for a week every month. They received further training every quarter. The information collected covered all the main social parameters, like population and health, employment, agricultural production, education, housing, and infrastructure. The results of the monitoring surveys were computerised for ease of analysis, and Bangladeshi staff were trained for this purpose.

To sum up, the Greater Noakhali experiment represents a new model for the monitoring and evaluation of people-centred projects, where monitoring acts simultaneously as an on-going management tool, and as the basic data collection system for evaluation, and where the whole process relies on participatory methods, with local staff being responsible for collecting and analysing the data. The terms for this kind of monitoring, 'effect monitoring' and 'impact monitoring', are now coming more widely into use. To quote Nielsen again, 'One might visualise the function of monitoring as covering the total spectrum from progress monitoring, through effect monitoring, to impact monitoring, while the functions of evaluation are represented by occasional studies and investigations' (Nielson, 1989). The danger with this approach is, of course, that it could signal a lapse back into the old 'monitoring and evaluation unit' syndrome, especially as impact surveys need to be planned over a long period of time and absorb substantial resources. The risk is that the 'evaluation tail will wag the dog of management', and resources that should have been used for short-term management needs will be pre-empted. It should still be possible to fulfil both needs simultaneously, with careful planning, but if this does not work the result could simply be a splendid evaluation report on a failed project!

Participatory Monitoring and Evaluation: Rhetoric or Reality?

The Greater Noakhali experiment was among the first of what has subsequently become a rising tide of experiments in the application of participatory methods in monitoring and evaluation. The Operations Evaluation Department of the World Bank has taken a keen interest in this development and in 1996 the World Bank published its influential *Participation Source Book* (World Bank, 1996) to encourage staff members to try out this new approach whenever possible. A short time before this R. Picciotto, the Head of the OED had published an article with a colleague (referred to in Chapter 5) suggesting a new approach to the project cycle based on the listening and piloting mode, rather than on the more proactive mode used up to that time. In 1996, Mr Picciotto invited me to address a staff seminar at the World Bank on this topic. I had been giving a lot of thought to the problem of reconciling traditional evaluation approaches with the new strand of thinking which involved participatory methods. It seemed to me that it could be possible to combine together the ideas then germinating about moving away from the holistic conception of a project towards focusing more on its components and treating each as a separate 'experiment', with the use of participatory methods and the new listening/piloting approach. This led me to produce the chart given on page 177 (see Figure 8.3) which illustrates how one might combine these various ideas in the monitoring and evaluation of a water supply programme.

The thinking behind Figure 8.3 is as follows. The project (or more accurately now the 'programme' because the project has been divided into several component parts) is no longer conceived as having a fixed shape but rather it begins (ideally following a problem tree type of analysis of the problem it is intended to address) with a loose outline of the proposed programme which will take the form of a series of experimental components (following the process approach style of project management). Each experimental component comprises a sequence of steps: listening, piloting and demonstrating, after which whatever emerges as the most promising line to follow will become the mainstream of the project—at least for some time, until it becomes necessary to repeat the process. Baselines would be especially important with this 'experimental' approach as the object is to test out possible solutions and one needs to have a clear understanding of the starting position. The experimental components will each be going on concurrently, each at its own pace, but of course with a lot of interaction between them, and they will be supervised by the project management which has considerable local autonomy to decide how the programme budget should be spent. All relevant stakeholders will be given a chance to become fully involved in each component. In the early stages there will be no well defined final destination for

Figure 8.3 A Suggested Participatory Approach to the Monitoring and Evaluation of a Village Water Supply Programme

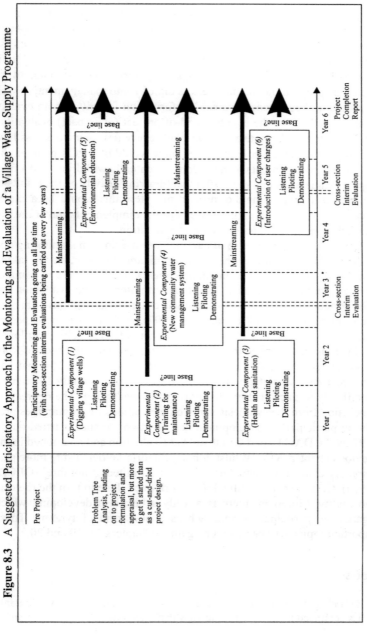

Source: Chart prepared by Dr Cracknell for World Bank Seminar on Participation, 1996.

the programme—only a broad statement of the ultimate goal. Time alone will show what eventually emerges from this process. It is an altogether more flexible, local stakeholder-focused, concept than before, and all the stakeholders will be thoroughly involved in 'learning-by-doing'. Monitoring and evaluation take place in a participatory fashion throughout the life of the programme, feeding results directly into management, as well as providing key ('benefit stream') information for any interim evaluations as well as for the eventual end-of-project (or impact) evaluation. Cross-section evaluations may take place every few years to assess how the programme as a whole is faring. There would be a PCR prepared by the project management when the donor eventually withdraws and a final impact evaluation some years after that (drawing heavily on the results of the previous impact monitoring). In my view this would be a major advance on the old 'blueprint' style of project implementation or the traditional 'three-week mission' style of evaluation.

The trend towards the use of participatory methods in monitoring and evaluation is undoubtedly the most significant change currently taking place in the field of aid evaluation. Robert Chambers calls it 'a major frontier', and he comments, 'Traditional monitoring and evaluation has been conducted by outsiders using their criteria and methods—this has been turned on its head' (Chambers, 1997). As is only to be expected with a new frontier, the territory on the other side is largely unexplored. To illustrate this I looked through the 632 references at the back of Robert Chambers' book *Whose Reality Counts?* and I found 154 that had some reference to participation in the title, but of these only 10 referred specifically to participatory monitoring and evaluation. The depressing conclusion from the synthesis study on evaluations of programmes promoting participatory development and good governance, carried out in 1997 by the DAC Expert Group on Aid Evaluation and mentioned in the previous chapter, was: 'Whilst donors' rhetoric favours using more participatory evaluation, actual practice is still limited, if not rare' (OECD, 1997a). Clearly there is still a lot of work to be done to turn the rhetoric into reality. Moreover, there is already a backlash developing which regards the participatory approach as a new kind of tyranny. These important topics will be taken up again in Chapters 18, 19 and 20.

Notes

1. It is rather curious that the World Bank Institute, a branch of the World Bank, has continued to promote the old view that monitoring and evaluation are so

similar that they can be treated as if they were virtually synonymous (Valadez and Bamberger, 1994).

2. This kind of monitoring, often using rapid rural appraisal methods, used to be dubbed 'quick and dirty', but happily that term has now dropped out of use. It was never fair to imply that the information obtained in this way was somehow inferior to the 'pure' information obtained from statistically impeccable sample surveys. It is information of a different sort, needed for a different purpose, and since it reflects the views and practical experience of the respondents it is just as valid as any other information. Furthermore, it is a technique which is far more likely to uncover unintended and unexpected effects than predetermined statistical surveys.

3. Team Technologies Inc. organises 2-day familiarisation courses on the computerisation of the logical framework. The computer packages also cover the problem tree, and various other techniques of project planning, including network analysis.

4. Henrik Nielsen, who is now with DANIDA, has incorporated this study, along with others he carried out later, into a compendium report that spans a decade of highly innovative activity in the field of decentralising the monitoring function, and switching responsibility for monitoring from the donor to local government impact monitoring (Nielsen 1998).

9

A Neglected Area: The Role of Organisational Dynamics and Organisational Learning in Evaluation

'The organizations which excel in the future will be those that discover how to tap people's commitment and capacity to learn at all levels in an organization'
(The Fifth Discipline, *Senge, P. [1990] quoted by Chambers, R. [1997]*)

'Knowledge comes, but wisdom lingers'
(Locksley Hall, *Alfred Lord Tennyson*)

'Knowledge itself is power'
(Religious Meditations: 'Of Heresies', *Francis Bacon*)

'Who is this that darkeneth counsel by words without knowledge?'
(*Job*)

"Where is the Knowledge we have lost in information?"
(The Wasteland and Other Poems, *T.S. Eliot*)

In recent years what is almost a new school of thought regarding aid evaluation has come into being. Its main exponents in Europe are a group of economists-cum-organisation experts located mainly in Scandinavia, and I have enjoyed working closely with them in several consultancies and collaborating with them on several articles. New ideas about aid evaluation have also been germinating in the United States and elsewhere. Some of these researchers concentrate on organisational dynamics (what makes an organisation tick), and others on the way organisations learn, and the significance of this for feedback. Each will be considered in turn.

Organisational Dynamics

Why Organisational Dynamics Matters

The principal theme of this new school is clearly stated in the introduction to a recently published book by three Swedish researchers, J. Carlsson, G. Kohlin and A. Ekbom, as follows, 'The way aid activities are being evaluated is primarily a function of organizational dynamics, and not a technical/administrative matter' (Carlsson et al., 1994). They note that the aid donors try to improve their project preparation methods, and systems of information dissemination, in the light of evaluation findings, but their basic conclusion is that this is not adequate in itself. They argue that effective feedback, and getting people to change their habitual way of doing things in response to evaluation findings, has to involve a thorough understanding of how organisations take decisions; how they set objectives; how they resolve internal conflicts; and how they learn. In other words, their thesis is that effective feedback is a function of organisational dynamics. That is why this chapter has been placed before the three chapters dealing with various aspects of feedback.

An organisation can be viewed as 'a social construct that thinks, learns, and acts through its members. An organization lives in motion and cannot be fully understood as a static phenomenon. It is made up of relations between its actors at different levels, both within and outside the organization. The dynamics of an organization are made up of how people co-operate, compete, or end up in conflict with each other' (Carlsson et al., 1994). In an organisation, each individual is motivated by various interests: some are related to the task he or she is currently performing in the organisation; some are linked to the individual's perception of his or her future career, and whatever might affect it; and some are related to the individual's personality and personal preferences (including his/her private life). These interests certainly affect how the individual acts in the organisation, and by appreciating them 'we can begin to understand...the motivating factors that underpin the varied styles of careerism, gamesmanship, task commitment, rigidity, "turf protection", zealousness, detachment, and free wheeling, that lend the politics of organizational life its detailed character' (Carlsson et al., 1994).

The way an organisation operates depends very much on how these competing interests interact, and especially on the reward structures that exist. The latter may well be inconsistent (e.g., speed of disbursement of funds *vs* high quality of aid), and 'a single organizational rationality is a very rare phenomenon, and is not a very useful point of departure for understanding what makes an organization tick' (Carlsson et al., 1994).

Coming down to specifics, the attitudes of the staff to evaluation findings will differ according to their role in the organisation. Thus senior management and professional staff will be interested in assessments of project performance, but the operational staff might feel threatened by these and adopt a more negative attitude. Neither operational staff nor professional staff are likely to be very interested in the public relations aspect of evaluations, whereas senior management will understand its importance and are likely to take a more positive stance. Having been a civil servant for most of my career, I am well aware of the importance of these motivating factors in understanding how an organisation learns, especially in relation to getting colleagues to act on evaluation findings.

Conflict and Coordination

Conflict and coordination are simultaneously present in most organisations. Even if an aid organisation presents a unified 'front' to the outside world, in practice, under the surface, it comprises networks of people with divergent interests. One such network usually comprises the well-trained and highly experienced professionals and technical experts who often enjoy considerable status and a degree of independence in the organisation, and who work closely with the recipients. Another will comprise the administrators and decision-makers who have strong systems of authority, while not always possessing the same degree of expertise, although they have a good deal of experience. Power becomes a crucial variable: some groups have more power than others, and so an organisation tends to evolve into a minority of leaders and a majority of led.

These factors may be subtle and not easy to tie down, but they have a major influence on how an evaluation activity is set up in the first place; how it carries out its work; and especially how receptive the organisation is to feedback. Understanding them is important for an effective evaluation system.

One important consequence of viewing the aid organisation not as a monolithic, wholly rational body but as a loose coalition of interests, often in conflict with each other, is that one ceases to expect the objectives of aid to be necessarily stated in a clear and unambiguous way. Within the organisation, people will have different perceptions of what the objectives of the organisation are in general, and this will extend to the objectives of particular activities. This of course can create very difficult problems for the evaluator, and is one explanation for the fact that so often the objectives of projects are not clearly specified, especially if the organisation does not use any such system as the logical framework.

To complicate further an already complicated situation, aid organisations do not operate in a vacuum. They are subjected to pressures from political parties, the treasuries, NGOs representing specific interests, private businesses, the general public, pressure groups on aid, the media, and of course the recipients of the aid. All of these are pursuing their own interests, yet somehow the aid organisation has to keep them in balance with the objectives it has set itself.

Organisational Dynamics and Evaluation

Against this background it is time to consider the role that evaluation as an activity can play. First, it is plain that evaluation takes place within a political context, 'The policies and programmes that are being evaluated are proposed, defined, debated, enacted, and funded, through political processes. The evaluation itself has a political stance because it makes implicit political statements about issues such as the legitimacy of programme goals and of project strategies, and the usefulness of various implementation strategies' (Carlsson et al., 1994). Evaluators need to concern themselves not only with programme objectives but with organisational objectives as well. And one of the most pervasive of organisational objectives, which affects almost all aid agencies, is the pressure to spend the funds allocated for aid within a given time frame.

The way evaluation results are received and acted upon will often depend on the status and function that the recipient of the evaluation results has in the aid hierarchy. Senior management will look to evaluations to help strengthen the organisation vis-à-vis its external environment, especially those authorities to which it is most accountable. But the operational departments are more likely to be looking to evaluations to safeguard their interests, especially vis-à-vis conflicts with other operational departments. In fact, the further away from the 'workface', the more dispassionate will be the recipient's viewpoint about evaluation results. Operational staff will be very concerned about efficiency of implementation, and performance assessments, and very aware of the impact that evaluation reports could have on their own career prospects. They tend to be less interested in impact aspects, whereas senior management will look to evaluations as early warning signals, guides to the effectiveness of policies and strategies, a source of new ideas and concepts, and as raw material for debates about future directions.

It is a common experience of aid agencies that often little notice is apparently taken of evaluation findings at the policy level, and this can be ascribed to the fact that evaluators often make the mistake of addressing only departmental goals, and tend to overlook the political ones. In practice, evaluation findings are only one among a number of inputs that go into the reformulation of aid policies. They have to be weighed against influences coming from outside the agency (such as pressures from specialist NGOs, or the media, or treasuries), as well as the power structures and delicate coordination/conflict balance within the organisation itself. This issue is discussed more fully in Chapter 11, but here it can be stated that evaluators are being naïve if they expect their findings to result immediately in the aid organisation changing its policy. Policy changes are the net result of the interaction of many influences, and sometimes evaluation findings may be used merely to legitimise decisions already about to be taken on other grounds. Carlsson, Kohlin and Ekbom quote an insightful observation of Cronbach's: 'What is needed (from evaluation) is information that supports negotiation, rather than information calculated to point out the "correct decision".' (Carlsson et al., 1994).

Evaluations of projects implemented in the participatory mode have shown that participatory techniques are unlikely to be successful unless the projects are linked to organisations that have the characteristics of 'learning organizations', that is, where there is a willingness to listen, to engage in dialogue and mutual learning, to be open to the need for change, and to possess a capacity for vision (see Blackburn with Holland, 1998).

Two Inferences

Where has this discussion of organisational dynamics brought us? Two important inferences seem to emerge. The first is that it must surely help to ensure that evaluations are directed at improving aid effectiveness (and not be hijacked by other considerations) if there is a sense of ownership on the part of senior management. This can be achieved if the evaluation unit's work is closely directed by a body such as the Projects and Evaluation Committee in DFID, and especially if this body receives the reports and decides what action is to be taken on them. The inevitable coalitions and conflicts between the power networks in the organisation will still be there of course, but they will make themselves felt within the body of senior management itself rather than impinging too directly on the work of the evaluation unit. There is more chance that the body of senior management will find a consensus that leaves the maximum scope for aid effectiveness to be the organisation's guiding light, and not other preoccupations.

The second inference is that it is vital for aid effectiveness to be at the forefront of the incentive/reward structures within the organisation. For example, if speed of disbursement of aid funds is seen as the main criterion of good aid management, aid quality will be forced into a secondary position and only token acknowledgement will be made to evaluation results geared to improving aid effectiveness. Staff will say Amen, and then go back to doing what they were doing before—trying to spend the aid funds within the time allotted. Aid quality is only likely to become the dominant target if there is strong political support from the top, and an appropriate reward structure. To quote von Metzsch, one time Chair of the DAC Expert Group on Aid Evaluation: 'An organization does not easily change, nor does it willingly become a learning organization. There must be incentive or pressure to learn from evaluation' (von Metzsch, 1995).

How an Organisation Learns

Second only in importance, for evaluators, to understanding what makes an organisation tick, is to understand how an organisation learns. This is obviously vital if the feedback of evaluation findings (discussed in the following three chapters) is to be successful.

Gradually evaluators have acquired a deeper understanding of how the organisations they serve 'work', and in particular, how they learn. They have become aware that communication is both an art and a science: it needs a lot of flair, persuasive ability and understanding of human nature. I often remind myself that evaluation is all about communication. After all, what is the use of evaluating something if you can not convince others that your findings are relevant and important? Yet I find very little reference in the literature to this aspect, and some of the evaluation articles, and evaluation reports I have seen are virtually unreadable. This is not a mistake that leading firms in the private sector have made. Many commercial consultant firms send their staff on expensive courses on group psychology and the art of communication: clearly they are in no doubt about the importance of this kind of training. But communication is also a science: it calls for well constructed systems, interlocking mechanisms, and a better understanding of what constitutes an organisation's learning process (see Figure 9.1).

Although they have seldom had any specific training in this field in the past, aid agency evaluators have found themselves acquiring new skills in communication and organisational learning. There is now a new breed of evaluators who have studied and done research on organisational learning, and are combining their skills with those of experienced evaluators to explore what has been till now a very neglected territory.

As Box 9.1 shows, organisational learning experts have drawn an important distinction between 'learning by involvement' and 'learning by communication', which has implications for evaluation feedback; and they have made a strong case for more research into how aid agencies 'learn how to learn'.[1] Both these learning methods are needed. And in addition, more research is needed on the effectiveness of the various learning linkages shown in Figure 9.1, including a study of knowledge structures.

Knowledge Structures

Every organisation possesses what is often called its 'conventional wisdom', that is a set of ideas, and commonly held truths, acquired largely through corporate experience, which guide people's behaviour. These comprise the organisation's 'knowledge structures'. An organisation can be flexible and capable of change only if new ideas can penetrate these knowledge structures. On the other hand, knowledge structures should not be blown about by every wind, otherwise the organisation will lack

Figure 9.1   Key Questions Concerning How an Organisation Learns

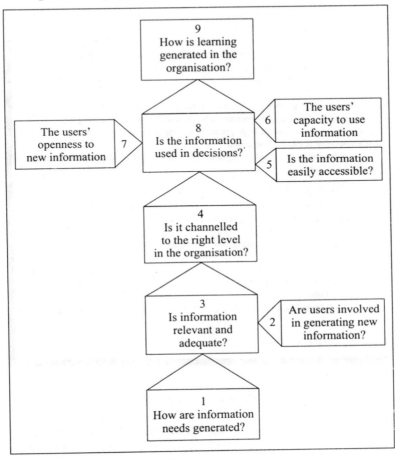

Source: Scanteam International (1993).

stability. Evaluators need to have an intimate understanding of the network of knowledge structures they are dealing with, and if feedback is to be successful they need to have a feel for the best way of presenting new ideas, new concepts, new ways of operating, etc., emerging from evaluation activity, to the appropriate knowledge structure. This is rather a far cry from the relatively straightforward process of conducting an evaluation, but it is the very stuff of feedback.

Box 9.1   How Evaluation can Help an Organisation to Learn

Hitherto very little study has been made of the processes whereby institutions learn. This information is vital if evaluation feedback is to be effective. There are basically two different processes of successful learning. The first is "Learning by Involvement", i.e. the aid agency staff actually being involved in evaluations in a direct way—planning them, participating in overseas evaluation missions, and handling the reports. The snag is that only a few people can be directly involved in this way.

The second is "Learning by Communication". People can learn in more passive ways, e.g., by listening, or reading. It has the advantage of reaching a far wider circle, but it needs to be of high quality to be effective, and even then the transfer of knowledge is likely to be small.

The advantages and disadvantages of these two modes of learning can be illustrated as follows:

Learning by Involvement	*Learning by Communication*
Reaches a few	Reaches many
Presupposes high absorptive capacity	Presupposes low absorptive capacity
Provides difficult inputs	Provides easy inputs
Emphasis on reliable and valid results	Emphasis on new thoughts and holistic perspectives
Action-oriented	The input may not be directly applicable
Programme officers take active part	The stimulus to learn is served by others
Often expensive	Can be cheap
Controlled close to the users	May be controlled centrally or outside the system

Source: Forss et al. (1994).

Openness to New Ideas

A recent review of the way the Norwegian Aid Agency, NORAD, learns from its evaluation activity, found that where evaluation findings were immediately applicable at the project level there was a rapid learning process. But where the findings were less specific, and related to broader areas of policy, often of an interdisciplinary character, the learning process was slow. In particular: 'New thoughts and holistic perspectives are among the least valued qualities of evaluation reports' (Samset et al., 1992). This is common experience among aid agencies, and it is understandable because changing an agency's basic policy in any direction is a far greater step than changing one's practices vis-à-vis specific types of projects. It also requires broad agreement on the part of all those who make policy. Yet if there is no openness to new ideas blowing in from evaluation work, there is a risk of the agency falling into a rut. There is a need for organisational cultures to be flexible and receptive to new ideas. To quote the same report again, 'Curiosity, experimentation and novelty of ideas, must be leading elements in the organizational culture' (Samset et al., 1992).

Motivation for Learning

Many studies have demonstrated that learning is unlikely to take place unless there is motivation in addition to the instinctive desire of most people to improve their own performance. Unfortunately, various factors may work in the opposite direction, that is causing learning to hindered rather than helped. For instance, staff are often under such great pressure that they can fairly claim that they simply do not have the time to read evaluation reports and other such 'improving' material. The survey of staff in NORAD, mentioned earlier, found that 94 per cent of the respondents complained that lack of time was the greatest obstacle to learning (Scanteam International, 1993). Even more important, the pressure in most agencies is to disburse the funds allocated for aid within a given time frame, which is sometimes as short as one year (this is often referred to as 'moving the money'), and failure to do this is deemed to be far more serious than failing to do everything possible to improve the quality of the aid. Placing emphasis on learning, at the expense of 'moving the money' could well damage a person's career prospects. In these circumstances it is not really surprising that feedback to improve quality and performance has not hitherto been given a very high priority.

How Knowledge is Generated and Used

As an aid evaluator in the ODA I found that increasingly my energies were being directed at trying to ensure feedback of the lessons from the growing stockpile of evaluation reports into the ongoing work of the Ministry. We tried many different ways of passing on the knowledge being acquired, but it was a very frustrating business. It is by no means an easy task to pass on knowledge in a form that busy colleagues can digest and utilise efficiently—one needs to understand the underlying organisational dynamics governing how corporate bodies absorb knowledge, as well as recognise the factors that facilitate or impede the process at the level of the individual. However, in spite of the difficulties, I never lost my conviction that this was one of the most important tasks that the evaluator had to tackle. I was therefore delighted when I was invited, in 1996, to participate in a three-person team being commissioned by the Expert Group on Development Issues set up by the Swedish Ministry for Foreign Affairs to carry out a research project on organisational learning, my role being to study the evaluation function in this context. I visited a number of bilateral and multilateral aid agencies, including Sida, ODA, BMZ, GTZ, DGIS (the Netherlands), WHO, IBRD, EDI (Economic Development Institute) and IFC (International Finance Corporation). Our report was published in 1998 as part of a new series of reports being issued by the Expert Group on Development Issues (Forss et al., 1998).

Our report covered such issues as the distinctive learning problems that aid agencies have (compared with most other bodies) in that the projects they fund are usually located thousands of miles away; also that they involve a great variety of stakeholders often representing very different cultures, and the overlapping and frequently contradictory nature of the goals and objectives of aid. However, we concluded that learning does indeed take place, albeit rather slowly (although the study of learning through evaluation showed that it had taken place faster in that area than in the other two areas we looked at, namely girls' education and technical cooperation). But the main problem we identified was not so much generating new knowledge as ensuring that the knowledge already acquired leads to improvements in aid performance.

We found that a lot of learning takes place internally through work contacts, etc. (although not often through contact with beneficiaries), but that often there needs to be an external spur, for example, from dynamic leaders who deliberately promote the learning process (as the President of the World Bank is doing), or from parliaments or as a result of pressure from the media or elsewhere, before learning takes place.

Once it is acquired, knowledge spreads through the organisation via a network of internal channels through the natural process of osmosis. However, increasingly organisations have come to feel that this natural process by itself is not enough and that it needs to be supplemented by more formal means of sharing knowledge, like for example systematic feedback arrangements, including the use of information technology. New styled 'knowledge centres' are being set up in some aid agencies to ensure that this happens, and internal organisational structures are being redesigned deliberately to facilitate the spread of knowledge—we described some of these in our report. New cadres of staff called 'knowledge officers' have been appointed in the World Bank, and new groups such as the Learning Group on Popular Participation have been established to encourage learning. In DFID a new Knowledge Policy Unit has been created with the following objectives:

- To improve the strategic direction of DFID's overall knowledge effort;
- to promote DFID's partnership objectives in the knowledge field;
- to enhance DFID's internal knowledge management and lesson-learning capacity;
- to advise on general knowledge issues and to maintain contact with other institutions;
- to improve DFID's performance measurement and evaluation of research activities;
- to improve knowledge dissemination and uptake (Clift, C., 1998).

We discovered that increasingly aid agencies are shifting from vertical information flow patterns to horizontal ones. Previously, that is before the introduction of decentralisation and the increasing use of the process approach, there was a more hierarchical system of management, from the centre to the periphery, and back up the line. This kind of management and information flow system has been called 'Apollinarian' after the Greek temple where the columns are only joined across the top (Blackburn with Holland, 1998). But today the communication flows tend to be more horizontal, with staff working in the field now wanting to exchange their experiences with others working in the same sector or in the neighbouring region. This change has important implications for feedback.

Computerised data systems are being rapidly developed, but it is interesting that many aid agencies are becoming dissatisfied with their existing 'disembodied' information systems and are now developing new ones. The search is on for new ways of preserving the link between information and the particular circumstances in which it was first obtained, and carefully recording the details of the people who first supplied it so that face-to-face sharing of information becomes possible.

We looked at the question of whether there was any evidence that all this activity on the organisational learning front was in fact leading to improvements in the quality of aid. Rather disappointingly we found that although learning was certainly leading to improvements at the project level there was less evidence of that happening at the strategic or policy level where there often seems to be a reluctance to accept the need for change. This kind of higher level learning is called 'double loop learning' in the literature, and research has found that it is far harder to achieve in most other fields of endeavour as well. One of the reasons for this in the aid field may be, as noted elsewhere, that aid agencies' internal reward systems do not encourage quality improvements but rather speed of disbursement: there is also a general tendency towards risk averseness, especially where sensitive political issues are involved.

The main conclusions to be drawn from our research can be summarised as follows:

- Learning involves listening and a sense of partnership. In terms of development aid it is indefensible for donors not to learn from their beneficiary partners.
- It is primarily of course individuals who learn, but organisations can also learn. What is important is that the organisation has incentives to encourage individual learning to be shared at the organisational level. New organisational structures are needed to facilitate this process and a learning culture needs to be deliberately fostered.
- Top management must be seen to be enthusiastic about learning, and ready to reward those who are motivated in this direction, and who motivate others.
- Old styles of top-down management need to be revised in the direction of 'bottom up' initiatives, more flexibility in response to experience, less rigid control systems and fewer fixed boundaries of responsibility, more encouragement of cross-cutting competencies, more fluidity in personal appointments so that there is more cross-fertilisation of ideas and experience, and more formalised arrangements for learning and follow up.

Organisational learning is still a relatively new subject, but there is no doubt that it will figure more prominently in the years ahead. A strong lead is being given by the private sector, where many large corporations and others take the subject very seriously, and if these profit-maximising organisations think it is worthwhile one can safely assume that it is also worthwhile for the public sector as well. For aid evaluators its significance in the context of the feedback of evaluation findings cannot be questioned. In short, I fully share Robert Chambers' optimistic observation that: 'We seem to be in the middle of a quiet but hugely exciting revolution in learning and action' (Chambers, 1997).

Note

1. The World Bank is taking 'learning-by-involvement' seriously: Senior staff are now being encouraged to gain first hand experience of working in a rural village or urban slum (Blackburn with Holland, 1998).

10

Feedback

Part One: Client Orientation of Evaluation Reports

'Of all the businesses by far,
Consultancy's the most bizarre,
For to the penetrating eye
There's no apparent reason why,
With no more assets than a pen,
This group of personable men
Can sell to clients more than twice,
The same ridiculous advice,
Or find, in such profusion,
Problems to fit their own solution.'
(Seen on the desk of a consultant in Botswana)

'Reading maketh a full man; conference a ready man; and writing
an exact man'
(Of Studies, *Francis Bacon*)

'Experience is not what happens to a man. It is what a man does
with what happens to him'
(Aldous Huxley)

Feedback has been defined by the DAC Expert Group on Aid Evaluation as 'a management term that covers: organising evaluation findings to guide future aid programme decisions, and necessary measures taken to deal with weaknesses found in the evaluation' (OECD, 1986). Feedback is the Achilles' heel of evaluation. It is clearly vitally important, because without it the whole evaluation process is largely a waste of time. If an evaluation report can be likened to the head of an arrow, then feedback would be the shaft: one without the other is useless. Yet ironically this is the branch of evaluation which has so far received least attention (Cracknell, 1993). Why should this be so? Perhaps it is merely a reflection of the relative newness of the subject.[1] Priority had first to be given to getting the whole show on the road: the first task of newly created evaluation units was to establish methodologies and to build a stockpile of completed evaluation reports. Only after these had been achieved were people ready to devote attention to feedback.

But that still does not explain why it has taken so long to give feedback the importance it clearly deserves. There must be deeper reasons. One may be the fact that feedback is an altogether different kind of operation from the carrying out of evaluations and the preparing of reports. To quote a fairly recent article on evaluation in France: 'In spite of the fact that understanding the world, and changing it, are very different, people are often strongly tempted to believe that the links between the two are natural or automatic' (Duran et al., 1995). Feedback calls for different kinds of skills (more those of the communicator than the analyst), and for a different kind of motivation. Planning and implementing an evaluation study is a challenging, rewarding and ultimately a very satisfying task. It has a clear structure—a beginning, middle and end: it involves teamwork, and it takes you to interesting places overseas. It is also a high-profile task; a report is produced and the evaluation team members usually have their names on the front cover. All this is deeply satisfying. But feedback offers none of these attractions. It is amorphous and hard to take hold of firmly (often no-one even seems quite sure whose responsibility it is): it involves seeming to put oneself in a superior position colleagues—'telling them their business': one is more likely to lose friends than to gain them, and if pursued too enthusiastically it could even threaten one's future career. Yet, as Eleanor Chelimsky has aptly commented, 'the courage to say what users may not want to hear is the characteristic of an evaluation function that keeps institutions honest' (Chelimsky, 1994). Small wonder then that evaluators have often taken the easy way out and have simply promulgated their reports, hoping that those who receive them will actually read them and act on the findings.

Unhappily, all too often the reports have remained unread, and little or no action has been taken. Some commentators have even suspected that the whole exercise is some elaborate front—a way of assuring potential critics in Parliament, the media, or the Treasury, that lessons are being learned and acted upon, even if they are not!

Fortunately the situation has greatly improved in recent years, and it is now universally recognised that feedback is not an automatic process. Just distributing reports will not do. Feedback has to be planned for, and organised, with as much care and determination as was required for the evaluation itself. A lot has been accomplished recently, but there is still a long way to go. The subject is so important that I have devoted three chapters to it. This first one deals with what might be called the 'raw material' of feedback, that is, the reports themselves and other evaluation findings, and considers the extent to which they meet users' needs. Chapter 11 deals with the organisational structures and mechanisms needed to ensure that the reports lead on to action, and Chapter 12 deals with the feedback of data through management information systems.

The usefulness of evaluation reports depends on two factors: first, the initial choice of projects or topics for evaluation (if these do not include topics that the agency staff are most concerned about the evaluation findings are unlikely to have much impact), and second, whether the reports have been prepared in such a way as to make them 'user friendly'. Very few donor agency staff actually have to read the evaluation reports as part of their normal duties (unlike feasibility studies or appraisal reports for instance, which have to be studied by all those responsible for preparing and approving new projects), and therefore they need to be written and presented in an attractive way. All too often evaluation reports are written without adequate regard to who the audience is, or what their needs are. In 1990, USAID carried out a study of the extent to which evaluation recommendations were presented in a way that would facilitate follow up action being taken, and they found that the proportion was less than half. One reason for this may have been that in two out of three evaluations no-one from USAID had participated in the evaluation (USAID, 1990).

Client Orientation

Too often in the past the evaluation programme was decided by the evaluation unit after only cursory consultation with operational colleagues, that is the programme was 'supply-led' rather than 'demand-led'. The need to ensure that there is client orientation in the planning of an evaluation programme has already been mentioned in Chapter 2, and suggestions were made for achieving this. Client orientation is vital for feedback because only if the evaluations address felt needs will people be likely to respond. To quote Jean Quesnel, former Chair of the DAC Expert Group on Aid Evaluation, 'when managers commission an evaluation, they also buy into the results and are more likely to use the recommendations provided by the evaluation for future design' (Quesnel, 1995). Dan Stufflebeam, Chairman of the Joint Committee on Standards in the United States, has argued that an evaluation 'should not be done at all if there is no prospect for its being useful to some audience' (Stufflebeam, 1980, quoted in Patton, 1997).

User-Friendly Reports

It is more important for evaluation reports than for reports of any other kind, that they should cater for the needs of the potential audience. This means that they should:

- be short and to the point;
- have a brief executive summary of not more than a few pages in the front, the main report not extending to more than about 40–50 pages, although there can be lengthy annexes containing much of the supporting material (survey results etc);
- be presented attractively—small print should be avoided, and there should be plenty of paragraph headings breaking up solid pages of text, and visual variety like photographs or illustrations (including a sketch map of the location of the project) can be useful;
- have a clear and comprehensive list of contents to facilitate quick access to relevant sections (bearing in mind that often the report will not be read from cover to cover but 'dipped into' for relevant information); sometimes an index would be useful;
- have a chapter on lessons learned, leading on to recommendations for action;
- contain annexes covering the terms of reference, people met, field visits made, acronyms, bibliography, and brief biographical details of the evaluators;

- describe the data and methodologies used;
- be sometimes tailored to meet the needs of specific users (some evaluation reports seem to be written with little thought to who the users might be, or what their interests are, for instance, there is often excessive emphasis on efficiency issues, many of which are project specific and have little relevance elsewhere, whereas there may well have been useful lessons relating to effectiveness, impact and sustainability that would have been of interest to a much wider audience); and
- should always ensure that certain key issues, such as gender, environment, sustainability, and institutional development, are not overlooked or ignored.

Some donor agencies, such as the Swedish agency Sida, take all these criteria very seriously, and they produce very attractive and readable evaluation reports, often with eye-catching titles like 'Aid under Fire' (referring to Swedish aid to Mozambique) or 'Sisterhood on Trial' (about the performance and linkages of sister industries in Tanzania). But other agencies, including, I have to say, DFID, produce reports (mainly for internal consumption) which may be excellent in terms of content, but which pay little heed to considerations of attractiveness or eye-catching style. A recent evaluation of participatory methods makes the same point: 'If feedback is to contribute to planning processes it must draw attention and excite' (Blackburn with Holland, 1998). I continue to be surprised and disappointed at the dull and unimaginative presentation of so many evaluation reports—one really has to be keen to bother to read them. In training courses I have run for evaluators I usually have a session where I get the participants to score a selection of evaluation reports according to their readability and capacity to excite attention. I think the participants are at first rather surprised that I should do this, but afterwards I hope they get the message that if you want people to read your reports you need to make them attractive.

Transparency

In a few agencies the reports are classified 'For internal use only', the main reason being the fear that the evaluators might not be as frank as they would otherwise be if they knew that the reports would be published. However, in most agencies these days, the reports are openly available to the public on demand (subject to the recipient countries giving their approval, which they usually do). This is another reason why they should be attractively produced, because the general public and the media have even less direct incentive to read them than the agency staff themselves.

Syntheses

In the early days of evaluation activity most of the evaluations were of individual projects. But it was soon found that these were of little value, other than to the staff immediately concerned with the project, because it was not possible to draw inferences of a general nature from only one project. So it became the practice to 'cluster' projects by sectors, and then to produce 'syntheses' of the findings, on the principle that if the same finding recurred in several places it was justifiable to draw a broad conclusion with some confidence. Today it is quite rare for individual projects to be the subject of evaluations by evaluation units, except as part of synthesis studies. For a while the practice was to continue with individual evaluations in their own right, but then to group the findings in an attempt to synthesise them. But now in some donor agencies, such as the Netherlands and DFID, the decision is first made about the sector or sub-sector to be evaluated, and then individual projects are selected for evaluation primarily on the basis of the contribution they are expected to make to the synthesis. Synthesis evaluations are far more useful all round (whether to the staff of the donor agency, the media, or academics and consultants) than are one-off project evaluations, and they have now become the norm.

Research Syntheses

A special kind of synthesis study is the 'research synthesis' (also known as meta-analysis). This is a synthesis of all the relevant research/evaluation findings relating to a specific topic. The initiative for carrying out such syntheses usually comes from a high level, like the Parliament, or Congress in the United States. A good description of the effective use of research syntheses has been given by Eleanor Chelimsky, until recently Assistant Comptroller General for Programme Evaluation and Methodology in the General Accounting Office, USA. Over a period of 14 years her department produced 280 evaluations, of which 30 used research syntheses as the main evaluative approach. The techniques can be summarised as follows:

- negotiate the specific policy issue with the relevant Congressional Committee;
- consider whether it is suitable for answering through a research synthesis;
- refine the issue and agree about the shape of the study;
- gather all relevant extant material from research, evaluations, and other sources;
- appraise the quality and reliability of the studies, and interview the authors;
- begin to synthesise all this body of information, and carry out a comparative analysis, combing the data and relating it to the policy issue;
- summarise the current state of knowledge on the issue;
- present the findings, orally and in writing, to those in Congress who requested it. (Chelimsky, 1995).

This is a good illustration of how already existing evaluation and research material can be synthesised to yield quick and useful (if not always complete) answers to specific problems. Because they can be completed in a matter of months they are especially useful for addressing policy issues that call for a quick response. Hitherto in many donor agencies there has not been enough feedback of this kind outside the principal stakeholders (that is, the donor agency and the recipient), and it needs to be remembered that the legislators, academics and the media are all stakeholders as well.

Often research syntheses are carried out before a project or programme is approved, as a kind of pre-investment study. The objective is to collect together whatever is already known about a subject, before a decision is taken to proceed with a proposed policy or programme.

However, with research syntheses of both types it has to be borne in mind that some of the information will be of doubtful quality, and caution needs to be exercised in using it. To quote a very experienced World Bank education expert, 'Many of the studies from which a meta-analysis must draw its information lack rigor. It is better to base decisions on one or two rigorous studies than to draw from 200 unreliable ones' (Psacharopoulos, 1995).

Other Types of Evaluation Reports

In addition to syntheses of project evaluations, there are a number of other types of evaluation in use. For example, as mentioned in Chapter 3, sometimes a donor agency will commission an evaluation of all its aid projects in one particular country. I participated in just such an evaluation of the European Commission's aid to Botswana where we had to evaluate no fewer than 23 projects in the space of only a few weeks (Cracknell et al., 1989). Another approach is to concentrate on a particular theme, such as an evaluation of food aid, or of aid by non-governmental organisations (NGOs), or of emergency relief. Yet another variation is to evaluate some aspect of aid procedure, such as the use of counterpart funds, the management of technical assistance, or the process of project identification. One donor agency, (the Netherlands) once tried a very grandiose evaluation— to assess the effectiveness of Dutch aid overall. But such ultra macro approaches are rare and have seldom proved very satisfactory. The important thing is to ensure that whatever the topic of evaluation, it meets the felt needs of at least some colleagues in the aid agency, that is the evaluation programme is truly client-oriented.

Tailoring Evaluation Reports to the Needs of the Users

Different audiences have different needs when it comes to evaluations. For example, the professional and technical advisers will especially appreciate the technical details and will use the results to sharpen their understanding of what makes for good or bad projects, and to recharge their personal memory databanks. But senior management is mainly interested in the policy/strategic implications; whilst the media are especially interested in the issues of accountability; and academic researchers and evaluation consultants (and evaluators in other agencies) will have a particular interest in the methodology used. Evaluation reports should be prepared with the needs of these different audiences in mind, so that they do not all necessarily have to plough through the full text to get what they want. This point was well expressed in a report on a Dutch Workshop in Islamabad as follows: 'It is not sufficient to define the output of an evaluation as a report only. The evaluation team should further articulate the evaluation's audiences and expected impact on different users, in order to arrive at the most effective means of shaping a final evaluation document which will be relevant to all parties concerned' (Frerks and Tomesen, 1989).

Keeping Jargon within Bounds

A glance at any recent professional evaluation journal will indicate the extent to which jargon has invaded the evaluation profession. Obviously jargon is acceptable as a convenient means of communication between professionals, who can be expected to master the language. But when it comes to communication between evaluators and those being evaluated and those who commission the evaluations, jargon is totally unacceptable. Sentences like the following, taken at random from a recent journal article (and acceptable in that context), are a great turn-off for anyone outside the charmed circle of professional evaluators/researchers:

A frame analysis enables the analyst to move beyond propositional claims, and how they are articulated in terms of the mode of discourse, to incorporate knowledge claims as cultural constructs.

The significance of this need to keep jargon within bounds when communicating outside the inner circle of initiates, came home like a blow between the eyes to a Norwegian evaluation research team, and it is very much to their credit that they had the honesty to admit it in a recent article. They were evaluating a major Norwegian programme to help small businesses, and when they presented their first interim report they were taken aback when those being evaluated declared that the report was 'not worth the paper it was written on'. The meeting to discuss the report was a major disaster, and when they searched for the reasons afterwards, they identified two in particular: 'The report was viewed as hopelessly academic in its present form', and 'our writing style was not acceptable' (Finne et al., 1995). They had not adequately consulted the intended beneficiaries, nor had they tried to express their findings in a way that the lay person could understand. Fortunately, they learned the lesson quickly and went on to complete a very satisfactory evaluation. But it had been, in their own words 'a ground-shaking experience'. As I have already emphasised earlier, evaluators, above all else, have to be communicators, otherwise their work is wasted: they must be communicators not only of the final results, but communicators throughout the process of planning and conducting the evaluation. Jargon has to be kept within bounds by the evaluator, just as a priest leaves his theological books in his study when he gets up into the pulpit to preach.

Recommendations in Reports

It is a cardinal rule that evaluation reports should always conclude with recommendations. It is not too difficult for the evaluator to pinpoint weaknesses or deficiencies (or positive points) in a project, but it is far more demanding to have to put forward recommendations for action. Recommendations are a vital component of any feedback system.

Some of the recommendations may relate to the specific subject of the evaluation, like ways of making the project more sustainable, or improving the distributional effects. Others will relate to the aid/development process more broadly. Unless there are representatives of the donor agency on the evaluation team, the report writers are likely to be reluctant to make recommendations about the agency's internal administration procedures as they may not feel competent enough to do this. That may not matter too much because the agency will no doubt have learned most of these lessons already through its monitoring system. More valuable are the recommendations relating to policies, strategies, concepts, and impact. These can have broader relevance, and when compared with findings emanating from other evaluations may suggest the need for important switches in emphasis in aid policies. The way in which recommendations are used to stimulate feedback at the policy level, for example, through the 'cover note system', are discussed in the next chapter.

Timeliness

Feedback is far more effective if the evaluation reports appear at a time when important decisions are being taken, and not afterwards. Of course this is very difficult to achieve because (as Figure 10.1 illustrates for one agency which is probably fairly typical in this regard) preparing for,

Figure 10.1 Production Time of Seven NORAD Evaluations

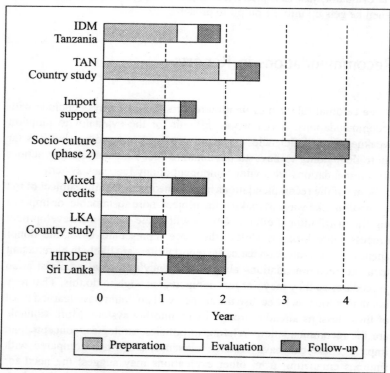

Source: Scanteam International (1993).

implementing and following up on, an evaluation takes from one-and-a-half to two years.[2] Obviously it is not easy to see that far ahead. It is essential to keep one's ear to the ground, trying to guess what topics will break surface as burning issues two or three years hence. Impact studies generally take considerably longer still, which is one reason why they can seldom be made to dovetail into important policy decisions: rather, they provide long-range feedback on broad strategies (like success of poverty alleviation) more than on specific policies. It may be desirable to speed up an evaluation, or to curtail its scope, if timeliness is crucially important. In the case of inter-phase evaluations, of course, timeliness is the most critical factor because decisions on a succeeding phase have to await the results of the evaluation of the current one.

Evaluation Summaries

Even if all the recommended practices for user-friendly reports are adhered to, the full report may not be read by its intended audience. Donor agency staff are usually simply too busy to read the reports unless they actually have to, whilst many other potential readers, such as the media, consultants and academics, are often satisfied with only a short summary (provided they can call for the full report on request). So many agencies now produce one-page summaries of the key findings, and distribute these widely, offering to send the full reports on request. This system works very well, and saves time as well as money (not to mention trees in the Amazon!). In DFID, for instance, most members of staff have been given a ring binder in which to house the one-page summaries called 'EVSUMs'. Each EVSUM carries at the top a classification of the sector (using an agreed international method of classification), and when they receive them the staff file them away in the appropriate section of the ring binder. As they do this they glance quickly at the other EVSUMs in the sector, and so build up a visual impression of the findings. Every time they have to deal with a new project they can look up the relevant sector in the ring binder, and find there a mini databank of findings from previous evaluations in that sector. They can always call for the full reports, but in practice they do not do so often, because of lack of time. This is another way in which a 'corporate memory' can be built up gradually.

Stockpile of Evaluation Reports

Each year that passes sees another accretion of say 20–25 evaluation reports to each donor's stockpile (or considerably more for the larger donors). Already these total many hundreds of reports for each donor, and many thousands for the donor community as a whole. Unless we are to be forever re-inventing the wheel it is crucial that everyone involved, evaluators and operational staff, recipients, media and others, have access to this stockpile. There are already excellent arrangements for ensuring this. Each donor keeps its own stockpile of evaluation reports readily available on demand, and in addition each agency has access to the evaluation reports produced by other agencies. They also have access to the computerised data records, both of the evaluation community at large, and relating to the operations of their own agencies, as described more fully in Chapter 12. There is now no excuse for evaluators failing to take fully into account the findings of other evaluations relevant to the project they are working on, and in their evaluation reports they should always state specifically how they have made use of this other material.

Sector Manuals, Office Procedure Manuals and Other Outlets

The evaluation reports themselves are not the only vehicle of feedback. Many aid agencies now extract the key findings from the evaluation reports and insert them into various kinds of guidance manuals. Typical are the 'sector manuals' in DFID, which cover most of the main sectors and which deal with issues related to the design and appraisal of projects in each sector, whether technical or economic. Sometimes the lessons are more procedural in character and call for a modification in the office's internal procedural guidelines. Sometimes they are related more to issues of policy, and the appropriate vehicle is the 'policy guidance note'. Some agencies, such as the Bundesministerium fur Wirtschaftliche Zusammenarbeit (BMZ), prepare annual summaries of the key lessons from their evaluation findings for publication, although in the case of Germany this is partly because they do not let the public see the evaluation reports themselves. So, by way of compensation, they arrange for these occasional summaries of distilled evaluation results to be widely published, both in English and French. Without communication channels of the various kinds described here, it would be difficult to ensure that the evaluation findings are made available to those who need to be aware of them.

Notes

1. To illustrate the fact that feedback is a relatively new subject, I can recall the gales of laughter at an international conference, not so many years ago, when the official interpreters translated the word feedback as 'retro-alimentation'! The French terms are 'retroaction', or 'effet de retour'.
2. The authors of a recent review of feedback procedures in the Norwegian aid agency NORAD, considered timeliness to be so important for effective feedback that they recommended that the time taken to carry out evaluations should be reduced from the present average of two years to only six months. Whilst this is a laudable aim, my experience is that it would generally be impractical, bearing in mind, in particular, the time it often takes to get approval for an evaluation, especially from the recipient country. To achieve 20–25 completed evaluations per annum, one needs to have a 'pipeline' of actual or potential evaluations totalling around 50 at any one time: this is to allow for the inevitable falling out of evaluations, for all sorts of reasons, before they can be implemented.

---11---

Feedback

Part Two: Mechanisms of Feedback

'To err is human, but to persist in error is inexcusable'
(Cicero)

'To err is human, but to foul things up completely requires a computer'
(Seen on a door at the Institute of Development Studies,
University of Sussex)

'The bearings of this observation lays in the application of it'
(Bunsby, Dombey and Son, *Charles Dickens*)

In the early days of evaluation activity it seemed to be assumed that the main task was to carry out the evaluations, and one could then rely on the reports being read, and acted upon, by the parties concerned. However, it soon became evident that this only happened at the project level, and even then not always. Moreover, feedback across the organisation, and especially at the policy level, occurred only if specific steps were taken to that effect. This experience has led evaluators, and experts in organisational learning, to look more closely into the ways in which organisations learn, and to look for more purpose-built ways of ensuring that follow up action is taken.

Feedback at the Project Level

Feedback at the level of the particular project being evaluated is to some extent automatic in the sense that the staff responsible for implementing the project can reasonably be expected to read, and act upon, any evaluation reports dealing directly with their projects (although even this has been disputed).

The feedback problem at the project level mainly arises in getting the information across to other colleagues working on similar projects elsewhere in the agency, or outside it. Such feedback will not take place of its own accord. It has to be specifically provided for, partly through such vehicles as those described in the previous chapter, namely, EVSUMs, sector manuals, and such like, and partly through mechanisms devised for this purpose. Thus although the evaluation unit should not take upon itself the responsibility for ensuring that action is taken on evaluation recommendations (that task properly belongs to the projects and evaluation committee, or whatever body is given this responsibility—see below), it should always have a keen interest in fostering what has been called a 'feedback culture'. This implies getting feedback institutionalised as a normal, almost instinctive, function within the organisation. Various ways of achieving this have been evolved. For instance, the evaluation unit can make a point of finding out what new projects are entering the organisation's project pipeline, and it can send the appropriate evaluation summaries to the desk officers responsible. This is a way of alerting them to the existence of the findings (and they may perhaps call for copies of the full reports if they think these may be useful), at an early stage in the setting up of the project. This procedure may be given added impetus if the office decides (as DFID, CIDA and USAID and some other agencies already do) that every submission for approval of a new project must contain a statement that the relevant evaluations have been consulted, and indicate how the findings have been taken into account. Some agencies also insist that someone from the evaluation unit be present when decisions about new projects are being taken.

Feedback at the Programme, Institutional or Sectoral Level

Above the project level there is usually a programme of which the project may be just a constituent part, or an institution such as a Rural Credit

Authority, which exercises broad supervision over the project. Feedback at this level is rather less direct than at the project level, because the staff are likely to be that much more remote from the project, and because not all the lessons relating to the project are likely to be relevant at the higher level. On the other hand, because this level of feedback is broader in scope, it offers more opportunities for feedback involving a much wider circle of people, and therefore has more influence. This is especially true of course at the sectoral level.

A very useful mechanism for ensuring that evaluation lessons are absorbed at this intermediate level is the holding of seminars and discussions centred on evaluation syntheses. These should include experts invited from outside the agency, representing for instance consultants, academics, and the media. The aim is to foster a wide-ranging discussion at the sub-sectoral or sectoral level, based on whatever evaluation syntheses may be available, that is, not merely those produced by the donor agency itself but also relevant evaluation reports and syntheses produced by evaluation units elsewhere. Some agencies try to hold these gatherings in the developing countries (for example, the European Commission often arranges meetings in the developing countries, to discuss basic principles emerging from evaluation findings). The Dutch, Scandinavians and Americans, among others, have also organised evaluation seminars of this kind. They help to ensure that the benefits are shared with the local experts, and with those currently working in related projects. Such seminars are of course also relevant for feedback at the policy/strategic level as well.

Feedback at the Policy/Strategy Level

The main problem in the area of feedback relates to feedback at the policy level (Cracknell, 1993). Unfortunately, the record of many donor agencies in this regard has been poor (OECD, 1990). This became very apparent to me when I was invited in 1990 by the European Commission to join with the then Head of the Evaluation Unit in DG VIII, Dr Hellmut Eggers, to carry out a review, requested by the Council of Ministers, of feedback procedures among the member states and the Commission. We found that only three member states had really effective feedback systems at the policy level, namely Germany, UK and the Netherlands. Their systems were different, although they had some features in common. In

Germany, the minister in charge of development drew up what was called a 'protocol' for each substantial evaluation, setting out the action that he proposed should be taken in the light of the evaluation. He reported this to the Bundestag, and undertook to tell the Bundestag in due course what action had actually been taken and with what result.[1] The German aid ministry estimated in 1990 that this procedure ensured the implementation of 80 per cent of evaluation recommendations (OECD, 1990). Reference has been made earlier to the senior committee of officials in DFID (the Projects and Evaluation Committee, PEC) which has the responsibility for approving major new project proposals, and which receives, and decides on the appropriate action to be taken upon, all evaluation reports. This dual function of the PEC (approving new projects and receiving evaluation reports on past ones) is seen as a very valuable form of 'instant feedback'. To quote the one-time Chairman of the PEC R. Browning: 'The insight into how projects work, which the study and discussion of evaluation reports gives us, helps us a great deal when it comes to considering new projects; and because we are the body which considers all new projects, the lessons are often very quickly applied' (Browning, 1984). The secretary to the PEC keeps track of the action taken, in the light of the Committee's deliberations, and reports back at six-monthly intervals. In the Netherlands the evaluation unit reports directly to the minister who decides (in consultation with his senior officials) what action should be taken, and how that action will be monitored, and reports back to Parliament.

In the World Bank, the Joint Audit Committee highlights, for the attention of management and the Board of Executive Directors, areas of the Bank's work in which changes in policy may be warranted (on the basis of evaluation findings), or where practice may be falling short of policy or operational guidelines (World Bank, 1994). Under the Bank's directives the Bank's management should formally respond to every OED evaluation, and the OED keeps a 'Ledger of Evaluation Recommendations, Management Responses and Actions'.

The common features of all these systems are:

- there is a senior body responsible for receiving evaluation reports and deciding what action should be taken;
- specific decisions are taken on the action required in response to the evaluation findings; and
- the subsequent action is carefully monitored and reported back to the senior body.

Most of the other member states, including the European Commission itself, at the time of our 1990 review, had no such system and formal feedback at the policy level was very weak.[2] Admittedly, the need for formal feedback arrangements is less in the case of small donor agencies like that in Denmark (DANIDA), which has only around 400 staff members who work mostly in the same building and who meet each other regularly. But even in these circumstances some kind of 'informally formal' system of feedback is needed. In larger agencies, where the staff are widely separated (for example, in DFID, where a substantial part of the staff are located at East Kilbride near Glasgow in Scotland, whilst the rest of the staff are located in London or in the Development Divisions), the need for formal feedback is much greater.

The Cover Note System

The three effective feedback systems described earlier depend heavily upon the staff of the agency translating raw evaluation findings into specific proposals for action. The Department for International Development has evolved a particularly effective mechanism for achieving this— the cover note (Cracknell, 1988b). Before a cover note can be produced the evaluation unit has to consult with relevant departments in the office to check whether they accept the relevance and accuracy of the findings, and especially what their views are on any recommendations. Out of this process emerges a consensus about the action that should be taken in response to the evaluation. Armed with this, the evaluation unit is then in a position to produce the cover note. This first of all summarises the main findings of the evaluation, and the recommendations made by the evaluators, and then puts forward specific recommendations for action based on the consensus reached with those colleagues most directly affected. The evaluation report is presented to the Projects and Evaluation Committee together with the cover note, but in practice it tends to be the recommendations for action put forward by the evaluation department that dominate the discussion in the committee. The committee does not itself decide finally what action should be taken with regard to specific projects or programmes, since operational responsibility must always lie with the relevant department which alone knows the full story, but it forwards its own recommendations for action to that department. However, when it comes to broad issues of policy, affecting perhaps general office procedure, these are within the competence of the committee and it will decide what action needs to be taken. The cover note is a crucial component of this feedback procedure, because the committee's time is necessarily extremely limited (it may have to discuss 2 or 3 evaluation reports at each meeting devoted to evaluation), and unless a lot of prior work has already been done to translate ideas into specific actions the Committee cannot operate effectively. Box 11.1 summarises the key features of the cover note system.

Box 11.1   The Cover Note System

Effective feedback of evaluation findings demands formal systems for the presentation of findings and recommendations to senior management. The Cover Note System is one such. It comprises a Cover Note attached to the evaluation report when it is presented to senior management, usually about 3/4 pages in length, and covering the following sub-heads:

1. Evaluation title, date and reference no.
2. Background to the project.
3. Main findings.
4. Summary of comments received from colleagues most directly affected, and associated bodies.
5. Recommendations for action:
   (a) those recommended by the consultants
   (b) report on Evaluation Department's discussions with colleagues on these recommendations.
   (c) the Evaluation Department's own recommendations for action, based on (a) and (b).

(The usual procedure is for there to be a follow-up, six months after the evaluation report and Cover Note were presented, to check what action has been taken.)

Feedback to Beneficiaries

A serious deficiency in the feedback procedures of virtually every aid donor is the way feedback to the beneficiary countries is neglected. Of course the evaluation team will have de-briefed the officials of the developing country where the project is located before they left, as a simple matter of courtesy. But the de-briefing that takes place, usually the day before the evaluation team leaves the country, is necessarily cursory in nature as the team will not at that stage have finalised their findings and may well be reluctant to discuss their likely recommendations with the recipients before they have submitted their report to whoever sponsored them. The evaluation report is generally sent to the beneficiary country for information, but usually only after it has been dealt with within the donor agency, and this may be many months, or even years, later. Even then feedback is not assured as there is evidence that the evaluation reports often do not percolate down to the actual project level, so that the people most directly concerned may never see them (Schaumburg-Muller, 1988).

Few donors have followed the example of the World Bank in asking the beneficiary country for its comments on the evaluation reports and then attaching these to the reports themselves when they are presented (although the Bank has found that the beneficiaries seldom in fact have any substantive comments to make). There are a few donors (mostly in Scandinavia) who have organised feedback seminars in the developing countries where the projects were located, and a few make a practice of allocating a small part of the budget for each evaluation to cover the feedback to the developing country (that is, a return visit by the evaluation team to present their report and to elicit reactions). Another useful way of involving the recipients in the evaluation process is to table evaluation results for discussion during the annual aid programme negotiations.

Apart from these initiatives, which are to be welcomed, it remains true that feedback to the beneficiary countries has hitherto been generally very poor, despite the fact that all donors pay lip-service to the need to foster the growth of evaluation systems in the developing countries. In the World Bank, for instance, this is listed as one of the responsibilities of the director general of the OED. This failure to involve the beneficiaries in feedback is doubly unfortunate because the local project managers and policy makers need above all others to profit from the findings of the evaluations (since they have to continue living with the projects long after the donor has left the scene). It is also important that the developing countries are encouraged, at every opportunity, to strengthen their own nascent evaluation capabilities. It is not surprising that the developing countries often regard evaluation as the special province of the donors, who they see as using this technique as a way of assuring their own tax payers that development aid is working. They are surely only likely to be reinforced in this view when they observe the rather cavalier attitude towards their interests, in this field, that so many donors adopt.

A relevant issue is the extent to which the developing countries should be involved in the actual carrying out of evaluations, but this is a major topic in its own right, with important implications for the future of the whole subject, and it is taken up in Chapter 19.

Follow-up Action

The question 'Who should be responsible for seeing that action is taken on evaluation reports?' was mooted in Chapter 4, and we must now address this issue. The experience of the last 30 years or so would tempt the cynical answer 'apparently it is no-one's responsibility', although that would certainly not be justified in the case of the agencies already mentioned that have specific arrangements for follow-up. I recall hearing a senior USAID official once complain at a meeting of the High-Level Group of the DAC in Paris, that most of his agency's evaluation reports finished up on colleagues' window sills unread, and I am afraid this has been the experience of all too many aid agencies over the years.

So whose task is it? First we can say that the evaluation unit should not take upon itself the responsibility for ensuring that action is taken on evaluation recommendations. This should be the task of the Projects and Evaluation Committee, or whatever senior body that performs a similar function. The evaluation unit should not try to become the conscience of the office as a whole. In any case it must always be the task of the department directly responsible for a project or a programme to decide what action should be taken in response to evaluation findings. As mentioned earlier the Projects and Evaluation Committee (or its equivalent) is not in a position to take decisions relating to the work of specific departments—only the department head can do that: the committee only takes decisions regarding broader strategies and policies that are cross-cutting.

However, if there is no such committee to recommend follow-up action, should the evaluation unit then have a more proactive role? In at least one agency the answer has been Yes. Thus a review of feedback procedures in the Norwegian aid agency NORAD states: 'The mandates of the evaluation units should extend to follow-up activities. A major part of the work on any particular evaluation should take place after it is finished and be concerned with introducing and developing its knowledge in the organization" (Scanteam International, 1993). Provided the evaluation unit's follow-up role is confined to 'introducing and developing knowledge' no doubt there would be general agreement that this is a suitable function for evaluation: the dividing line seems to be between such a function and that of actually ensuring that action takes place. Evaluators do not have the detailed knowledge of how the operational departments are running their affairs to be able to press them to take any particular course of action. If they tried to usurp the proper responsibility of the latter in this way they would soon lose their credibility and the confidence of colleagues. The evaluation unit might possibly share some responsibility for monitoring and evaluating whatever follow-up action is taken (for example, in advising on methodologies), but it should not assume primary responsibility for the follow up itself.

Having said that, one has to admit that if some of the ideas now being discussed about evaluators becoming more involved with the stakeholders, even to the point of them becoming 'negotiators' (as discussed in Chapters 19 and 20), come to fruition, the question of responsibility for follow-up takes on a rather different complexion. It may be that with socially-oriented projects, where participatory evaluation is practised, the 'within-project' feedback has to be instant. It takes place as an integral part of the evaluation process itself, and cannot be separated from it. Similar difficulties arise vis-à-vis the evaluation of process approach projects as described in Chapter 6. These types of evaluation raise difficult questions about the true role of the evaluator, which are taken up more fully later on. Even so, however, for the many evaluations where participatory evaluation techniques are not appropriate, follow-up of action taken on recommendations remains the responsibility of senior management and not of the evaluation unit.

A common experience of most aid evaluators is that their evaluation recommendations do not immediately (if at all) lead to action at the strategic or policy-making level. The reasons for this are discussed later (Chapter 15).

Feedback Outside the Agency

So far the discussion has been about feedback to the two parties most immediately concerned, that is the donor and the recipient. But what mechanisms exist to facilitate feedback to the other parties involved, like the Parliament and the media (representing the taxpayers), consultants, private sector businessmen, and academics? In some countries, feedback to the press is not very well organised and comprises mainly the distribution of short evaluation summaries, but some donors, such as NORAD and DANIDA, make a practice of presenting their evaluation results at press conferences where the evaluation team is represented. The holding of seminars, to which representatives of the various interested parties are invited, was mentioned in the previous chapter. In addition, some donor agencies, such as DANIDA, make special provision for members of Parliament, leading academics or consultants, and representatives of private sector businesses and trade unions, to participate in evaluations organised especially for them. The aim is to give them some direct feedback which gives them a 'feel' for development aid and which is altogether independent of the evaluation work of the ministry's evaluation unit. Some agencies encourage journalists (and sometimes provide them financial assistance) to visit overseas projects, for example, when a minister or a senior aid official is visiting the project, so that they can write first hand reports of what they have seen. This kind of feedback may not be technically very expert, but in terms of public relations it can have a great impact.

Informal Feedback

So far the discussion has been exclusively about formal feedback, as if this is the only kind of feedback that matters. But that is not so. There is always a lot of informal feedback going on all the time. For example, there is informal feedback whenever members of staff talk to each other about their work or their travels, and especially when staff from the agency's head office in the developed country pay their regular visits to projects overseas. Informal feedback is probably at least as important overall as formal feedback. But, in the nature of things, it is not easily monitored, nor can it be readily channelled in any particular direction, and therefore it does not render formal feedback unnecessary.

Use of Evaluations in Training

A much neglected aspect of feedback hitherto has been the potential use of evaluation reports in training the staff of donor agencies, and of course the staff of institutions in the recipient countries. Evaluations are excellent for training because, unlike project appraisals, which are concerned very much with projections and forecasts, evaluations are concerned more with documenting and analysing what has happened. They have the ring of truth about them, and are more down-to-earth than appraisals, which tend to be heavily economic in character. But at the same time they generally involve the use of a wide range of economic, social science, and anthropomorphic techniques. In addition, they comprise an ideal basis for training in logical framework methods, and I have on many occasions used evaluation reports as raw material for logical framework seminars. In the case of the Norwegian aid administration, a 'School of Development Cooperation' has been set up to systematise learning, and monitoring, and evaluation reports constitute an important input into its curriculum (Scanteam International, 1993). In the World Bank, evaluators from the OED also participate in the training seminars for participants from developing countries run by the World Bank Institute, and they use these occasions as opportunities to disseminate evaluation findings and to give training in evaluation methodologies.

Notes

1. On a recent visit to Germany, I found that this system is now only rarely activated, which seems a pity when one considers how effective it was.
2. I was very pleased to find, when visiting the Evaluation Unit of DG VIII of the European Commission recently that a new system has now been introduced (which I was told was in direct response to our report, so evaluations do sometimes have an impact!). This involves a newly created policy support group whose task is to receive evaluation reports and to recommend, and monitor, whatever action it is agreed should be taken on them.

12

Feedback

Part Three: The Role of Management Information Systems

'When you can measure what you are speaking about, and express it in numbers, you know something about it, but when you cannot measure it, when you cannot express it in numbers, your knowledge is of a very meagre and unsatisfactory kind'

(Lord Kelvin, 1883, quoted in Management by Objectives, Civil Service College)

'Now what I want is Facts... Facts alone are wanted in life'
(Mr Gradgrind, Hard Times, Charles Dickens)

'Truth is never pure, and rarely simple'
(The Importance of Being Earnest, Oscar Wilde)

'Experience is in the fingers and head. The heart is inexperienced'
(Thoreau)

Data Rich but Information Poor

Every individual maintains a personal stockpile of information in his or her own memory, and generally this is not just a haphazard jumble of odd facts and figures but a carefully sieved and sorted inflow of facts that are mentally classified for quick retrieval. Similarly, every technical expert in an aid organisation keeps a personal databank of key parameters (e.g., cost per student place, square feet of hospital space per patient, man-hours required to grow certain crops, etc.), as well as a databank of a less statistical kind comprising experience gained in implementing aid policies.

An organisation does not automatically have such a corporate memory—it has to create one. The personal databank of each individual in the organisation is not available to the corporate body as a whole, except through such occasions as meetings and seminars when information can be shared. Moreover, when individuals leave the organisation they take their personal databanks with them. An organisation has to establish a corporate memory bank rather in the same way as an individual does, that is by the careful sieving, storage, and classification of information. At first the emphasis was on a statistical corporate memory, so that at least the organisation was able to track what it was doing in a numerical sense, and that has been the main emphasis in many aid agencies up to now. But more recently the main thrust has moved towards a corporate memory geared more closely to the management needs of the organisation.

Donor agencies have made significant advances in recent years in the introduction of management information systems (MIS). Their primary purpose is to improve the flow of information available for internal management purposes, but an important secondary role is to enable the agency to provide key information about its activities to outside enquirers (e.g., Parliament, pressure groups, media, etc.). An MIS should serve the following functions:

- Provide critical decision-making information in a timely, useful and cost-effective manner;
- help project administrators manage resources to achieve the desired development objective within the prescribed time-table;
- track the flow of project inputs, activities, and outputs, for accounting and planning purposes;
- assist managers to modify project activities within the parameters of the project system;

- serve as an early warning system to signal serious deviations from expected project implementation, and thus to prompt selective interventions;
- report progress and identify problems to be solved (Frerks et al., 1990).

A legitimate criticism of these systems is that up to now they have been 'data rich but information poor', or, as Widstrand has put it, 'Most often large scale organizations have data banks, but no institutional memory: they never seem able to draw on earlier experience' (Widstrand, 1990). As Patton has pointed out, our age can store information but does not know how to use it (Patton, 1997). In short, the existing management information systems yield a lot of factual data about such things as the number of projects the agency is handling; where they are located; how much is spent on them, etc.; but they (as yet) do not provide much information about whether aid operations are successful or not, and why.

Evaluators obviously have a vital interest in such management information systems. They find the data itself useful, because it helps them to assess how representative their evaluation programmes are of the agency's work as a whole, in terms of type, size, and location of projects, etc. Representativeness may not be the primary concern in the selection of projects for evaluation, but it must always be there as one of the relevant criteria, so the evaluator needs to be able to test whether the programme is satisfactory in this regard. But even more important, evaluators appreciate that as management information systems are further developed, from the provision of bare factual data to the provision of more qualitative information, so they will provide valuable avenues of communication for evaluation findings throughout the organisation.

Another advantage of the aid agency having a computerised management information system, from the evaluator's point of view, is that it makes it possible for a consistent approach to be adopted at all stages of the project cycle. As mentioned earlier, most agencies are now introducing procedures for tying the logical framework into the existing standardised monitoring forms, and into the PCRs, so that they comprise an integrated computerised monitoring framework. Typical of these is DFID's computerised information management system that was introduced in 1992–93, and which is illustrated in Figure 12.1. Data generated from the office forecasting spreadsheet (the 'OFS' in Figure 12.1) is fed into the MIS, whilst information also flows in the opposite direction to the country strategy paper. Of greater importance from the evaluation point of view, however, is the information stream that begins with the

Figure 12.1 DFID's Information Flow System

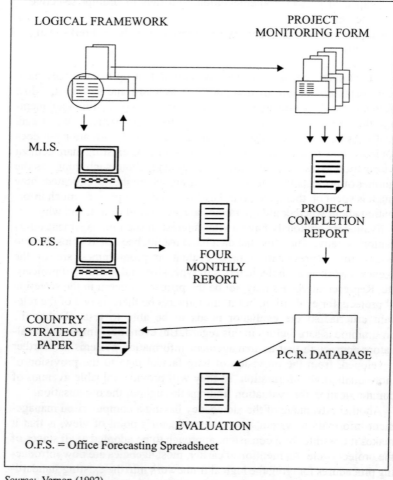

Source: Vernon (1992).

completion of the logical framework. The links between each stage of the project cycle, namely the appraisal stage (when the logical framework is prepared), the implementation stage (when monitoring takes place), and the PCR stage, are automated so that the key project data generated in the initial logical framework are carried through on the computer to the two succeeding stages. Not only does this save having to copy out all this basic information time and again, but it also ensures that the same criteria that were used in the logical framework are also used in the monitoring process. When the project has been completed, instead of the project officer having to scour through old files trying to find the relevant information, it is automatically brought forward on the computer and fed into the PCR. Similarly, if the project is eventually evaluated the same basic project information, and criteria, are used. The latest development is that DFID has set up an Intranet (i.e., an internal version of the Internet) and the EVSUMs have been put onto it: the PCR database will also be put on it in due course. But this is just a staging post on the journey towards an even more comprehensive data storage and retrieval system, which is known as PRISM. In a speech to the UK Evaluation Society in December 1997, Mr George Foulkes, Parliamentary Under Secretary of State, DFID, announced that EVSUMs would shortly be available on the Internet (Foulkes, 1998).

Information Flows in a Typical Project Cycle Management System

The Department for International Development can be regarded as reasonably typical of a medium-sized donor agency. The project level information flow begins with the drawing up of the project memorandum, which sets out all the key information about the project, including the logical framework and the work plan, and possibly an activity chart. Once implementation is under way the following information flows take place:

Project Reports

These are carried out by non-DFID staff, for example, contractors implementing projects. The form used compares project progress with what was planned in the original project memorandum, at the activities and output levels of the logical framework (all projects of £250,000 or above have to have a logical framework matrix). The respondent has to report on various practical aspects, such as staff changes, visiting consultants, trainees, equipment and books, comments on the inputs/activities in general, and, most importantly, comments on the risks and assumptions in the logical framework, and whether these have caused any problems. The key factor is that the project reporting system is now geared closely to the logical framework, whereas in the past it was left to the contractor to more or less decide for himself/herself what to report on.

Monitoring Reports

These are prepared by DFID staff, often stationed overseas. They focus on progress in achieving outputs and purpose in the logical framework, and they also look at the assumptions. They make use of the indicators set out in the logical framework. It will be noted that these monitoring reports have moved up a notch in the logical framework hierarchy of objectives as they are concerned both with the achievement of outputs, and of purpose. They tend to be more concerned with objectives than with the physical implementation of the project. The frequency of monitoring missions can vary from a period as short as every 3 months, to annual visits. Again, the key point to note is that the monitoring is geared closely to the logical framework, but in this case they are capable of recommending changes to the Logical Framework matrix if they think these are called for. When reporting on project progress (both at the purpose level and at the goal level) respondents have to apply the rating system described in Chapter 7: these ratings are an important input into the MIS.

Reviews

These are carried out by DFID staff, jointly with other stakeholders. They are particularly concerned with progress at the project purpose and project goal levels. They can also provide useful information on aid effectiveness and impact. The Evaluation Department of DFID is intimately concerned with the conduct of these reviews. It issues guidelines on methodology, and its staff may participate in them when they form part of the agreed evaluation programme for a synthesis study. These reviews are considered to be particularly important in the case of process approach projects, because of the need to modify the design of the project as implementation proceeds. All reviews of projects over £500,000 are sent to the Evaluation Department which will then extract information for synthesis reports from time to time.

It will be observed that there is no mention of the participatory approach to monitoring in the above, but this is because DFID expects arrangements for this kind of monitoring to be worked out with the beneficiary stakeholders and local implementing agencies, during the initial project design stage, in conjunction with the recipients. It is difficult to introduce standardised procedures for these monitoring exercises in advance.

Policy Information Marker System (PIMS)

The policy information marker system (PIMS) is an information system that DFID has devised to enable it, among other things, to marshal, at very short notice, whatever information is available about certain topical and politically sensitive topics. It enables the minister, or the senior officials, to respond virtually instantly to any request (including requests from the DAC or other international bodies) for basic information about DFID's involvement in these key sectors. The information is also very useful for policy debate within DFID, and for monitoring, aid management and project design purposes. Every bilateral aid project with a commitment value of over £100,000 has to be considered for a PIMS marker.

The system incorporates a scoring mechanism related to the extent to which each project is targeting DFID's priority policy aims. This greatly enhances the usefulness of the PIMS for the Evaluation Department because it provides a valuable pointer to the projects that are geared most closely to meeting the ministry's priority policy objectives, and which would therefore be good candidates for evaluation. The system was reviewed in 1997 to bring it into line with DFID's new priorities. There are now 33 markers, clustered in three main groups, as follows:

Policies and actions which promote sustainable livelihoods

- Sound social and economic policies
- Access of poor people to land, resources and markets
- Human rights
- The removal of gender discrimination
- Training and skills development
- Reducing the illicit drugs trade
- Direct assistance to the private sector
- Good governance
- The prevention and resolution of conflicts

- Business partnerships
- Rights of the child

Better education, health and opportunities for poor people

- Lower child mortality
- Essential health care
- Effective universal primary education
- Post primary education
- Safe drinking water and adequate sanitation
- Emergency and humanitarian needs
- Lower maternal mortality
- Reproductive health services
- Literacy, access to information and life skills
- Food security
- HIV/AIDS

Protection and better management of the natural and physical environment

- National strategies for sustainable development
- Sustainable agriculture
- Efficient use of productive capacity
- Urban development
- Sustainable forest management
- Integrated management of water resources
- Protection of the global environment
- Energy efficiency
- Biodiversity
- Desertification, land degradation and drought mitigation

Other markers:

- Knowledge generation

International Sharing of Information

Thanks largely to the role played by the DAC Expert Group on Aid Evaluation, there has always been a lot of sharing of evaluation results between the various donors. At first this was on an informal and unorganised basis, but gradually it became more systematic, and this process was taken a stage further when, in 1988, the Expert Group set up a Feedback Database to help the members tap into each other's databases more easily. Box 12.1 describes how this database works.

Box 12.1   DAC's Feedback Database (CIDA)

In 1988 the Expert Group on Aid Evaluation of the DAC set up a computerised inventory of evaluation reports, which is run, on behalf of the Group, by CIDA. By September, 1990, it had registered 2148 abstracts from evaluation reports, the leading sources being: USAID (499), CIDA (332) and the World Bank (269). By region, 35% dealt with development in Africa, 27% in Asia, and 17% in Central and South America. By sector, 20% were in Agriculture, Fishing and Forestry, 10% were in Education, 7% were in Transport, and 6% were in Health: the rest were scattered among the other sectors.

The Database was originally designed as a simple hard-copy bibliographic tool, comprising: the title of the evaluation, author, date, language, and a short description of the nature and content of the report. However it was soon decided to expand the latter and also to add planned future evaluations. So that member states do not have to go to CIDA every time to access the Database a scaled down version of it has been developed and has been distributed in disk form. It was not envisaged that Third World governments would use the Database. The system was evaluated in 1991, and it was decided to continue it: also that access to it should continue to be restricted to members of the Expert Group. In October 1991 it was decided to allow UN specialised agencies to have access to it, and in 1992 on-line access was provided on an experimental basis.

Sources: Development Journal (1990); OECD (1993).

In addition to the DAC Database, CIDA maintains a comprehensive internal management information system of its own. The main findings are extracted from monitoring reports and evaluations and incorporated into the computerised data bank. For a decade or so now it has been possible for CIDA desk officers to flash onto their computer screens the complete life history of any project in summarised form, beginning with the main elements of the logical framework (showing the objectives, and inputs and outputs of the project), and continuing with the summarised results of monitoring missions and evaluations. This is an information system, rather than just a data system. Other donors, like DFID, are still some way off from achieving this level of information reporting. But, as stated earlier, they have already made provision for the key findings of monitoring missions (and project completion reports) to be put onto the computerised MIS, and it will not be long before this is extended to include the key findings from PCRs and evaluations as well.

Management Information Systems in the UN Family

The United Nations

During the 1980s, when the bilateral aid agencies were developing their management information systems, the United Nations (UN) agencies also began to move down the same road. Hitherto they had established excellent statistical services, but these did not go far enough, as they did not provide any indication of the extent to which the organisation was achieving its qualitative objectives. In 1980, the director general for Development and International Economic Cooperation of the United Nations called for the establishment of 'an institutional memory to facilitate the systematic storage and retrieval of country information and the results of past experience' (United Nations, 1980). As a result, the United Nations Development Programme (UNDP) developed a project institutional memory system (PIM) which is an extensive computerised catalogue system, listing all the agency's projects according to their principal characteristics. It did not, however, contain any indication of the results of the projects, so it still fell short of what the director general had sought.

UNIFEM

Since then, other UN agencies have been evolving their own management information systems, but none of them have attempted to incorporate qualitative information about project success or failure to the same extent as the United Nations Development Fund for Women (UNIFEM) has. The reason for UNIFEM being at the forefront of this development is that, of all the UN operational funds, it alone is mandated to demonstrate that direct action in support of women in the Third World is crucial for successful development. UNIFEM also wanted to demonstrate that a new focus on quality-of-life, and gender issues, could be a helpful counterweight to what they considered to have been an excessive emphasis on purely economic objectives of development. Because of this concern, UNIFEM was keen to build an institutional memory that went well beyond purely statistical recording and which covered the qualitative impact of the agency's operations in a way that would enable macro conclusions about the usefulness of the agency's activities on behalf of women to be drawn.

For this purpose UNIFEM realised that it had to rely basically on the flow of information that came from the on-going monitoring and evaluation processes. Up to that time a mass of this kind of information had been collected, but it had not been processed and stored in such a way that it was readily retrievable; nor had any attempt been made to analyse it in terms of the impact of UNIFEM's activities in general. To fill this gap, UNIFEM devised, with the help of a consultant, an ingenious knowledge bank, which identifies certain indicators of project impact in such a way that they are comparable across projects. The model provides a defined and workable set of 'common denominators' to enable disparate development project inputs and outputs, occurring in different timeframes, to be compared (Silvert, 1990). Box 12.2 briefly describes this intriguing approach to a qualitative information system, which is both 'data rich and information rich'.

Other UN Information Systems

Most of the larger aid agencies have now developed automated data reference systems. Typical of these is the keyword system developed by the World Bank (the 'evaluation textbase'), and similar systems developed by USAID and other agencies, whereby data is entered into the database under carefully selected key-words aimed at pinpointing the most relevant topics and findings in each report. Apart from the intensive labour input involved, the main problem with this is that it is difficult to encapsulate many of the most significant findings in just one word or phrase. Retrieval of information is not easy, and may require a lot of practice, and more time than most hard-pressed aid administrators ever have. It is not surprising therefore that evaluations of the effectiveness of such systems have shown that they tend to be used more by researchers and academics, than by aid administrators. If the information is not available, quickly and without too much effort, on their own computer screen, the aid administrators will tend to make do without it.

Box 12.2   UNIFEM's Knowledge Bank

UNIFEM was the first UN operational fund to devise an information system that enables qualitative information on the results of agency projects to be stored, processed and retrieved. Its computerised "Knowledge Bank" comprises two tiers as follows:

Tier I: *Information Baseline System.* This comprises factual information about projects, e.g. where they are located, size and type, etc, as well as information flowing from on-going monitoring and evaluation processes.

Tier II: *Effectiveness/Impact System.* This is the innovative part of the system. Impact is not measured by an overall indicator of impact, but rather by a ranking (or rating) of directionality (i.e. positive or negative outcomes), and the amount of impact that the projects have had on the participants within the time-span of the projects. These rankings are made by a Review Committee comprising three very experienced assessors (the choice of three is to avoid the risk of stale-mate), who do their rankings and then list their reasons. The former are susceptible to computer processing, whilst the latter can be retrieved through descriptor codes.

The two tiers are inter-dependent, each reinforcing the other. The system enables UNIFEM to present an impact analysis of completed project/programme support activities in a qualitative and measurable form, as well as indicating how participants' situations have changed as a result of UNIFEM's activities.

Source: Silvert (1990).

Evaluations of Database Systems

Several UN agencies have now carried out evaluations of their database systems, and these have shown that in many respects too much information in a databank is as hard to cope with as too little, especially if it is out of date or largely irrelevant. Staff who have taken the trouble to utilise the databanks only to discover that the information is ten years old, or relates to technologies that have become redundant, may well not bother to try again. Therefore it is important to keep the databank material relevant and up to data. This was the main conclusion of a detailed review of NORAD's systems of corporate memory in 1993: 'We would like to warn against creating a completeness which also gives access to old, irrelevant material automatically. This will create an over-complex and impractical situation which will drastically reduce the relevant use' (Scanteam International, 1993).

The International Labour Organisation (ILO) is another agency that has recently evaluated its experience with its database system. It was in 1986, when the volume of the ILO evaluation reports had reached the stage where they could no longer be handled on a card index system, that a new computerised evaluation database called 'PROGEVAL' was established. The aim was to enable the ILO staff to have quick access to the lessons learned from the ILO evaluations. It contains well over 1500 bibliographic references to evaluation reports of all kinds.

In 1993 an evaluation of PROGEVAL was carried out, and it was discovered that the system was not being widely used—or even known about (only 28.5 per cent of respondents had heard of it) despite the efforts of the evaluation unit in the ILO to publicise its existence (ILO, 1993). Project managers working in remote locations could only make use of PROGEVAL during their rare visits to the ILO field offices. On the other hand, the evaluation found that a high percentage of ILO officers in the field, as well as those at the headquarters, were using personal computers. This has led the ILO to consider putting PROGEVAL data onto diskettes for use in personal computers, with particular attention being paid to the identification of suitable menu-driven software to enable the data to be retrieved. Eventually, as CD-ROM readers become more widely available, these diskettes could be phased out.

The ILO has carried out cabling work at the headquarters to provide officials with on-line access to all databases in the house via the International Labour Information System (ILIS). Coinciding with this the evaluation unit has launched a campaign to increase staff awareness of the evaluation database. According to the 1993 evaluation, the information in PROGEVAL appears to be meeting the expectations of staff. Most highly appreciated were the evaluation reports emanating from ILO itself: less interest was shown in the evaluations carried out by other UN, or non-UN, agencies. Understandably (in view of their lack of instant access to other sources of data) the staff in the field generally indicated greater interest than those at the headquarters. The respondents said that they used the information mainly in connection with project preparation and formulation, but also for drafting terms of reference. The evaluation reports were also valued for the lessons they contained, especially the 'evaluation highlights' which were produced from the evaluation reports indexed in PROGEVAL.

As regards improvements to PROGEVAL, the respondents suggested that the information should be 'supplemented with full texts of documents ranging from evaluation guides and formats to specimens of "good" examples of project documents and project design elements such as statements of objectives, examples of indicators of achievements, descriptions of outputs and activities, etc.' (ILO, 1993).

Are Automated Data Systems Cost-Effective?

It is probably true to say that the agencies that have invested most heavily in automated data systems have been somewhat disappointed with the results, set against the costs. One of the leading agencies in this field, CIDA, has now realised that it relied too heavily on automated data systems in the past and it is now attempting to correct this imbalance by emphasising that informal feedback mechanisms, such as briefing sessions and seminars, should be seen as important complementary sources (OECD, 1990). There is no doubt that in terms of getting someone to change their accustomed practices, or to revise their ideas and philosophies, an ounce of face-to-face dialogue is worth a pound of automated data. The latter will always have a place, especially for staff working in isolated locations and without access to libraries or easy communication with professional colleagues, but it can never be a substitute for personal interchange.

Part 4

Impact,
Empowerment,
Stakeholder Analysis and
the Participatory Approach

Robert Picciotto, concluding his article commemorating the work of one of aid evaluation's best known pioneers, Albert O. Hirschman (The New Role of Development Evaluation in Rethinking the Development Experience—Essays Provoked by the Work of Albert O. Hirschman, [1994] L. Rodwin and D.A. Schon [eds], Brookings Institution and Lincoln Institute of Land Policy) wrote as follows:

The new development agenda has shifted the focus of evaluation in directions previously explored by Hirschman. His evaluative methods are calculated to irritate, surprise, and sow seeds of doubt; and in the ensuing puzzlement, he has often brought people together by undermining the certainties and dogmas that divide them. In short he has sought to contribute to the reform cycle through contrarian means. The evaluation profession is fast catching up. Within the framework of visibility and disappointment, evaluation contributes to the channelling of information and the encouragement of participation to convert the energy of public protest into constructive learning and reform. Now that the social dimension of development is receiving more attention, cost-benefit analysis is being enriched by multidisciplinary impact assessments, and participatory evaluation techniques are yielding their own contrarian findings. In time, Hirschman's surprising ideas will be included in the basic tool kit of evaluators not only because of their conceptual appeal but because they will be found to be helpful in facing up to reality.

Impact Evaluation

'One of the generally amiable idiosyncrasies of man is his ability to expend a great deal of effort without much enquiry as to the end results'

(John K. Galbraith)

'Man is a short-sighted creature at best'
(Colonel Jack, *Defoe)*

'Experience comprises illusions lost, rather than wisdom gained'
(Joseph Roux)

In recent years, impact evaluation has become important because donor agencies have become aware that projects that appeared to have been implemented effectively at project completion often seem to run into severe difficulties later on. Moreover, it became evident that in many cases it was not the target populations (usually the poorer people) who were benefiting most but rather the richer people who were in a better position to capture for themselves the benefits of the development aid.

Characteristics of Impact Studies

An impact study is hardly concerned at all with the process of aid delivery: it is assumed that the monitoring procedures and PCRs will have yielded adequate information on that. Rather, it is about the impact of the project on people, on the environment, on the economy, and on the social and political structure where the project is located. As discussed in Chapter 7, it also considers the unintended impacts, as well as the negative impacts that are so often an inescapable consequence of many development projects. An impact study will nearly always focus especially on the impact of the project on target groups. The distributional effects will be carefully studied. In the case of a dam project, for example, the impact study will concern itself with the distribution of benefits (and disbenefits) among the populations living both above and below the dam, as well as those benefiting from the power generated or from the water for irrigation. The expected distributional effects will certainly have been considered at the appraisal, but probably rather superficially. This is so partly because the key parameters will tend to be the economic rate of return of the project as a whole, and partly because the required information will not be available before the project starts. One of the key functions of impact studies is to throw light on distributive effects (or re-distributive effects not foreseen in the appraisal), so that they can be taken into account more effectively in future appraisals of similar projects.

Despite the obvious need for them, impact studies are still not all that common. This is because they absorb a lot of resources, take time to implement, and need to be conducted in full cooperation with the beneficiary country where the project is located, especially when language problems are involved. The typical procedure is for an impact study to follow on from a normal ex post evaluation mission which is concerned mainly with looking at the factors of sustainability and reporting on the extent to which these have been satisfactorily covered in the project design and implementation. Such a team, which usually spends only a few weeks in the country, and usually does not speak the vernacular language, cannot carry out an impact study by itself. All it can do is to make arrangements for an impact study to be carried out by a research institution in the developing country itself. This would nearly always involve a random sample survey of some kind, and so field investigators will need to be appointed and trained in what they have to do. The field survey may well take up to six months to complete and then the results have to be computerised and analysed. The impact study report is often written on a joint basis between the institution carrying out the impact study and the evaluation team appointed by the donor agency that had recommended it.

The above procedure was the one I adopted, with my Finnish and Zambian colleagues, in the impact evaluation of the 'Practical Studies in

Zambian Schools' project in 1994. This project, which was funded by FINNIDA (Finnish International Development Agency) lasted from 1974 to 1990: the impact study was carried out in 1994 (Cracknell et al., 1994b). Box 13.1 describes how this impact study was planned and implemented.

Box 13.1 Impact Evaluation of the 'Practical Studies in Zambian Primary Schools' Project

The Finnish aid agency FINNIDA funded this project from 1974 to 1990. The aim was to establish the teaching of practical subjects (i.e. carpentry, metalwork, craft skills, etc) in all Zambian primary schools. A series of on-going evaluations were carried out every few years, and the final ex-post evaluation took place in 1994. This concluded that the project had been only partly successful, mainly because the Zambian parents preferred their children to learn academic subjects so that they would at least have a chance (small though it may be) of getting a modern-sector job with relatively good wages, but also because many of the tools had been stolen, workshops had not been completed, and teachers had been transferred to teach other subjects. However the evaluation team noted that there were signs of a change in parental attitudes, as a result of the long process of economic decline and the consequent fall in wage levels in the modern sector. They recommended that an impact study should be carried out to throw light on this aspect in particular.

The impact study was planned and implemented as a joint exercise between the Finnish evaluation team (comprising 2 donor representatives and one Zambian), and the University of Zambia who would be responsible for the field work. Structured interview guidelines were drawn up and 18 third-year social science students were engaged and trained in interview techniques, They visited 448 teachers, 971 ex-pupils, 1010 parents, and 182 employers. The results were computerised and analysed by the University, and the impact study report was prepared jointly.

The report confirmed what the evaluation team had observed, namely that a very significant shift in parental attitudes had taken place during the last few years in favour of children learning practical subjects in school. This change affected not only pupils and parents but also teachers, and to a lesser extent, employers as well. It is now possible for a trained carpenter or plumber to earn a better living than a junior office worker—and far more chance of finding employment. The chances of success for the project in the future are therefore much enhanced, although this "window of opportunity" is unlikely in fact to alter the present situation very much because of the extreme shortage of funds in the education sector as a whole.

The impact study cost only about $ 10000, yet it provided valuable new insights, gave useful experience to Zambian researchers, and constitutes a database that will prove very helpful to the Zambian Ministry of Education in future years.

Source: Cracknell et al. (1994b).

The World Bank's Approach to Impact Studies

The World Bank started carrying out annual impact studies (mainly of agricultural projects) as far back as 1979, most of which involved attempts, through the use of socio-economic surveys, to assess the impact on the target beneficiaries. However, the Bank decided to move more decisively in this direction as a result of the review carried out in 1985 of completed projects and already mentioned in Chapter 1 (World Bank, 1985). This showed that many of the projects that had been successfully implemented a few years previously, with good rates of return, had run into difficulties and were then yielding only a poor economic rate of return. In 1993, the Bank set up an interim Working Group to prepare guidelines for impact studies, and they commissioned an English economist, Professor John McInerney of the University of Exeter, to assist them (World Bank, 1993). Because these are expensive and time consuming the Working Group recommended that only selected projects should be subjected to impact evaluation and the criteria it recommended were:

- There should be lessons of value for future projects.
- There should be sufficiently good documentation to make an effective impact study feasible, especially as regards the target population: the PCR rating should be at least satisfactory.
- There should be no overwhelming methodological or procedural problems, for example, inability to identify a relevant impact indicator.
- Ideally there should be some special features that might enhance the value of the project for impact evaluation—examples might be: projects that exemplify best practice; projects with inherent uncertainties that need investigating; projects of special innovative interest; and projects that are especially costly.

The Working Group suggested that there were two approaches to impact evaluation—the exploratory approach and the explanatory approach. The latter attempts a systematic explanation and quantification of the changes being analysed, and this would involve using experimental methods, like control samples. The exploratory approach, on the other hand, accepts that the full experimental approach is likely to prove very demanding in time and resources and opts for a simpler technique which involves documenting the changes that have occurred without trying to establish a control. The Group recommended that the Bank should adopt the exploratory approach as being the more practical and realistic one: 'With a large number and variety of projects to evaluate for impact, and a growing demand for impact study findings, a methodology and procedures which lead relatively quickly and reliably to more informed decisions is to be preferred to a small number of rigorous explanatory research studies which will often fail to deliver' (World Bank, 1993).

The Group identified four steps in an impact evaluation as follows:

Identification: Noting whatever changes (impacts) have taken place that can be attributed to the aid agency's intervention. These impacts may be intended, associated (i.e. linked in some way to the project, but only indirectly—these are often unintended impacts); accessory (i.e., impacts for which the project was only partly responsible); or unrelated (i.e., no obvious link with the project is apparent, but one needs to check).

Measurement: Trying to quantify or assess the significance of the changes (impacts). Participatory rural research methods will generally be most appropriate for this purpose.

Attribution: Trying to establish the causes of the changes, especially the extent to which they can be attributed to the aid agency's intervention.

Assessment: drawing together all the threads, and forming a judgement on the impacts in relation to the aid input: making recommendations for future aid activities of a similar kind.

As a guide to identifying likely impacts, the Group recommended categorisation into five 'impact domains': technical impacts, economic impacts, socio-cultural impacts, institutional impacts, and environmental impacts.

Impact Studies and the Beneficiaries

As stated earlier, a crucial element of any impact evaluation is the impact of the project on the intended beneficiaries—the target population. This is of prime importance because experience has shown that often projects fail to benefit the poorer people for whom they were mainly intended. However, this is not enough by itself. One cannot be content merely to focus only on the impact on the intended beneficiaries: one must also study the impact on all the people affected by the project—whether intended beneficiaries or not. Only in this way can one hope to pick up the unintended impacts, and the disbenefits of the project. This is the main reason why the impact evaluation process cannot be reduced to a standard series of steps, as if it were some kind of mechanical procedure. A restless, investigative, stance is essential—a determination to study all the ripples created in the pool by the stone of the aid intervention wherever they may lead. What is clear is that the impact evaluator will be much assisted in this task if there has been conscientious impact monitoring during the life of the project.

One of the biggest advantages of impact evaluations is that they generally involve the officials and direct beneficiaries of the recipient country in the carrying out of the surveys. Thus not only is there a useful transfer of skills in the field of survey design and implementation, but all the results remain in the developing country and are available for further research, especially by university or research institution personnel. The Zambian impact study described in Box 13.1 yielded valuable information that the Ministry of Education badly needed for its own management purposes, and the fact that one of the three members of the impact evaluation team was a senior official of the Zambian Ministry meant that he was fully aware that the information existed and was in a position to make sure that it was used. Impact evaluation reports are of great interest to other donors as well because they throw a great deal of light on significant socio-cultural, environmental and other factors which are of common concern.

Timing of Impact Studies

It is not easy to decide what is the right time to carry out an impact study, and it probably varies in any case from project to project. If it is carried out too soon after project completion there may not have been time for the full impact to be felt. But if it is left too late other factors, not related to the project, may distort the picture. The World Bank Working Group recommended around five years after project completion as a rough guide. However, World Bank projects tend to be much larger and more multifaceted than many other projects, and so a shorter period might well be more appropriate for less complicated projects.

Second and Third Round Effects

One of the more difficult conceptual problems of impact studies is to decide how far to go in following the ripples of a project outwards. Every project has not only a direct impact on the beneficiaries, and others closely linked to it, but also an indirect impact on an ever widening circle of people. For example, if an agricultural project leads to substantial increases in farmers' incomes, they in turn will want to spend most of that increased income, and how they decide to spend it will have an effect in all sorts of directions. To investigate these 'second round', or even 'third round' effects (sometimes called 'spread effects' or 'multiplier effects'), the World Bank in the early 1970s initiated a major study of the Muda Irrigation Project in Malaysia (Bell et al., 1972). This found that these indirect effects were highly significant in terms of the wider economic and social impact of the project. For every dollars worth of paddy rice produced, it was found that another 75 cents worth of downstream benefits had been created (e.g., in construction, retail sales, restaurants, etc). Most farmers had a high leisure threshold and they began to hire labour as soon as their own income rose above a modest level. In fact, the increase in the wages of the landless workers in the region actually exceeded the increase in the incomes of the farmers themselves.

A similar situation occurs on the other side of the project equation—the inputs side. The agricultural project will cause more inputs, such as fertilisers, feeds and equipment, to flow into the area, and this will increase the incomes of the traders. These backward and forward linkages form an important component of impact studies, but it is not easy to decide how far down this road the evaluator should attempt to travel. The World Bank study just quoted was very expensive (as it involved many extensive field surveys), and time-consuming: it was really just a 'one-off' to explore the situation in a typical project. It would not be reasonable, or even possible, given the constraints on resources, to expect these wider impacts to be studied in any depth as a matter of course. Generally speaking, it can be assumed that such effects will occur, and they need only be studied if they are expected to be of an unusual nature.

Distributional Effects

Some of the problems of carrying out impact evaluations arise from the need to assess the distributional effects—especially the impact on the poor. These people are usually the least accessible members of society, and the least articulate. They seldom keep records, and generally only speak their own vernacular language. They are hard pressed just to survive, and field investigators are not always welcomed with open arms. Winning the confidence of poor people is not an easy matter and it cannot be rushed. Impact studies do not easily fit the pattern of a three-week evaluation mission. Even getting to the more remote parts of the country can add greatly to the cost of the study, and can take an inordinate amount of time. Finally, the host country may well be reluctant to let outsiders contact the beneficiaries directly for fear of generating aspirations that cannot be satisfied, especially if the evaluators are trying to contact poor people who were not direct beneficiaries of the project but who were affected by it—possibly in an adverse way. Many of these problems apply to any evaluation, whether of an impact type or not, and they are discussed more fully in Chapter 16 in relation to the evaluation of poverty alleviation projects.

Impact on Women

In recent years, the impact of aid activities on women has been a topic of particular concern, but again the problems of measurement are acute. Few published statistics differentiate between men and women, and often the men presume that they can always speak on behalf of the women. This makes contacting women directly very difficult. I once attempted to evaluate the impact of a Nordic project concerned with cooperatives in Kenya on women. Even with the help of a Kenyan colleague it was an extremely difficult task. The women would not volunteer information if there were men present, and the men did not take easily to the idea that the women had a right to ventilate their own ideas. In Moslem countries the difficulties are almost insurmountable, unless there is a Moslem woman on the evaluation team. Over the last few years, I have been a team leader of an evaluation of a major European

Union-funded project in Egypt, and it was only because we had a lady sociologist on our team that we were able to make any direct contact at all with the women in the rural communities of the Delta. Even so, she had to be almost aggressively insistent on seeing the women alone as the Egyptian men could not understand why this should be necessary.

Impact Indicators

The choice of appropriate indicators is a crucial part of every impact evaluation, and at least some of them should be chosen by the beneficiaries of the project themselves. For the most part the indicators chosen will be specific to the project being evaluated and are just as likely to be qualitative as quantitative. In addition, there are likely to be some general indicators reflecting improvements in the overall living standards of rural people. If possible the indicators should be applied not only to groups affected by the project but also to those not affected, so that a comparison is possible.

Purely by way of illustration, the following is a list of indicators of income and living standards, suitable for impact evaluation, prepared by the World Bank:

Examples of Indicators of Income and Living Standards

- changes in household income (often hard to assess);
- changes in cash income from a particular crop or activity (usually easier to collect than total household income);
- changes in levels of expenditure (i.e., as proxies for income);
- changes in selected types of expenditure (e.g., education or health care);
- use of cash and changes in expenditures by different members of the household;
- levels of food consumption;
- quality of housing, number of rooms and type of construction, i.e., as indicators of economic circumstances;
- amount and quality of land held securely;
- access to potable water supplies;
- access to electricity;

- access to sanitary facilities inside or outside the house;
- household furnishings, possessions and consumer goods;
- availability and quality of accessible public goods, such as roads, schools and health centres;
- numbers of children in school (World Bank, 1993).

Administrative Aspects

Historically the high cost of impact studies has been one reason why so few of them have been carried out. It is important to find ways of reducing the cost, for example, by making greater use of local institutions and consultants, and by adopting the exploratory rather than the explanatory approach. Savings could also be made if it became customary to build in impact indicators from the very start of a project rather than waiting till it is evaluated, and to extend the monitoring process to include the collection of this kind of data. The World Bank estimates that an impact study should cost between $60,000 and $120,000, depending on the extent of local fieldwork required (World Bank, 1993), but it must be kept in mind that World Bank projects are typically much larger than those of most other aid agencies.

—————— 14 ——————

Evaluating Sustainability

'Experience teaches slowly, and at the cost of mistakes'
(James Anthony Froude)

'Sustainability is in many ways the ultimate test of development efforts. It requires not only that a project be successful in achieving its objectives during the project life but also that the benefits it generates continue beyond the time of the donor's involvement—the durability of success'
*(*Sustainability in Development Programmes, *DAC Expert Group on Aid Evaluation)*

'An optimist is a guy that has never had much experience'
(Don Marquis)

The Factors of Sustainability

The concept of sustainability is so central to the whole process of project cycle management, and therefore for monitoring and evaluation, that it deserves a chapter of its own.

Sustainability was defined in a review of the subject carried out by the DAC Expert Group on Aid Evaluation (OECD, 1989a) as follows:

A development programme is sustainable when it is able to deliver an appropriate level of benefits for an extended period of time after major financial, managerial, and technical assistance from an external donor is terminated.

Donor agencies' universal concern with sustainability springs from the same source as the current emphasis on impact evaluation, namely the realisation that many projects turn out to be unsustainable once the aid component comes to an end. A project may even achieve its immediate objectives (e.g., the construction of a road to open up a natural resource), yet may not be sustainable without government support. There are many reasons for the lack of sustainability: the project may be starved of funds to meet recurrent costs, because the government has not made, or cannot make, adequate financial provision; the project may suffer from inadequate management ability once the well trained and experienced expatriate manager leaves; the government may give the project low priority once there is no longer any question of aid funds being involved. Whatever the reasons, the end result, in a depressingly high proportion of cases, is that the projects cease to operate effectively, or even fail completely, a few years after the donor's involvement has ceased.

In the past it seems to have been assumed that the donor's chief role was to establish an economically and technically viable project, and that if this was done the project would automatically be sustainable without any special measures being needed to ensure that it was. But as the feedback from evaluations and impact studies began to yield evidence of widespread post-project failures, donors became aware that provision for sustainability had to be built into the project cycle right from the start and at every subsequent stage.

In April 1990, the World Bank published the results of an analysis of 557 Bank supported operations. It found that 15 per cent were judged unlikely to be sustainable; 52 per cent were judged likely to be sustainable; and the rest were judged either marginally sustainable or uncertain. Africa had the lowest percentage of projects classified as likely to be sustainable (32 per cent), and Asia the highest (65 per cent) (World Bank, 1990). Ever since the publication of this report the World Bank has given major emphasis to sustainability factors in all its evaluation work.

The DAC Expert Group on Aid Evaluation published the results of a study of the factors of sustainability in 1989 (OECD, 1989a), and this suggested that there were seven factors. These seven factors form the subject matter of this Chapter.

First Factor: Need for a Strong Recipient Country Government Support

Unless a project continues to have adequate support from the recipient country's government it is unlikely to be sustainable. Sometimes donors take the initiative in fostering projects that fit their own criteria for aid well, like projects in the field of poverty alleviation, or environmental protection, but which may not carry the full support of the government which may have priorities of its own. If the donor makes it clear that it will only give aid for projects in certain selected sectors the recipient country's government is likely to accept the aid since otherwise it might not get any at all. But as soon as the aid stops the project is left starved of resources because the host government never gave it any priority in the first place. Another possibility is that by the time a project is completed there may have been a change of government and the newly appointed minister now responsible for the project may not give it the same level of priority so it gradually withers on the vine. It may not always be possible to guard against this eventuality because one cannot usually foresee when such a change of government will take place. But if it is seen to be a possibility at the project appraisal stage it might be possible to select for aid funding a project that is less liable to be overturned if a political change takes place.

One of the reasons why agricultural and rural development projects often show up badly from the sustainability point of view is that they often involve institutions operating at very different levels, some at the grassroots level, and some nearer the national level. Often these are at loggerheads with each other, and this does little for sustainability. A similar situation often prevails in education and also in health.

Second Factor: Need for Adequate Local Managerial Ability and Effective Institutions

Managerial ability is one of the scarcest resources in most developing countries, and it is very likely that once an expatriate manager leaves, and a less experienced local manager takes over, the project will run into problems. The solution is not to keep the expatriate manager permanently in post but rather to plan several years ahead for the eventual hand-over of management, which means giving training, especially on-the-job training, to whoever is destined to take over the management.

Closely allied to the need for managerial capability, is the need for strong institutional support (e.g., in the government and quasi-governmental bodies that may be destined to have ultimate responsibility for projects), and this again usually boils down to the need for skilled personnel. As the complexity of aid-funded projects tends to increase the demand for human capital becomes more critical for sustainability.

The evaluation of institutional development (sometimes called 'capacity building') has assumed much greater importance in recent years as many donors, notably the World Bank, have elevated this topic to the front rank of their development priorities. Every World Bank evaluation now has to assess projects not only in terms of sustainability in general but also in terms of institutional development in particular. At a seminar on evaluation in 1994, the representative of the Inter-American Development Bank reported that 'The experience of the IDB indicates that institutional factors often determine the success or failure of development programmes', and this is the common experience of other donors as well (OECD/IDB, 1994).

A whole new branch of economics 'new institutional economics' has arisen, which does not simply accept the existing institutions as given but looks into the question of how they came into being, and whether they are appropriate for current needs. It is now widely agreed that effective institutions are as important to a country's development as is the possession of natural resources. Criteria for effective institutional development which recognise the need for the government to provide certain basic services and physical infrastructure have been evolved, whilst at the same time leaving enough freedom for the private sector to develop in its own way. Clague has identified three types of information needed for evaluating institutional development:

- information on business people's perceptions on how well government agencies·are performing;
- information on the types of contract that are in use in business and types that are not;
- • information on how particular bureaucracies function (Clague, 1995).

DANIDA has had more experience in evaluating institutional development than many other agencies, and it has identified three key issues that need to be evaluated as follows:

- the integration of international assistance into national and local institutions (it is vital to check that donor involvement has not introduced dislocations or biases);
- the sustainability of the institutional arrangements (e.g., well-meaning donors can supply too many experts, so that an institution may be crippled when they leave);
- the effectiveness of the instruments and measures applied for capacity building (OECD/IDB, 1994).

A key finding from the experience of most evaluators of institutional development is that donors should be cautious about sponsoring new institutions, and should rather strengthen the existing ones if they can.

Third Factor: Need to Choose Technologies Suitable for the Recipient Country

It often happens that, because aid is tied to the supply of equipment from the donor country, Western type technologies, that are not appropriate for the recipient country, are used. They may not have the expertise to repair and maintain the equipment, nor may they have the foreign exchange with which to buy replacement parts. Moreover, perfectly adequate local technologies are often available: they may require more labour, but as a rule labour is not a scarce resource. I once visited a complicated computer-controlled pumped water supply installation in Botswana which was not really needed because a simple gravity feed system would have done the job almost as well and without any of the complications of the Westernised system. The European engineer in charge said that as soon as he went the local authorities would revert back to a simpler system, and the computer system would no longer be necessary. Unless appropriate technologies are employed, aid projects are unlikely to be sustainable.

Another problem is that small developing countries find themselves having to cope with a variety of different kinds of equipment supplied by different donors. I recall walking along the platform at Dar es Salaam station and noting that locomotives from at least four different countries were being used. The burden of having to train engineers to service these four types, and keeping stocks of spare parts, is one that poor developing countries could well do without: it is a frequent cause of non-sustainability of aid.

Fourth Factor: Need for Socio-cultural Compatibility, Local Participation and Gender Awareness

The widespread failure to relate aid projects to the socio-cultural circumstances of the recipient countries is one of the most common causes of post-project failure. The problem is that aid projects are often planned and implemented without adequate consultation with the principal beneficiaries. The project planners tend to assume that they know best what people want, and they do not bother to ask them first. They may have implemented a similar project successfully elsewhere, and they assume that what works in one place will work in another, or perhaps they are simply trusting their own judgement. Another factor is that asking the intended beneficiaries what they want is not actually as easy as it sounds. Often there are language problems, and it takes time to organise attitudinal surveys, especially if they have to be held in conjunction with a local institution. Meanwhile there are usually considerable pressures to push ahead with the project because the politicians (at both ends) are impatient and want to see the project being executed whilst they are still in power! Whatever the reason, the fact is that projects are often designed 'for' people rather than 'with' people, so that when the aid dries up the projects may collapse.

A particular deficiency in much project planning hitherto has been a failure to consider the role of women (OECD, 1989c). In most developing countries the women play a key part in all agricultural and rural activities. They are far more than wives and home-makers. They do much of the farm work in the fields; they collect firewood and help with the keeping of small livestock; and often they take part in petty trading. Projects involving rural communities are very likely to fail unless the women have been thoroughly involved in the initial planning, and continue to be given an important role throughout the process of implementation.

The recognition of the need to consider the role of women as an integral part of development, has been one of the most significant advances in the last decade, a decade characterised first by the establishment of 'Women in Development' (WID), that is, singling out women's issues for special attention; and more recently by the broadening of this concept to 'Gender and Development' (GAD), that is, women are now being seen as an integral part of any development strategy: both men and women being viewed in their socio-cultural and political contexts. Evaluating gender aspects involves two key concepts: gender *roles* (e.g., women's reproductive role), and gender *needs* (e.g., women's need of access to basic facilities like water, health care, and jobs, or their need to have a more equitable status in society). The concept of 'empowerment' is a powerful one in this context, just as it is with poverty-oriented projects. Up to now most evaluations have focused on their internal agency procedures regarding women's issues, rather than on the impact of projects on women, and the indicators used reflect this, for example, the number of women participating in training courses, agency staff gender awareness, etc. The Commonwealth Secretariat is the most gender-aware aid agency I have worked with, and there is hardly an activity that the Secretariat engages in where the gender awareness factor is not carefully monitored, but it too has difficulty in evaluating the gender impact of its projects in the recipient countries.

However, although the need for broader impact measures is now generally recognised, there are great difficulties in achieving this. A first step is to try to get the basic statistics disaggregated by gender, but despite the many attempts that have been made, little real progress has been made. Another step is to develop suitable indicators to measure gender impact more directly, for example, the extent to which women have access to credit, or control their own assets, or have political rights, etc. Participatory rural research methods are being used to throw light on such indicators as these, for example through gender disaggregated participatory mapping, transects, wealth or well-being ranking, and matrix ranking (Moser, 1995). Evaluation techniques in this area are still in the exploratory phase and many different methods are being used.

The proportion of evaluations covering gender issues is rising all the time. A study of 1315 evaluation reports, selected on the grounds that they contained direct or indirect discussion of the effects on beneficiaries, by the DAC Expert Group on Aid Evaluation, found that whereas in 1989 only 14 per cent of evaluations contained full discussion of gender issues, by 1993 that had increased to 37 per cent (OECD/CIDA, 1994). However, the report found that the quality and depth of gender discussions in evaluations still left much room for improvement. One problem is that if gender was not specifically mentioned in the project's original objectives it was often ignored, or treated only superficially, in the evaluation. The study's main finding was that it was the way the project had been prepared in the first place that had the most effect on whether gender issues were taken adequately into account. Thus if the socioeconomic factors had been thoroughly appraised in a participatory manner, with target groups shaping the design of the project, then there would be adequate recognition of gender issues subsequently. This led the report authors to recommend that gender consideration should be incorporated fully into every stage of the project cycle.

It is not enough to state in general terms, in the terms of reference for appraisal, monitoring, or evaluation, that gender issues have to be taken into account. They have to be specified in detail. The assessment of DAC members' WID policies, carried out by CIDA in 1994 on behalf of the DAC, which has just been quoted, proposed that the terms of reference, at each phase of the project cycle, should specify the following in particular:

- women should be identified as members of the target group;
- the role of women, as producers or decision takers, should be described;
- the participation of beneficiaries (men and women) in the early stages of the project cycle should be established;
- the gender strategies to be adopted by the project should be described;
- the gender-disaggregated data to be collected as the project proceeds should be stated;
- the plans for sustainability, in a gender disaggregated manner, should be summarised;
- the impact on women's workload should be monitored;
- the constraints to participation faced by women should be noted (OECD/CIDA, 1994).

If these key factors were incorporated into the terms of reference for the operations at every phase of the project cycle it would go a long way to ensuring that gender issues were more adequately covered.

The substantial progress made so far in WID/GAD issues has been due in large part to the work and influence of the DAC Expert Group on Women and Development, a sister group to the Expert Group on Aid Evaluation, and the two groups have worked together very successfully over the years. The dedication and commitment to the cause displayed by the Expert Group on Women and Development has helped to overcome the reluctance on the part of all but a few donors, at least in the early days, to adopt a positive stance on gender issues. However, it has to be recognised that insofar as that reluctance sprang from an instinctive feeling that attitudes to women are deeply embedded in the cultural soil of a country, and that those attitudes are unlikely to be changed as a result of pressure from donors with quite different cultures, it may have had some justification. This indeed is recognised in the OECD/CIDA Report of 1994: 'Some donors expressed concern with the possible imposition of donor values upon Third World women as an example of supply-driven development—an approach which could undermine long-term benefits and increase the risk of unanticipated negative impacts on women' (OECD/CIDA, 1994). I can echo this warning, having worked quite extensively in Egypt and other Moslem countries, and having personally encountered the attitudes of Moslem women to their own inferior status: they do not necessarily seek equality with men, and may well identify their status with ancient religious or cultural traditions. This is a highly sensitive area, and the CIDA/DAC report wisely concludes: "The challenge faced by GAD and WID is to promote the integration of women, taking culture into account, but without reinforcing traditional paternalistic patterns of behaviour" (CIDA/OECD, 1994).

Fifth Factor: Need for Projects to be Compatible with the Environment

In recent years, the environment has become a major factor of sustainability. If a project is implemented without adequate prior consideration of its likely impact on the environment it might actually do more harm than good, and might not be sustainable. This is of course especially true of projects relating to the exploitation and management of natural resources. Not so long ago it was possible, for example, for large dams to be constructed without adequate prior analysis of the likely impact on the environment, so that the ecology of the river basin has been permanently changed in ways that fundamentally affect the livelihood of large numbers of rural people. Sometimes forests have been cleared without sufficient attention being paid to the environmental effects, or to the need to ensure that the resource is renewed.

A special study of the problems of evaluating environmental issues was carried out by the DAC Expert Group on Aid Evaluation in 1989 (OECD, 1989b). It concluded that the aid donors still have a long way to go before environmental issues are adequately covered, either in appraisals or in monitoring/evaluation. Considerable progress has been made since then, but the basic problems still remain. One of the difficulties is that environmentalists have only quite recently been appointed to donor institutions, and they have hardly had time as yet to ensure that the subject is well covered. Perhaps understandably these specialists tended at first to engage in dialogue with other environmentalists in other agencies rather than in trying to build a closer relationship with the non-specialists in their own agencies, especially the economists. The DAC survey even considered that the subject was at that time still a 'ghetto', and that this isolation had to be broken down.

Up to now it has been the multilateral agencies that have advanced further in this field than the bilateral donors, mainly because they have been subject to more pressure from public opinion. They also have the advantage of close liaison with the United Nations Environment Programme (UNEP) and other agencies such as the Centre for Development Information and Evaluation (CDIE) in USAID which have fostered new attitudes and advised on appropriate techniques.

As to the extent to which environmental issues are adequately covered in evaluations, the DAC survey revealed that all the 10 member states, and 6 multilateral agencies that responded were disappointed with what had been achieved so far. Although standard terms of reference for evaluations nearly always include reference to the environment, in practice evaluators often have little to say about environmental aspects. In some cases this may be simply due to the fact that in a good many projects the environment is not an issue (e.g., institution building, manpower, food aid, health projects, or many research projects). The Swedish aid agency, Sida (previously SIDA) calls these 'environmentally neutral projects', but it warns that: 'A group of projects which at first sight appears environmentally neutral, but whose focus can cause environmental effects, form a grey zone which should be considered carefully. This type of project includes: education, vocational training, research, disaster relief, institutional support, and rehabilitation of existing infrastructure' (SIDA, 1994a). The failure to cover environmental issues adequately in evaluations is partly due to the fact that even where environmental aspects are relevant they were not properly covered at the appraisal, so there was no baseline data to build on. But often the main reason is simply that the evaluators themselves are seldom equipped for the task. It seems to be the case that only when there is an environmentalist on the evaluation team (or doing the monitoring) are the environmental issues dealt with adequately. Carrying out an environmental appraisal requires some training, whilst carrying out a more rigorous environmental impact assessment is a skilled task and it seems that only specialists are capable of doing them.

Sida recommends that the first step in any evaluation is to decide whether the project is 'environmentally neutral', or 'environmentally consequential' (bearing in mind the possibility of there being a grey zone as mentioned earlier). For the former, the evaluator needs to ask only one question: 'Have any positive or negative environmental consequences been noted?', and if the answer is Yes, to note what these have been, and what measures were taken to deal with them. But in the case of the environmentally consequential projects, the following procedure is recommended. First establish whether an environmental impact study has previously been carried out. If the answer is Yes, the evaluator then establishes what environmental changes have taken place that can be attributed to the project, and what has been done to deal with them. If the answer is No, the evaluator will have to try to build up a picture of what the environmental situation was when the project began, and then to assess what subsequent changes have taken place. Figure 14.1 illustrates this process (SIDA, 1994a).

Figure 14.1 Procedure for Evaluation of Environmental Projects

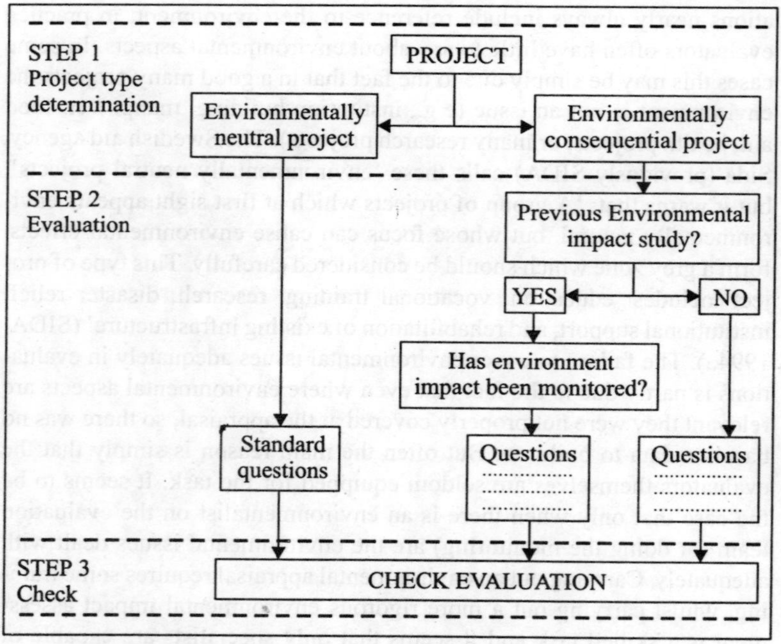

DFID has established a procedure for dealing with environmental issues throughout the project cycle, which also uses a process of 'initial screening' to establish whether environmental aspects are likely to be significant or not, and if they are it recommends that either an environmental appraisal should be carried out at the project appraisal stage, or (if environmental aspects are very significant) an environmental impact assessment (ODA, 1992). Both approaches emphasise the great importance, with environmentally significant projects, of carrying out some kind of prior assessment of the environmental situation, otherwise it will be very difficult later on to evaluate the environmental impact. On the other hand, because these can be expensive, it is equally important to establish in advance whether they are really needed.

One of the weaknesses in this area is that there seems to be inadequate linkage between environmental impact assessment and cost-benefit analysis. It is important that the costs and benefits of preventing environmental damage should be assessed in economic as well as physical terms: for example, methods of controlling harmful effluents may also enhance productivity, so there could actually be a commercial benefit to offset against the cost. The two methods most commonly used for calculating the economic impact on the environment are:

(a) calculating the effect on production of a particular environmental factor; and

(b) calculating what it would cost to put right any environmental damage caused as a result of the project.

Often the necessary technical knowledge, for instance, what the environmental impact of a proposed project may be, is missing. In logical framework terms, this means that there are few reliable indicators for measuring environmental factors, and a lot of research will be needed to establish them. In the meantime, in an attempt to side step this problem, attention is now turning to 'surrogate' methods of valuation. These are derived from observing what humans actually do. For example, if they are prepared to walk a long way to collect clean water it suggests that they value the product highly, and might therefore be willing to pay for it to be protected, or brought nearer their home (ODA, 1992). Another approach is to link environmental issues to pricing policies. For example, it is possible, through the price of a product, to influence customer behaviour in an environmentally friendly way. Thus a premium on leaded petrol will persuade more drivers to choose unleaded petrol. It is also possible to pursue a policy of 'the polluter must pay', through economic and pricing policies (Winpenny, 1991).

Another technique which has been used is to invite a group of experts to 'score' a project using pre-selected environmental criteria—sometimes called the 'Delphi technique' (Winpenny, 1995). Economic techniques such as cost-benefit analysis and cost-effectiveness have their place, but the general view is that environmental issues embrace a much wider area of concern, including socio-cultural, institutional and distributional aspects, and that any evaluation method must assess these wider impacts as well as the strictly economic ones.

Winpenny emphasises the importance of distinguishing between those projects with direct environmental objectives, and those that have indirect environmental impacts. He suggests that the latter cause particular problems. One reason for this is that there is a tendency to turn a blind eye to adverse environmental impacts, because these would reduce the expected rate of return. Examples of adverse impacts are: build-up of resistance to pesticides; contamination of water in aquaculture fisheries; spread of waterborne diseases; siltation of reservoirs; and soil erosion. The depletion of natural capital like the cutting down of natural forest, is often ignored, because the environmental effects may not be immediately apparent and may only work themselves out over a long period. There are also difficult problems of whether to apply the normal time discount rate, when the exhaustion of natural resources may be irreversible unless stemmed in time.

Winpenny recommends the 'LPDM approach', that is, listening, piloting, demonstrating, and mainstreaming, already described in Chapter 5—see Figure 5.4 (Winpenny, 1995). This would involve the stakeholders in a more integral way, that is through the 'listening' phase, and then through the piloting of small trial projects to learn lessons before replicating the projects on a larger scale. It is an approach very much in line with current thinking about the need to involve the stakeholders more. However, piloting may not be very practical if the environmental impact takes years to make itself evident. Moreover, one can see problems in the case of a major dam project for instance where the environmental impact may be problematic yet there is no obvious way of piloting on a small scale. There could also be ethical objections to carrying out pilot projects with potentially adverse environmental impacts.

A particular problem with environmental issues is that under severe stress ecologies can break down completely, and this can make an assessment of the risks in the logical framework a crucial, but very difficult, matter. Sensitivity analysis may have a special role to play in this context.

A complicating factor is that environmentalists sometimes tend to claim that their subject embraces virtually everything, including issues that are covered elsewhere, for example, in the evaluation of social or cultural impact, and perhaps paradoxically this may reduce their influence in the organisation. A similar thing happened with the physical planning development experts a decade or so ago who began to claim that planning embraced virtually everything, so that in the end no-one took much notice of them.

What is now urgently needed is more attention to the environment in monitoring, to ensure ultimate sustainability; and also better feedback of information on the impact on the environment of completed projects, including more ex post environmental impact assessments. As more of this kind of information becomes available it should be possible to better assess the economic, as well as the social, implications of projects that have significant environmental implications. Until everyone is better informed on these aspects, there is a risk that environmental issues could remain the poor relation of development—starved of resources and skilled personnel, and always a prey to tokenism.

Sixth Factor: Need to Ensure that the Project will be Financially Viable

All aid projects are subjected to rigorous economic analysis, with the main emphasis being on social cost-benefit analysis. A vast amount of effort has gone into the search for ways of improving project appraisal techniques. But it has now come to be realised that there was probably overmuch emphasis on social cost-benefit analysis and not enough on financial cost-benefit analysis. Thus if a project showed a satisfactory rate of return, using such techniques as border pricing, shadow wages etc, it was considered worthy of aid financing. Very little attention was paid to the actual cash flows: it was simply assumed that if the financial rate of return was significantly less than the economic rate of return the government would make up the difference. But in practice governments often were not in a position to do this, with the result that as soon as the flow of aid money ceased the projects were starved of cash and soon ran into difficulties. A typical case is a power station, where the social cost-benefit analysis would be calculated on the basis of an economic rate being charged for the power supplied (i.e., regardless of what the actual power tariff was). This took no account of the well known fact that governments in many developing country try to keep electricity rates low, with the result that the power authority is often too short of money to be able to fund even basic maintenance and repairs. This problem can be resolved if the likely financial deficit is foreseen and effective remedial action built into the project design. Donors have favoured the introduction of user cost changes to ensure that beneficiaries pay for the services they receive, and thus the supplying agency is kept solvent. Experience has shown, however, that this kind of resource mobilisation often depends heavily on strong community participation beforehand. The World Bank review of sustainability, referred to earlier, commented that for many projects 'sustainability has been determined by the capacity to compete for scarce financial capital available in the income or savings accounts of governments' (World Bank, 1990).

Seventh Factor: Need for Robustness in Project Design to Cope with the Unexpected

The only certain thing about project planning is that the future is uncertain, and not all the forecasts will work out as planned. Some degree of robustness in project planning is desirable to avoid project failure occurring as a result of the unexpected. In logical framework terminology, as mentioned earlier, if the degree of risk in the last column of the matrix appears to be unacceptable then it is necessary to redesign the project to cut down the risk element, even if in doing so the economic and financial rate of return is reduced.

Planning for Sustainability

When the importance of these seven factors of sustainability came to be fully recognised the main donors searched around for means of ensuring that they were provided for in a systematic way during project design and implementation. The European Commission (DG VIII), for instance, commissioned a special study on how this might be achieved, and the consultants came up with some very complicated ideas, but in the end the Commission settled for the simple but very effective mechanism of the integrated approach described in Chapter 5.

However, it is increasingly coming to be recognised that this kind of advance planning for sustainability is unlikely, in itself, to be enough. Sustainability will often depend upon, among other things, a continued flow of information vital for successful management. Whilst the donor was involved, this may have been ensured through the monitoring function, but once the donor leaves the resources (and expertise) may be lacking, and monitoring, especially impact monitoring, may fall away. To quote a Dutch workshop report: 'Since the impact of projects often occurs only after donor sponsoring has stopped, a system of evaluating impact after project termination is needed. This is probably one of the most important measuring tools for the sustainability of projects' (Frerks et al., 1990).

Equally important, as a means of fostering sustainability, is the need for donors to stand by with relatively small amounts of aid, so that they can respond to appeals for help some time after their main involvement has come to an end. Often this will involve only a short mission by one or two experts, or a series of such measures, or sending project staff for further training, but these could be vital for sustainability.

But above all, sustainability depends upon the responsiveness of management to the challenges that face it. As Hirschman pointed out, over 30 years ago, challenges produce responses, and provided this goes on happening it is not essential for project planners to get everything right from the outset (Hirschman, 1967). But this of course assumes that managers indeed have the skills to face up to crises as they come along, and this in turn points to the need for the fostering of capacity building and the ability to solve problems. Whether aid donors can do much to help recipients solve their management problems is a moot point: management skills are more often caught than taught. But at least they can put their weight behind any locally inspired initiatives to promote such skills, and can try to engender a cultural environment that rewards enterprise and initiative. The more aid donors can contribute towards these ends the more chance there is that aid projects will be sustainable.

The seven factors of sustainability are now incorporated into virtually all terms of reference for new evaluations, and are usually systematically covered in monitoring procedures. The DAC Expert Group on Aid Evaluation has promulgated guidelines on how they should be covered in the terms of reference for evaluations. These ensure that the eventual evaluation reports will generate information on each factor on a comparable basis, thereby enabling the international aid community to establish a really useful databank on sustainability.

15

Sectors Presenting Special Problems in Evaluation

Part One: Technical Cooperation, Research and Development, Good Governance and Policy-Level Evaluation

'If any ask me what a free government is, I answer, that for any practical purpose, it is what the people think it is'

(Letter to the Sheriffs of Bristol, *Edmund Burke*)

'Government, even in its best state, is but a necessary evil: in its worst state, an intolerable one'

(Common Sense, *Thomas Paine*)

'All government, indeed every human benefit and enjoyment, every virtue, and every prudent act, is founded on compromise and barter'

(*Edmund Burke*)

There are a number of sectors or types of projects that present special problems to evaluators, and they form the subject matter of this chapter and the following one.

Problems in Evaluating Technical Cooperation Projects

Proximate and Ultimate Effects

Some technical cooperation projects consist of technical back-up to engineering or construction projects, and these on the whole are straightforward and do not constitute a problem for evaluation. The main problems arise with the substantial block of technical cooperation that comprises institutional and human capacity-building assistance, such as training, experts, linkage arrangements with teaching institutions, etc. Here the main problems relate to the fact that technical assistance generally does not have a direct pay-off: it involves training or some other form of skill transfer that is intended to augment the stock of human capital, but it is likely to be some time before the benefits are actually realised. Because of this difficulty, evaluations often take the escape route of simply measuring the achievement of the immediate outputs of a project, such as whether the candidates were successfully trained, or experts satisfactorily completed their assignments, or institutional strengthening arrangements were implemented. These have been called the 'proximate effects' (Cassen et al., 1986). Much more difficult to assess is whether these trained people went on to help their country's development in the way that was intended; or whether the experts transferred skills that were in turn put to effective use; or whether the institutions generated skills that were applied effectively for the country's development. These are called the 'ultimate' effects. It is usually impossible to attribute these ultimate effects, with any certainty, to a specific piece of training, or the influence of a particular expert: they are 'joint products'. The achievement of the ultimate target will depend upon many other factors quite outside the scope of the project being evaluated; for instance, the trainees may find better paid jobs abroad, or the counterparts trained on the job by an expert may be posted to altogether different kinds of work where their training is not needed. In these circumstances how is the effectiveness of the technical cooperation to be judged?

The difficulty of attributing effects to causes in the field of training is one of the main reasons why most aid donors have cut back, or completely eliminated, those kinds of technical cooperation that aim to give a general technically-oriented education rather than more narrowly based training for a specific skill, usually for personnel associated with large aid-funded projects, that is 'project related training'. Others have criticised this policy on the grounds that it reduces the flexibility of the developing countries' access to training assistance, and that generalised skill training is more likely to yield benefits over the lifetime of the person trained, than narrowly focused training.

Early evaluations of technical cooperation focused almost exclusively on the proximate effects, but in the last two decades or so attempts have been made to cover the ultimate effects as well. For example, some evaluations of training have involved meeting study fellows some time after they have returned to their own countries, usually in their own places of work. Their employers and colleagues may also be interviewed at the same time. I once led a team of evaluators who visited Indian study fellows in their work situations in many Indian towns and cities, and we found the results to be of much greater value than if the evaluation had concentrated only on the training received, rather than on how it was put into practice (ODA, 1982). Follow-up evaluations of this kind have now become far more common, and they are often combined with tracer studies, which are surveys designed to find out to what extent the trainees have used their training in a work situation.

Economic Approach to the Evaluation of Technical Cooperation

There has been a lot of discussion in the evaluation literature, as to whether an economic rate of return can be calculated for technical cooperation projects in the way that it can for most capital aid projects. Back in the 1970s, the World Bank carried out a major exercise attempting to calculate such a rate of return for education projects in Kenya. It cost a lot of money, and the results were certainly interesting but despite all the resources used it was still difficult to say with any certainty what the economic returns were, or to what extent they could safely be attributed to the educational inputs (or were perhaps more a reflection of innate abilities). That approach has seldom been adopted since, although there are a few technical cooperation (TC) evaluations that have used economic criteria, such as the ODA evaluation of an open university project in Pakistan (Collister et al., 1979), or another ODA evaluation of the training given to Indian railway workers, which showed that one of the trainees had been able to suggest an improvement in fuel efficiency which had led to an estimated saving of £3.9 million in fuel costs, compared with the £6000 cost of the training (Hume, 1990).

One of the leading commentators who favours an even more determined attempt to quantify the benefits, is Professor Paul Mosley. In a paper to an evaluation workshop in Lysebu, Norway, in 1990 (Mosley, 1990) he urged that much greater efforts should be made to estimate the economic value of the outputs of TC projects, and also that a comparison should be made of the cost-effectiveness of the particular kind of TC input being evaluated and the various possible alternative ways of achieving the same objectives. The latter is virtually never done in TC evaluations (presumably one reason being that it would involve the evaluator in the collection of a lot of economic data not directly related to the actual inputs being evaluated). At the very least, Mosley argues, one should look into the question of whether a study fellow brought to a developed country for training might not more economically have been trained in his own or a neighbouring country. For example, an evaluation of ODA assistance to the Indonesian Institute of Public Administration found that parts of the project's training activities could have been organised in Indonesia for less than one third of the cost of organising them in London (Lowcock and Watson, 1988); or possibly a particular programme of training in a third world institution could have been planned more cost-effectively. To take another example, anyone evaluating a British aid project which involves sending British experts to a developing country should also take into account the indirect costs, such as housing, that the host country might have to meet, as well as the direct costs, and compare the situation with what it might have been if an expert from elsewhere had been engaged, but this kind of comparison is virtually never done. Mosley recommended that at least 25 per cent of TC evaluations should be carried out not less than three years after the termination of the operation, so that some assessment of impact can be made. The British Council routinely follows up British aid funded trainees one to two years after their return, but maybe this period should be extended to three years (despite the concomitant risk of failing to make contact with them after such a long gap). Mosley also recommended that all evaluations of training should involve interviews with the trainees' employers. He concludes: 'The sensitivity and detail with which eventual USERS of a TC process, rather than simply the trainees themselves, are probed is probably the best test of professional competence in this difficult and under-researched field'. As indicated in the previous paragraph, Mosley is pushing against an open door, as most donors are now trying to do this, although there is still some way to go.

New Approaches to TC Evaluation

An important contribution was made to the debate on quantification of the results of TC projects, when the then Head of the ODA Evaluation Department, and a colleague, presented a paper to the Action Aid Conference on the effectiveness of British aid for training in 1990 (Morris and Lowcock, 1990). They first pointed out that the use of the project framework for all ODA projects helped to ensure better evaluation of TC projects because the objectives, and criteria of success, now had to be established at the beginning of the project. They then described some of the new approaches to economic quantification that were being tried out in ODA. For example, there is the 'switching value' technique, whereby the minimum increase in output (e.g., worker productivity arising from a training project) that would be needed in order for a pre-determined rate of return to be achieved is calculated. This level of output is called the 'switching value'. The evaluator then judges, on the basis of experience he has gained elsewhere, whether this level is likely to be achieved. Another is a scoring system which assigns numerical scores to a completed project under each of a number of criteria, such as implementation performance, benefits created, sustainability, and impact. These are added together to give a score for the project as a whole, and this can be compared with scores for other similar projects. Finally, they describe a method that quantifies the economic costs and benefits as far as possible whilst stopping short of attempting a full-blown cost-benefit analysis. Thus the first step would be to calculate the costs of the training—this is straightforward. Then one systematically lists the expected outputs and effects, using a standard check-list approach. Finally, one compares the two, and in some cases the results will be 'clear cut' (i.e., outstandingly successful, or outstandingly unsuccessful), and in others it will be less obvious. In the latter cases, one cannot take the evaluation much further, but at least the clear-cut cases will have been identified, and they could yield important lessons. To sum up, the method involves the following steps:

- calculate cost per unit
- systematically list the effects per unit
- judge whether these effects are:
  - worth significantly more than the costs
  - worth significantly less than the costs
  - or can't say!

It may seem to be a bit messy, but the results could highlight important lessons for TC policy.

Some of the problems of evaluation of TC arise from the fact that each donor is approaching the subject from its own point of view. Colclough, in a paper to the same Lysebu workshop mentioned earlier, put forward the interesting suggestion that one of the UN agencies (the obvious candidate would be the United Nations Development Programme) might take upon itself the task of evaluating TC, from the viewpoint of the recipient rather than the donor. 'Shifting the locus of analysis to the recipient, and using personnel from a range of different agencies, together with local staff, would refocus the criteria for evaluation strongly upon the developmental impact of TC projects and programmes. Matters of agency politics would be downgraded in importance in comparison with the present system' (Colclough, 1990).

Despite the difficulties of economic assessment, technical cooperation is generally considered to be the most effective of all forms of aid, and this is supported by a wide range of evaluation studies. The Cassen Report *Does Aid Work* (1986), quoted above, contains a reference to a World Bank study of 95 completed technical cooperation projects involving TC aid to institutions, which found that 36 per cent achieved 'substantial success', 51 per cent were 'partially successful', and 13 per cent had 'negligible' results. These good results seem to be a fairly typical picture of evaluation findings in this sector.

Problems in Evaluating Research and Development Projects

Peer Group Review

The evaluation of research and development projects raises a number of special problems. For instance, the researchers are likely to be so pre-eminent in their particular field that it may be difficult to find a generalist evaluator with enough understanding of the context of the research to be able to evaluate it. One solution commonly adopted is 'peer group review', that is, getting other researchers working in the same field to comment. A variant of this is the 'panel of experts' approach that has been used by DG XII of the European Commission (Georghiou, 1995). These panels comprise experts in the technical field itself, experts from other fields, users of the results, and others with management and science policy experience. Generally, this system has worked well, although a review in 1988 found that it was 'liable to confuse its mission between evaluation of the researchers in the programme, and its correct target, which is the value added by the programme as a system of research' (Georghiou, 1995). A second difficulty was that 'A panel, unused to evaluation, may not be able to ask the right questions, and to remedy this it was proposed that guidelines should be drawn up'. I was commissioned by DG XII in 1991, together with a Belgian colleague, to carry out this review of evaluation procedures used in the Commission, and to prepare suitable guidelines (Sensi and Cracknell, 1991).

The main criticism of the 'panel of experts' system of evaluation is that the members of the panel, whether researchers or users, are likely to be biased in favour of research resources being steered towards their sector, and they may even hope to benefit themselves in the future. To meet this criticism, great care has to be taken in the selection of the members of the panel to try to balance the need for expertise against the need for independence, and to ensure that the whole process is transparent and open to public debate.

Another criticism is that although the panels have been competent to examine the technical quality of the research, they have not been so successful in reviewing the economic and social aspects. However, these are relatively minor criticisms, and the general opinion in the European Commission is that the panel approach has been very successful. Peer group review, of which this is one example, is likely to remain a distinctive feature of the evaluation of research and development.

Applying the Logical Framework to Research and Development Projects

Turning from the general to the particular, there is a special problem when it comes to the application of the logical framework to research and development projects. With research and development projects, the element of uncertainty is much greater than with other projects, and indeed the search for solutions to problems is central to the whole exercise. This kind of uncertainty is not something to be avoided if possible (which would normally be the case with other projects) but has to be accepted as an integral part of the project. Research, and to a lesser degree the application of research findings, is essentially a matter of experimentation. One tries various different approaches in the hope that at least one of them will prove successful. It is a characteristic of research and development (R&D) projects that just one successful 'strike' among a lot of failures can often justify the whole enterprise. But even if none succeeds, one has at least added this negative finding to the general stock of knowledge, and adding to the stock of knowledge is what research and development is all about.

The problem that arises is—how does the evaluator cope with this kind of 'risk' in the context of the logical framework? Whereas the risks usually entered in the right hand column of the matrix are those that one would avoid if possible, in the R&D case there is no question of trying to avoid them because they are an integral part of the project. Similarly, there are problems with the objectives and with the indicators of performance. These cannot be set out with any certainty because of the many unknowns. It would be absurd to establish rigid indicators when the result of a specific intervention is as yet unknown. Instead of 'If (a) then (b)', it is a case of 'If (a), then we think it should be (b) but it could also be (c) or (d)'. The solution to this dilemma is to develop the idea of 'milestones', that is, one needs to identify a series of sequential steps, or objectives, but only the first one or two of these can be launched upon with any assurance and indicators set. The subsequent steps are best regarded merely as useful milestones, or guideposts, on the way to achieving the ultimate objective of the research. They give some indication of how the project manager sees the project evolving, but the actual path the project takes will depend upon what happens in the first few stages. As to the risks, these are not to be avoided, or even to be minimised, as they are inseparable from the project design. Instead, the best approach is to assess the degree of risk involved in moving from one milestone to the next. This will help the project manager (and others above him) to monitor carefully what is happening as the research moves through its various stages. As with TC evaluation it is messy, but at least it is better than trying to apply rigid evaluation methods that are likely to fail and could cause researchers to lose confidence in the approach altogether.

Problems in Evaluating Good Governance

The State—Help or Hindrance?

In the 1980s a major change took place in the way the role of the state was regarded. Previously it had been seen as a prime mover in development, but from the 1980s onwards it has been viewed more as a constraint. Now the emphasis is on trying to ensure that the state keeps to its proper sphere, and leaves plenty of room for the growth of the private sector and quasi-government organisations or NGOs where appropriate. It is another application of the principle of subsidiarity—let the state do what it has to do but do not encourage it to expand into other areas. At the same time, the donors have come to realise that in the past, poor governance had a severe adverse effect on aid-funded activities; so during the last decade or so good governance has become a high priority with donors. There are now many projects and programmes aimed directly at improving governance, whilst even with other projects and programmes it is recognised that good governance may be a necessary condition for success. Therefore evaluating good governance is now an important task facing evaluators.

However, it is by no means an easy one. Although most people have a general idea of what good governance means (e.g., free and fair elections, adherence to human rights, freedom of association, etc), there is no universally accepted set of precise criteria. Moreover, many people are now less sure than they were, even a decade ago, as to what the criteria should be. To take one example: it seems to be generally assumed that multi-party systems are more likely to lead to good governance than are one party systems. However, research has shown that democratic governments have generally been weaker and less forceful in the pursuit of their goals than authoritarian ones, and have supported greater inequalities (although they may have been able to protect civil and political rights and freedom of association) (Healey and Robinson, 1992).

Another complicating factor is that if political parties are split on ethnic lines (unfortunately politicians often have no compunction about playing the ethnic card where it suits them), and free elections are likely to bring into power one of the larger ethnic groups, which may then totally ignore the interests of other ethnic minorities, is this an advance towards good governance or not? In short, may there not be some inconsistency, in a situation of ethnic rivalry, between free elections and human rights? Perhaps the latter need to be enshrined in the governance of the country before free elections can really work.

Some commentators believe that only when there is an independent and robust indigenous business class, to act as a counterweight to political influence, is democracy likely to flourish (e.g., it was the coalition between the urban middle and business classes with the trade unions that brought about a peaceful change of government in Zambia).

Is Democracy Always Good for Development?

According to Healey and Robinson (1992), there has not yet been enough empirical research to indicate whether in fact liberal and competitive regimes are more favourable to development than more authoritarian ones. Those who have researched into this issue are themselves divided. Some have found that authoritarian regimes encourage stability, and even reduce inequalities. Others see democratic systems, and economic and social development, as mutually reinforcing. Yet others take the view that neither interpretation is correct, and that in fact the nature of the political regime is not the main factor affecting economic and social development. Such uncertainty makes it very difficult to suggest straight-forward criteria for evaluating good governance. If there has to be a trade-off between economic and social growth, and freedom of association, etc., who is qualified to make such a judgement other than the people themselves?

Some researchers believe that the tendency to regard the development of the country as the highest goal of government is a rather dangerous one, since it can generate expectations far ahead of any possible means of satisfying them, which erodes people's confidence in the government and eventually a military coup is likely to take place.

Experience has shown that any evaluation of governance has to be embedded in a thorough understanding of the socio-cultural setting, that is, what has been described as the 'soil' in which development takes place. Some soils foster the growth of good governance—others do not. Research results indicate that government works best in socio-cultural settings comprising many horizontal civic associations, that is settings where there exists a 'civic culture'. The main socio-cultural variables have been identified as: mechanisms for dispute resolution; tolerance of outsiders; attitudes towards resources; the legitimate locus of authority, including the separation of powers; and organisational boundaries (i.e., where does a person's allegiance lie?) (Klitgaard, 1995).

What makes the evaluation of governance so sensitive is that it necessarily involves the notion of legitimacy. Culture is a 'process of social groups contending for legitimacy, the state being one of the more powerful forces in the struggle' (Partridge, 1995). Most bilateral aid donors, and indeed many international agencies such as the World Bank, mostly have to work through governments, and therefore may seem to be in support of those in authority, whereas it is commonly accepted that the main development challenge today is to empower the poor and powerless who are the local stakeholders of many aid funded projects. Any evaluation of governance must take cognisance of the need to incorporate all the stakeholders in the process of development.

There is at least one area where there seems to be a measure of agreement. Most researchers agree that political instability is bad for a country's development, as it deters investors and forces people to take a very short-term view of the future. Of course, it is not always clear what the proper inference from this should be. The causes of political instability can be many and various. Some argue that authoritarian rule is itself a basic cause of political instability, because it denies people the opportunity to protest and drives dissent underground. But others argue that democracy can also be a cause of political instability, because it provides a platform for opponents of the government who can whip up opposition, often in very dubious ways. Also, as indicated earlier, one of the most potent sources of political instability, in Africa especially, is ethnic rivalry, and there is plenty of evidence that political leaders are prepared to use it for their own political advantage regardless of the consequences. This points to the need for ethnic tolerance to exist before democratic institutions are likely to work satisfactorily. Possibly the growth of interest groups, such as trade unions or business associations, which tend to cut across ethnic boundaries, may help to create a more receptive climate for democracy.

There still remain many unresolved issues. Some would argue that democratic values and human rights are basic needs of people everywhere, no matter what their cultural background, and donors should do what they can to ensure that they have them. But others would take the view that these need to grow naturally from the cultural 'soil', and cannot easily be transplanted from outside.

In view of all the problems discussed above, it is not surprising that many observers are sceptical of the prospects for democracy in Africa: 'For Sub-Saharan Africa it is difficult to take a sanguine view of prospects for the revival of elected assemblies to provide the basis for increased legitimacy, to check the excesses of executive power, to debate policies, and to make laws' (Healey and Robinson, 1992).

How can we find a way out of this morass? What criteria of success or failure should the evaluator use? If we are genuine about wanting to listen to the beneficiary stakeholders, we should surely give greater emphasis than hitherto, to what kind of governance the local people themselves want than to what the aid donors think is in their best interests. The evaluator would do well to avoid making sweeping generalisations, or too many value judgements. Rather, it would be better to focus on a clear description of all the factors, political, economic, social and cultural, that have a bearing on 'good governance' in the actual circumstances of the case being evaluated. In particular, the evaluator would be well advised to concentrate on the positive factors making for good governance, rather than try to evaluate the punitive measures taken by some donors in an attempt to coerce the government of developing countries into carrying out particular policies. These positive factors fall into two categories as follows:

Public sector reforms

- promoting better management of the public sector;
- encouraging civil service reforms;
- pushing for greater accountability and transparency in government;
- strengthening the legal system and training the police;

Political reforms

- training journalists and promoting a free press;
- supporting human rights groups and other civic and non-governmental organizations;
- providing election monitoring;
- encouraging constitutional reform;
- assisting new political parties (IDS, 1995).

The last word on this difficult subject may be left to Healey and Robinson, who conclude their review of governance with these comments:

> On balance where does this leave us? Certainly there can be no assurance that political liberalisation or multi-party democracy will also ensure better economic management. Governments which no longer monopolise power, and are obliged to be more responsive to the effects of their actions on their citizens should, as a result, formulate policies which are better adapted to changing conditions and needs, and are more credible and workable. Nevertheless, such governments will have to negotiate conflicts of interest more openly and skillfully, and handle the pressure of increased popular expectations in the context of limited state resources. The prospect for a combination of greater political freedom and competition with

improved economic management, seems most likely under conditions where excessive expectations are not encouraged, where the skills and morale of the bureaucracy can be rapidly improved, and where those who hold power seek institutional mechanisms effectively to control overall public expenditure or its monetary financing (Healey and Robinson, 1992).

Problems of Policy-Level Evaluation

Policy Evaluation a No-go Area?

Some donor agencies take the view that their evaluation units should not attempt to evaluate development aid policy directly, as they do not believe there is any scientific and impartial way of evaluating policy.[1] The argument is that policy is simply what emerges from an elaborate process of give and take between competing interests. It is what it is, simply because of the balance of factors at the time when the policy decisions were taken. Therefore, it is argued, it cannot be directly evaluated. All the evaluator can do is to evaluate the **Effects** of a policy, and indirectly this provides feedback that would enable the policies themselves to be evaluated. However, other donor agencies do not see any difficulties in direct development aid policy evaluation, and are happy for their evaluation units to tackle policy issues head on. In fact, some agencies, as mentioned earlier, have two evaluation units, one concerned with macro policy issues and the other concentrating on project level issues.

As regards the policy environment of a project within the developing country itself, the tendency hitherto has been to take this as given as much as possible. However, the trend towards structural adjustment financing (and the associated practice of the donor attaching conditions) is drawing the donors more and more into close involvement in the macroeconomic policies of the recipients. In fact, it is impossible to evaluate this category of aid without forming a judgement on the recipient countries' policies and the way they are being implemented. So far the recipient countries seem to have accepted this, but it raises the question of whether the evaluators should not also be free to form a judgement on the policies of the donors, for example, regarding possible commercial and political objectives of aid; the relevance of aid tying, and other items on the donor's 'hidden agenda'. Should the evaluator be free to comment on what are often conflicting policies of the donor? These are very sensitive issues and may well be beyond the evaluator's competence. For instance, it is not self-evident that the commercial linking of aid necessarily operates to the disadvantage of developing countries as a whole, if the existence of such a policy is a necessary condition for public support for an aid programme in general. Such macro policy issues, however, are usually outside the scope of any one evaluation exercise.

Another factor that is drawing evaluators closer to policy issues is the trend towards syntheses. These usually relate to whole sectors, and inevitably there has to be a focus on the policy being pursued by the recipient in that sector, as well as on the broad sectoral policy of the donor. For this reason it is important that the recipients are full participants in the evaluations that feed into the synthesis reports, as well as in the seminars held to discuss the findings. Indeed, the debates on sectoral policy that syntheses generate could be among the most valuable outcomes of this kind of evaluation.

'One of the Rowers'

A common complaint of evaluators who have undertaken major evaluations of policy issues, is that often very little notice seems to be taken (at least in the short term) of the results. This leads to considerable frustration on the part of the evaluators (especially if they come from outside the aid agency), but it is now coming to be realised that evaluation results are only one input into policy making. Often the other influences (political, social, economic, etc.) are more important: also policy changes take a long time to work themselves out, and may take place some years after the evaluation findings, that provided the initial impetus, were presented. All that can be hoped for is that the evaluation findings will at least be taken into account when policy changes are made. Also, if the evaluators are able to participate in the discourse leading up to policy decisions, that is as much as they can reasonably expect: 'There cannot be a direct relation between the evaluation done and the policy lessons learned' (van de Knapp, 1995). The Head of the Evaluation Unit of the International Development Research Centre in Canada expressed it well when he said, in answer to a question about how his unit operates, that it was an actor in the activities being evaluated, and that 'The IDRC evaluator is like one of the rowers on a rowing team, rather than an observer watching from the shore' (IDRC, 1996). It is vitally important for the evaluators to understand what the potential user's needs are and to be able to present the findings in a way that addresses those needs as directly as possible. Patton, the arch exponent of utilisation focused evaluation, accepts that even if evaluation findings do not lead directly to action they can still serve a useful purpose: 'Evaluations seldom lead directly to concrete decisions—they provide additional pieces of information in the difficult puzzle of programme action, permitting some reduction in the uncertainty within which any decision takers inevitably operate' (Patton, 1997).

'The Lion and the Calf'

In some respects the debate on the scope for policy evaluation is academic because there is no way of entirely avoiding policy aspects, even if the intention is to do so. The projects, being in the public domain, were themselves the outcome of political decisions, and they remain subject to political pressures throughout their lives. Even the work of the evaluator, and the eventual report, have powerful political implications, and may be used to attack or defend political decisions. The issue is therefore really one of degree, and revolves around whether policy issues should be tackled head-on or taken into account only when they impinge unavoidably on the project being evaluated. It has not been easy for policy-makers and evaluators to learn how to work together. As Eleanor Chelimsky, President of the American Evaluation Association remarked, in her address to the first Conference of the European Evaluation Society in 1994: 'I'd advise any evaluator to remember that when the lion and the calf lie down together, the calf isn't likely to get much sleep' (Chelimsky, 1994).

Note

1. The UK Treasury does not have any problems with policy evaluation. In 1988, it produced a guidance manual on *Policy Evaluation* (Treasury, 1988). The Treasury is primarily responsible for oversight of the policies of government departments, rather than for projects or programmes. The manual states: 'Although in this Guide we use the term "policy evaluation", the advice also applies to the evaluation of programmes and projects.'

16

Sectors Presenting Special Problems in Evaluation

Part Two: Poverty Alleviation, NGOs, Small States and Structural Adjustment

'When poverty comes in at the door, love flies out at the window'
(Old proverb)

'Love in a hut, with water and a crust, Is—Love forgive us—cinders, ashes, dust.'
(Lamia, Pt 2, Keats)

'Carelessness in small things leads little by little to ruin'
(Ecclesiasticus—The New English Bible)

Problems in Evaluating Poverty Alleviation

Why is Poverty Alleviation so Seldom Evaluated?

Considering that most donors have put poverty alleviation at the top of their development policy agendas for many years, it is surprising how little attempt has been made to evaluate projects in terms of their impact on the poor. As mentioned earlier, the Real Aid Group in the UK (notably Professor Paul Mosley) has been one of the foremost critics of the aid donors on this score. Probably one of the reasons for this situation is that a direct assessment of changes in the poverty level is extremely difficult, as Mosley himself discovered when he attempted to evaluate a poverty-focused ODA aid project in Peru (Mosley et al., 1984). Not only is it difficult to get accurate information about personal incomes (even very poor people are reluctant to divulge this kind of information), but in fact it is difficult, if not virtually impossible, to select an appropriate unit for measuring changes over time. Should one consider only the income of the farmer himself, or of the farmer and his wife, or should the family be included, or even the whole 'household' (i.e., those living in the same house, whether members of the family or not)? The latter would seem to be appropriate, but in fact it is like a jellyfish, constantly changing its shape as members come and go.

All the standard terms of reference for evaluations require evaluators to consider the impact of development aid on the beneficiaries, and often refer specifically to poor people, but because of the practical difficulties evaluators have generally steered clear of attempting to quantify the incomes of poor people directly. To quote Mosley: 'Out of thousands of evaluation reports which have so far issued from the aid agencies, the number which measure how far the poor have benefited from the project can be counted on the fingers of one hand' (Mosley, 1987). Instead of direct measurement of income, the tendency has been to look for proxies of income, such as ownership of a bicycle or a radio, or whether there is a tin roof on the house. Yet even these present considerable difficulties because no two communities are exactly alike in this respect. One community may spend its increased income on food, but a neighbouring one may prefer to spend it on the house. When I attempted this approach in rural Java I was surprised by the differences between one village and even a neighbouring one. Usually expert sociological advice is needed in the choice of suitable proxies. There is also the problem that poverty is sometimes absolute (e.g., not having enough to eat) and sometimes relative. In the latter case, poverty alleviation becomes more a matter of reducing inequalities, whereas in the case of absolute poverty it becomes a question of survival.

The Search for Suitable Indicators

The use of proxies is not an altogether satisfactory solution to the problem of measurement—although it may often be the only practical one for members of an evaluation mission spending only a few weeks overseas. The plain fact is that measuring the impact of a development project on target populations cannot be satisfactorily done during a short mission. Therefore, attention has been turning more towards the use of baselines to establish what the socio-economic circumstances of the target population are before the project starts, and then to specifically monitor the impact on those groups, as the project is implemented, using participatory methods (i.e., not waiting till the project comes to an end). Hopefully, as these techniques are further developed, the evaluation of poverty-focused development aid will be much improved. Box 16.1 describes some research aimed at developing a new approach along these lines.

It has to be remembered of course that increasing the income of poor people may not be the only, or even the main, objective of a poverty-oriented project. Research in Rajasthan in 1988 found that increases in per capita income did not figure prominently among the farmers' own criteria for wellbeing (Baulch, 1995); while research in Bangladesh has revealed that the number of female-headed households, rather than attempts to measure income directly, was the most reliable indicator of poverty (Hashemi and Das, 1994). A common objective of poverty-focused projects is to 'empower' poor people so that they can better stand up for themselves in their relationships with the more powerful people in the community. Such projects are likely to comprise measures to foster commercial activity, self-education, formation of labour unions, etc. In other words, it is essential to evaluate poverty-focused projects against the people's objectives, and these will not always be income related.

Another important distinction has to be drawn between what has been called 'transient poverty' (e.g., resulting from policy reforms) and 'chronic poverty' (Penalver, 1995). Projects aimed at addressing the former need to be evaluated bearing in mind the transient nature of the poverty.

Finally, it has to be remembered that research has clearly demonstrated that there is a strong link between growth in the economy at large and the reduction of poverty. Therefore, in evaluating projects aimed directly at the alleviation of poverty, it is important not to overlook the indirect contribution to achieving this objective arising from projects aimed

Box 16.1 Methods and Indicators for Measuring the Impact of Poverty
Reduction Interventions

The problem of selecting suitable indicators for measuring progress with poverty-oriented projects led the ODA, in 1992, to commission a project on this topic to be carried out by the aid charity Action Aid. The objectives were: to examine existing indicators; to suggest suitable alternatives that take more account of the participants' own perceptions of their wellbeing and status, and to propose new approaches to impact evaluation of poverty-oriented projects.

The examination of present indicators used by NGOs found that because of the lack of any agreed definition of poverty, most NGOs focused on output indicators rather than on impact. Where indicators were used, these were seldom discussed with the participants themselves: there was a major difference between involving beneficiaries retrospectively in evaluations, and their participation from the appraisal stage onwards. The research team's conclusion on this phase of the study was that in participatory impact assessment: 'There is more rhetoric, and work at conceptual levels, than there is real practice and experience. The major area for further work needs to be at the project level in order not only to work with communities to identify indicators, but also to collect information over time and monitor how they use these indicators' (Goyder, 1995).

The Action Aid research is now concentrating on new methods of 'negotiating' appropriate indicators for poverty focused projects with the intended beneficiaries right at the start of the project. The word 'negotiating' is the appropriate one because the research has already demonstrated that there are a number of interest groups in poor rural communities with sometimes conflicting objectives. There are also conflicting objectives when the other stakeholders are brought in, so choosing indicators can prove to be a highly sensitive process involving delicate negotiation between interest groups. Action Aid suggests the 'identification and reconciliation approach' (described below) to help groups of people to identify their own indicators.

Stage	Task	Output
1. Exploration and presentation	Group discussion	Visual data
2. Categorisation	Identify and categorise areas of change	Visual data
3. Review categories	Analysis of visual data categories	Agree
4. Define elements/indicators	Dialogue: staff and group leaders	Group level indicators
5. Integration of 'group' indicators into 'community-based' indicators	Meetings between group leaders	'Community indicators'

Source: Goyder (1995).

primarily at increasing economic growth. It could well be that the latter are actually more successful in reducing poverty than the former. Even if it is concluded that in the short term (i.e., within the immediate objectives) projects aimed directly at poverty alleviation should have priority, it should be borne in mind that in the longer term (i.e., within the scope of the wider objectives) the best hope for a lasting improvement might be promoting economic growth.

I began this section by noting the scarcity of evaluations of poverty alleviation, and the criticisms levelled at aid agencies on this score. The latter must have had some effect because in 1997 DFID commissioned a major evaluation of its support to poverty reduction, to be carried out by three development research institutions in the UK. The hope is that the results will help to operationalise the intentions in the 1997 White Paper to give even higher priority to poverty alleviation. The European Commission (DG VIII) has also launched a major evaluation of poverty alleviation projects, so it seems that the evaluation community has reacted positively to the criticisms made. Poverty reduction was also the main theme of the annual conference of the Development Studies Association in Bradford, 1998.

Problems of Evaluating NGOs

How do you Evaluate a Mosaic?

The topic of poverty alleviation evaluation leads on naturally to how NGOs evaluate their activities (since they are par excellence geared to helping the poorest). The main problem that faces the NGOs is that their aid programmes are like an intricate mosaic of very small projects that (unlike most mosaics) do not always comprise any obvious pattern. It would be prohibitively expensive to attempt one-off evaluations of specific projects, except for a few large ones, so self-evaluation has generally become the norm. A great advantage that the NGOs have over most official aid agencies is that they have a substantial presence in the field— it is from there that the aid activities are controlled, not from headquarters. This means that participatory monitoring and evaluation techniques are feasible and indeed they are widely practised. But like any other type of donor agency the NGOs also have a need for some accountability. Admittedly this is less a problem for them than for most public sector aid agencies because when members of the public donate money to a charity they usually assume that the funds will be well spent (since they do not usually pass through the hands of possibly corrupt local officials), but in any case their individual contributions are so small that they would not think of trying to check on how the funds are used. Nevertheless, the NGOs themselves feel a need to be accountable, and the large ones at least have now set up their own evaluation systems. The larger NGOs now routinely conduct external evaluations to supplement the self-evaluation system—either external in the sense that they are carried out by staff of the NGO's own evaluation unit (who will have had no previous connection with the object being evaluated), or by consultants hired from outside, or perhaps a mixture of the two. These external evaluations tend to look at selected individual projects or programmes chosen because they are reasonably representative of the NGO's activities.

Other Characteristics of NGO Evaluation

Because of the volunteer ethos of most NGOs there is an understandable reluctance to apply very rigid standards of evaluation, either in terms of the success or otherwise of the project, or in terms of staff efficiency. In particular, there is no general enthusiasm for applying elaborate techniques such as cost-benefit analysis or the logical framework, although the larger NGOs are now making use of some of these techniques mainly because of pressure from official aid agencies that are contributing funds. Riddell, in 1990, described NGO evaluation as 'minimal, discrete and marginal' (Riddell, 1990). It has certainly improved since then, but that description is still broadly applicable. I became personally aware of the importance of an understanding of the ethos of working for an NGO when I participated in an ODA-funded evaluation of the Voluntary Services Overseas Scheme. The senior officials of the charity were very anxious to make sure that I understood how different their approach to overseas aid was compared with that of civil servants and I had to respect that.

NGO staff are usually paid considerably less than those working for official aid agencies, although they often have as much responsibility and work under great pressure. The charities often pride themselves on keeping administrative costs down to a minimum but that does not leave much room for evaluation work. Part of the attraction of working for an NGO (and one reason why gifted people are prepared to work for them) is the lack of bureaucracy and the loose central control. Coming from a typical Whitehall Department as I did, where there is a definite hierarchy and a certain respect for rank and position, I was astonished to find, when I evaluated a project for a leading NGO, that the youngest and least experienced member of staff was listened to with as much attention as the oldest and most experienced. In such a liberal working environment it is very difficult for those working at the headquarters to impose a demanding management system on those working in the field. Evaluations have to be handled extremely sensitively.

Furthermore, NGO projects and programmes often lack clearly stated objectives and criteria of success: many are simply aimed at 'helping the poor' in some ill-defined way. This makes systematic evaluation very difficult.

Finally, another factor affecting their dedication to evaluation work is that they are even more anxious than are the official aid agencies to assure the public who donate the funds that these are being directed to the right ends and that they are effective. They are not keen to have any publicity about their weaknesses or failures and there is always a risk that evaluations could expose them.

A Specifically NGO Approach to Evaluation

After having evaluated a number of NGO projects, Riddell, in 1990, used this experience to promote what was a specifically NGO approach to evaluation. Instead of their trying to use the more sophisticated methods then being developed by the official aid agencies he suggested that it would be adequate simply to apply the seven key questions listed in Box 16.2.

Since then there has been a considerable improvement in the NGO track record on evaluation, partly because they have been under pressure from official aid agencies that are contributing increasingly to their funding to use better evaluation methods, and partly because the NGOs themselves have been caught up in the general movement towards more transparency and accountability. However, there is still a lot of room for improvement as was shown by the results of a review carried out by an independent consultant (Smillie, 1995) which was itself one of the inputs into a major synthesis evaluation commissioned by the DAC Expert Group on Aid Evaluation which reported in 1997. The report covered 240 projects in 26 developing countries. It found that NGOs were in general achieving their immediate objectives (90 per cent or more of projects

Box 16.2 Seven Key Questions for Evaluating NGO Activities

Riddell found that few NGOs have the resources, time, or skills, to conduct so-phisticated evaluations comparable to those of the official aid agencies. Moreover they have a reluctance to engage in quantitative statistical exercises. He therefore set himself the task of devising a much simpler system of evaluation that would be appropriate for their circumstances. Rather than depending on a lot of factual information his approach relies more on qualitative judgement. It simply comprises the following key questions:

1. Has the project been successful in achieving its objectives?
2. Has the overall economic status of the intended beneficiaries been enhanced following the NGO intervention?
3. Have the benefits of the project been distributed equally between different groups of people - richer, poorer; men, women; landed, landless?
4. Has the change in economic status of the beneficiaries been due more to the influence of other non-project factors or vice versa?
5. Has the project been executed efficiently—that is, were the costs appropriate to the range, level and distribution of benefits?
6. Do the results of the project provide grounds for believing that this type of intervention can be replicated so that the benefits can be spread more widely? Specify these.
7. (a) If the NGO is still involved in the project, is a date set for withdrawal, and is withdrawal likely to lead to any particular problems?
   (b) If the NGO has already withdrawn, did this lead to any particular problems? In general, what are the prospects for project sustainability?

Source: Riddell (1990).

had achieved their immediate objectives), but there was a lack of evidence of impact, and a tendency for the NGO projects and evaluations to focus on outputs rather than objectives. It found that most NGO projects did reach the poor (though often not the poorest), but analysis of target groups was rare. There was a lot of evidence of major improvements in living standards and health status as a result of NGO projects. However, financial sustainability was usually very doubtful, and future prospects for many projects were poor. The report argued that rather than trying to make a blanket assessment of NGO interventions it would be more effective in future to direct evaluation work at isolating those factors which contribute to NGO success in different sectors and circumstances (OECD, 1997b). One of its principal conclusions was that evaluating the impact of NGO projects had proved to be extremely difficult mainly because the NGOs themselves had made very little attempt to do this. It commented:

'There is a pressing need to improve both methods of assessing impact, and impact itself'.

NGOs as Pioneers of Participatory Methods

As stated earlier, NGOs have a great advantage over official aid agencies in that they are already implementing aid in a general participatory manner, and they have naturally developed their evaluation systems along these same lines. I have referred earlier to the occasion when I joined an OXFAM staff member (an Ethiopian), in a remote part of eastern Ethiopia, in an exercise involving the application of logical framework methods in monitoring a soil erosion control project. This was done using a variety of visual and hands-on techniques, and the results were very impressive indeed: they clearly proved to me that it is possible to combine fairly sophisticated techniques like the logical framework with participatory methods. In this particular case, the OXFAM staff member had been well trained in the logical framework approach at Wye College and was an expert in its use, whereas others might not have that advantage; nevertheless it shows how NGOs can be at the cutting edge of new methodology.

Charities Evaluation Services

In 1990, ODA carried out an evaluation of NGO activities (Cameron and Cocking, 1991), on the basis of which the authors recommended that NGOs should improve their project management systems; strengthen their evaluation capabilities; pay rather more attention to cost-effectiveness and sustainability than hitherto, and share their evaluation experiences more widely. The authors recognised that the smaller NGOs cannot be expected to establish their own evaluation units, and they suggested that there was a case for this function to be supplied as a common service for any charity that wanted to use it. Shortly afterwards the Charities Evaluation Services was created, with help from many private and official bodies, including the Foreign and Commonwealth Office, and since then it has been providing valuable evaluation expertise and services to a variety of charities. Another major synthesis evaluation of NGOs carried out by the ODA in 1995 showed that although significant progress had been made there was still a need for NGOs to improve their project management, and particularly the monitoring and evaluation of projects (Surr, 1995).

Problems of Evaluating Projects in Small States

Every evaluation takes place in a political context to some degree or other. In large states it is seldom that the political aspects dominate the evaluation, but in small ones this is more the norm than the exception, and the evaluator has to learn how to cope with this problem.

Box 16.3 describes a recent evaluation of an educational reform programme in a small state—Belize. Such a sector-wide project, in a state of only 200,000 people, is inevitably highly political (Eyken et al., 1995). Indeed, the more all-embracing the project, the more certain it is that it will have a strong political connotation. In a small state the political

Box 16.3 Evaluating Educational Reform in a Small State: The Importance of Understanding the Local Setting

In 1992 Belize began a seven-year $ 12.64 mil programme to upgrade its entire primary education system. The project comprised in part the physical upgrading of the country's primary schools, and in part the raising of the proportion of trained teachers from 45% to 80% by the year 2000. A link was established (funded by the ODA) between the School of Education, University of Bristol, and the Government of Belize, and the former was invited to evaluate the project's initial impact. Their report stresses the supreme importance of understanding the local setting when carrying out an evaluation in a small state.

Belize is a tiny country in the grip of acute political tensions between those who look to the United States as their main ally and trading partner; those who look mainly to the Caribbean region; and those who favour a continuation of the British connection: "These political tensions lie very close to the surface of educational reform, shape their content, and influence their direction".

The evaluators quickly realised that they could not distance themselves from such political issues—rather the reverse. They were central to what was happening in the education field. So they decided to thoroughly brief themselves on the local situation as the essential basis for the evaluation: "We read all the national papers, and talked to journalists, trade union leaders, feminist movement activists, and those involved in previous educational reforms. We talked to politicians, both in the Government and in opposition. We sought above all to understand the underlying spurs to reform. We talked to outside observers, both from the Caribbean and those undertaking voluntary service in Belize. We read the history of the country, its novels, poetry, political tracts. All this was taking us very far from the business of evaluating the project, yet in the end that project had to be placed in a political context.... An evaluator must look beyond the project, place it in its setting, and seek to explain the actions of the principal actors".

Source: Eyken et al. (1995).

factor is exacerbated due to: the highly personalised nature of society; the lack of transparency as decisions are often taken on a personal basis and are usually poorly documented; the lack of specialists which means that decisions are often taken more on political than on professional grounds; and the inevitable blurring of the distinctions between politicians and civil servants. Eyken, Goulden and Crossley suggest that a methodology might be worked out to measure the relative importance of such political factors. For instance, 'It may be possible to map the intensity of relationships between central administrations and educational managers through the frequency of their correspondence or communications, the number of times they meet, and the responsibilities for specific tasks'. The authors conclude that in acutely political situations like this 'the evaluator may have to discard the conventional methods and approaches of the professional evaluator, and simply concentrate above all on being able to understand and explain what has been happening'.

Problems of Evaluating Structural Adjustment Financing and Sector, Programme or Commodity Import Support Aid

The increasing trend away from project aid to various kinds of non-project aid, such as structural adjustment financing, and sector, programme or commodity import support programmes, has some important implications for evaluation. Increasingly, as Figure 16.1 shows, many aid activities, although still controlled by the donor, are no longer identifiable as emanating from that donor. This is because the aid funds are handed to an intermediary institution like an NGO, a trade organisation or a research association, which then spends the money according to its own programme. In these circumstances, the donor has to rely on the intermediary institution carrying out its own evaluations. Many aid activities are hardly controlled by the donor at all, even indirectly. These include the four types of aid that are the subject of this section, and they present even greater problems to the evaluator.

With project aid, the donor is involved throughout the project cycle, usually in a fairly detailed way, especially if the integrated approach is being used. Often the donors have staff located in the field who can monitor and evaluate the projects. Generally speaking, the smaller the recipient the more directly the donor controls the aid.

Figure 16.1 Characteristics of Different Types/Categories of Aid Activities

	Largely Donor Controlled	Largely Recipient Controlled
Aid activities identifiable as emanating from the donor	Projects or programmes Country programmes Regional programmes Volunteer services	Concessionary credits Mixed credits Export promotion
Aid activities not identifiable as emanating from the donor	Implemented by NGOs Implemented through other institutions e.g. trade organizations or research associations	Balance of payments support Commodity import support Structural adjustment Programme aid

Source: Cracknell et al. (1994).

However, in the case of non-project aid, the responsibility has been passed almost completely to the recipient government. Field staff are no longer needed (to the same extent at any rate) to supervise the aid, and there is little if any possibility of the donor identifying in detail how the funds are used. How does one evaluate this kind of aid?

The first thing to be said is that inevitably much greater reliance has to be placed on the accountability of the institutions in the recipient country handling the aid funds, and on any evaluations that such institutions carry out. The donor's own evaluation emphasis has to switch from the project level to the broad policy level. Yet most donor evaluation units do not have much experience in evaluation at this level. Not only must the donor strengthen its own capacity to carry out this kind of macroeconomic policy evaluation but must also at the same time strengthen the recipient's capacity as well.

Of course this switch in emphasis raises difficult questions regarding the independence of the evaluations, and their credibility to the donors. There has to be a trade-off between the need for a degree of independence on the part of the recipient, and the need for relevance and credibility. It can be a risky strategy from the donor's standpoint: 'The consequence of the aid administration having an evaluation system largely governed and influenced by people and units with implementation responsibility may greatly reduce confidence in aid' (Cracknell et al., 1994).

But to return to the question of what techniques can be used to evaluate this kind of non-project aid, the DAC Expert Group on Aid Evaluation reviewed the experience of the member states in 1987 (OECD, 1987), and they highlighted some of the difficulties. The two main problems they identified were (*a*) the intrinsic fungibility of non-project aid (the donor can use it to fund a project that would have been funded from the recipient's own resources anyway, and that releases funds for other purposes), and (*b*) the virtual impossibility of establishing cause and effect relationships between the aid and its possible macroeconomic or sectoral impacts.

A number of brave attempts have been made to evaluate these kinds of non-project aid, and various techniques have been tried. For example, comparisons, largely qualitative, have been made between countries where structural adjustment reforms have been vigorously implemented and those where they have been implemented less effectively. Also, sophisticated macroeconomic models have been constructed in an attempt to identify and quantify the effects of certain variables associated with structural reforms on economic growth rates (along the lines of some of the macroeconomic models developed in the UK and elsewhere to study the effects of the European Commission's Structural Grants). The Dutch carried out an evaluation of 49 companies in developing countries that had benefited from commodity import support and this revealed some disquieting results. Much of the aid was going to large oligopolistic companies and served to strengthen their competitive position vis-à-vis the smaller companies. The study concluded that the net foreign exchange effect was negative, that is, the countries could have done better by importing finished goods. Three Swedish researchers, Carlsson, Kohlin and Ekbom, recently published a critique of evaluations of commodity import support schemes in which they note that most of the studies focused on the 'delivery' aspects rather than on the impact, that is, they concentrated on such aspects as: how the allocations of foreign exchange were made; which industries benefited and how; and the extent to which pressures for quick disbursement at the donor end influenced the way this kind of aid was given. The authors point out that although these aspects were indeed important in relation to the way commodity import support schemes were at first organised, they are less relevant now that non-project aid has expanded into sectoral or macroeconomic and structural adjustment financing. Now the key issue is whether evaluations can assess the impact of these policies at the macroeconomic level, but very few evaluations of this type have been carried out (Carlsson et al., 1994).

Evaluations of the impact of commodity import support aid need to cover two aspects, namely, the direct impact on the economy, and the indirect impact through the operation of the counterpart funds system (i.e., the local funds generated for the government when it sells the foreign exchange). Carlsson et al. describe some of the methods used to evaluate the macroeconomic effects of non-project aid. These include the use of three-gap models following Bacha (1990) and Taylor (1990),[1] based on the two-gap model (i.e., investment-savings, and trade gap) developed by Chenery et al.; the third gap being the fiscal balance. They also describe the alternative approaches used by Mosley and Toye (Mosley and Toye, 1991). These comprise three different methods. The first is simply a cross-sectional comparison between the countries that have had World Bank structural adjustment loans, and those that have not. The second is a cross-sectional regression analysis, involving multiple regressions, to analyse the qualitative influence of programme lending in relation to other influences on the macroeconomy. The third approach abandons any attempt at cross country comparisons and relies on a single country simulation model in which the 'without project' is constructed as an imaginary situation. This can be done either for a whole national economy or just for a sector.

An interesting contribution to this debate was made by Branson and Jayarajah at the 1994 World Bank Conference on Evaluation (Branson and Jayarajah, 1995). They used a policy assignment model to conduct a cross-country evaluation involving 55 countries. Their conclusion was that when a macro framework is introduced early on, and subsequent policy decisions are based on it, the chances of success, and of sustainability, are much improved.

As to the evaluation of counterpart funds, these have seldom been evaluated, and in fact, bearing in mind the fungibility usually associated with them, any attempt to evaluate their effect on the economy is likely to prove very inconclusive. I commissioned such an evaluation in the ODA some years ago but the results were not very useful. Donors could reduce fungibility by establishing conditions on the use of counterpart funds, but they are generally reluctant to do this as it could be seen as an infringement of the recipient's sovereignty.

This brief review has highlighted the problems of evaluating these non-project forms of aid. Probably it is true to say that the difficulties of evaluating the impact of commodity import support aid on macro economies are so great that, to quote Carlsson et al. again: 'The traditional focus of the evaluation system on commodity import support delivery in many ways is optimal. It is related to the immediate objective—

procurement of goods, which is the only level where it is both theoretically and practically possible to evaluate success or failure'.

Note

1. These three-gap models are discussed in Carlsson et al. (1994). They quote extensively from Bacha (1990) and Taylor (1990).

17

International Cooperation in Aid Evaluation

'What we are now seeing is a general blurring of the boundaries between different evaluation traditions which have often existed in relative isolation and even ignorance of each other'

(*Editorial by Elliot Stern in Volume I of the new journal,*
Evaluation, *July 1995*)

'There is nothing more difficult to arrange, more doubtful of success, and more dangerous to carry through, than initiating change'

(The Prince, *Machiavelli*)

'As the world becomes more politically diverse and complex in the 21st Century, evaluators will be called upon to exhibit considerable courage in the normal pursuit of their work'

(Evaluation for the 21st Century, *Eleanor Chelimsky and William Shadish*)

Evaluation is an area where there has been close donor cooperation from the very beginning, and the degree of cooperation is increasing all the time. This is no doubt mainly due to the fact that the subject was a relatively new one, and all the donors were learning-by-doing at roughly the same time, so that sharing experience with the various methodologies that were being tried out seemed to be a natural thing to do. Moreover, the resources allocated to evaluation were at first extremely limited and it was evident that only if evaluation results were pooled and compared would it be possible to draw broad conclusions on development issues.

OECD/DAC Expert Group on Aid Evaluation

The lead in donor cooperation in this field was given, early on, by the OECD (DAC) which was one of the first aid organisations in Europe to begin to tackle some of the methodological problems of evaluation, as early as 1969 (OECD, 1969). The DAC also organised a series of informal seminars for European evaluators, the first being in Berlin in 1966, and this was followed by seminars in Wassenaar (the Netherlands) in 1970, Amsterdam in 1973, and Copenhagen in 1975. Eventually, in 1980, a DAC Sub-group of Correspondents on Aid Effectiveness was set up, and joint activity began in earnest.

Right from the very beginning of its work, the Correspondents Group ran into the classic problem of priorities between the accountability objective of evaluation and lesson-learning. The members of the DAC, at that time, were reeling from the effects of retrenchment forced on the donors by the oil price shock, and were trying to justify expenditure on aid. So they looked to the Group to provide an answer to the question 'Is aid effective?', that is, their emphasis at that time was on accountability. However, when the members of the Group turned to their evaluation findings in an attempt to answer this question, they found that most of their evaluations had been geared to lesson-learning: they had not been randomly selected, but were biased towards projects that encountered particular difficulties, or that were unusual in some way. They could not be regarded as representative of aid activities in general, nor were they comparable with one another because there had been no coordination between the evaluation units as regards what the evaluations should cover. most covered only aid delivery although a few did attempt to assess impact, some included environmental and gender aspects but most of them did not. At that time, each agency was more interested in the way it, as an aid organisation, was operating, rather than on aid effectiveness in general.

Although the final outcome of this first joint activity by the Group was very disappointing, in that the answer to the question raised by the DAC could not be given, the experience had been a very valuable and seminal one. The Group had found the experience of working together very formative and stimulating, and they saw great opportunities in the future for improving their evaluation work by sharing experiences and by engaging in joint activities. So they were very keen that the DAC would decide to retain the Group. They were afraid that the negative results from their first assignment might lead the DAC to terminate the group. But they need not have worried. By that time the DAC had realised the great importance of having a more permanent and highly professional evaluation capability, and rather than terminate the group they decided, in 1982, to turn it into an Expert Group on Aid Evaluation with an assured future. The Expert Group was given a new remit, which omitted the previous requirement to report on the overall effectiveness of aid, and instead focused more on distilling operational lessons from evaluations. This was an important change which gave the Group a clear directive for its future work. 'Freed from the pressures to demonstrate aid effectiveness, the Group could now focus on improving aid effectiveness by learning from past experience' (OECD, 1993). The Expert Group's new tasks were:

- strengthening the exchange of information, experience and cooperation between national, and as appropriate, multilateral evaluation units;
- contributing to improved aid effectiveness, by attempting to distil from evaluation studies operational lessons for project and programme planning and design, for consideration by the DAC;
- examining the feasibility of launching a set of joint or coordinated studies, undertaken by interested members, of aid effectiveness in a major sector, such as agriculture, or possibly in particular countries;
- seeking ways to promote and support developing countries' evaluation capabilities.

The next 10 years saw impressive progress in improving evaluation procedures in a number of directions. First, it was decided to build on the work that had already been done in the abortive attempt to assess the global effectiveness of aid, by distilling useful operational lessons from the existing stockpile of evaluation reports. This led to the 'Lessons of Experience' report in 1984 (OECD, 1984) which was well received by the DAC, and helped to ensure that the Group would have a mandate to continue its work. This was followed, a year later (by which time I had become Chairman and so had a special interest in its work), by another influential report on evaluation methodologies (OECD, 1986). This was not an attempt to standardise procedures—it was far too early for that (if indeed it will ever be appropriate), as members were still experimenting with different methods. Rather, it was intended to encourage and guide the exchange of information and ideas on methodologies. It contained a list of definitions of terms (drawn up in consultation with the Joint Inspection Unit which had earlier issued its own definitions of terms), and this has since proved very useful in avoiding potential terminological confusion. The compendium was again well received within the DAC, and the Expert Group was by now firmly established with a challenging agenda ahead of it.

As is evident from the number of times reference has been made in previous chapters to the work of the Expert Group, it has had a major influence on the development of the subject, on a global scale. It meets twice a year in Paris, and comprises evaluators, usually at the level of unit head, from all 18 bilateral donors, in addition to observers from the multilateral aid agencies. All three regional development banks, as well as the World Bank, are invited to attend, as are the OECD Development Centre, the UNDP, and (since 1992) the European Bank for Reconstruction and Development. An excellent working relationship has been established. In the words of a one-time Chair of the Group, Klaus Winkel, 'The Group has played a significant part in the emergence of what can now probably be described as an international evaluation community' (Winkel, 1990).

As a result of its experience over the first 10 years or so, the Group realised that evaluating aid delivery was never going to yield valuable answers to the kind of questions that people would be asking, and so they decided to switch the emphasis towards the impact of aid. Also as a result of the difficulties already encountered, the Group decided to try to coordinate, at least in some degree, the members' evaluation activities: all the members agreed to include in future terms of reference for evaluations certain standard clauses, covering a few high priority topics, as a minimum. Another outcome of this first phase of activity was that the Group agreed to share information on proposed new evaluations, so that the risk of duplication (and excessive burden on the recipient countries) could be avoided.[1] This decision in favour of transparency of evaluation findings has set the tone of the Group's work and has been followed ever since.

The Group's next step was to focus on a series of selected issues of common interest, for example, the role of women (sometimes on a collaborative basis with the Expert Group on Women and Development), sustainability, maintenance, environment, feedback, non-project aid, technical cooperation, the role of NGOs, and technology choice; the reports that resulted from these have been extensively quoted in previous pages. Another development was to stimulate the growth of evaluation in the developing countries, and to facilitate more interchange of ideas and information with these newly emerging evaluation units: a number of seminars were held for this purpose. The Group also moved into the area of training for donor evaluators, and as part of this initiative I was invited to run a week-long training course at Hornbaek in Denmark in 1992. There were around 20 young evaluators from all the main aid donors, and development banks, and we had a most stimulating week.

The sharing of information was taken an important step forward when CIDA offered to be responsible for the computerised databank system described earlier (Chapter 12). This is a very good example of the way the Group has been able to coordinate its work and avoid wasteful duplication.

In 1988, the UK presented to the Group the results of a major evaluation of the effectiveness of UN agencies, which introduced the concept of a 'litmus test'. The Group considered the possibility of adopting this approach and extending its activities in this direction, but eventually shied away on the grounds that in many agencies the multilateral agencies are the responsibility of finance/treasury departments, and also because it was feared that it would take the Group into areas that were beyond its competence.

The Group has also worked on preparing a set of 'principles for evaluation and development assistance', which have now been formally approved by the DAC (OECD, 1991a), and have taken their place alongside the principles for project appraisal (adopted in 1988), and the principles for programme assistance, and principles for technical cooperation.

Finally, the Group has laid the foundations for joint evaluation exercises, although so far, apart from joint evaluations of UNICEF, WFP and UNFPA, only limited progress has been made, perhaps because the European Union has also initiated joint evaluation activity among the member states (see below).

Future Work Programme of the DAC Expert Group (now called a Working Group)

The Working Group has a full programme of future activities that should keep it busy for the next few years. This includes the following main areas:

- inventory and analysis of rating systems;
- enhancing the evaluation inventory (CIDA databank);
- developing a framework and indicators for assessing progress in implementing women in development policies;
- studying methodologies and results of country programme evaluations;
- organising further informal seminars on an ad hoc basis (one was held in the USA in 1995 and another in Australia in February 1996);
- organising joint training sessions for evaluators from member countries;
- developing an evaluation framework for poverty alleviation programmes;
- completing the joint evaluation of programmes promoting partic-ipatory development and good governance;
- synthesising lessons of successful development cooperation projects;
- synthesising results of NGO evaluations;
- promoting the planning of more joint evaluation studies;
- synthesis work on the evaluation of such topics as emergency aid, environment, private sector development, and institution build-ing; and
- reviewing progress to date with helping the developing countries to improve their own evaluation capacities, and organising more country case studies and workshops.

The European Union

A second important forum for donor coordination is the regular gathering of heads of evaluation units of member states of the European Union. This tends to duplicate the work of the Working Group in some respects, but it has the advantage that there is a bond uniting the participants (as fellow members of the European Union) that is tighter than that in the Working Group, and therefore they are better able to organise joint action. This may explain why one of the first substantive joint evaluations (of food aid) was planned and carried out within the European Union coordinating group rather than by the Expert Group.

The UN Family

In the early 1980s, various UN agencies gave a useful lead in the stimulus of evaluation activity, and in the development of concepts and methodology—particularly the Joint Inspection Unit (an unfortunate title, because the word 'inspection' is studiously avoided by almost all evaluators, implying as it does an emphasis on fault-finding and policing, that is at variance with the image that evaluators want to generate). In 1979, the Joint Inspection Unit published a very useful *Glossary of Evaluation Terms* (JIU, 1979), and three years later it organised an inter-agency meeting in Geneva, to which representatives of the bilateral donors were also invited, and this was the beginning of a fruitful relationship with the UN family. I remember delivering a paper at that meeting in which I was somewhat critical of the prevailing practice in the UN agencies in favour of built-in evaluation, on the grounds that 'project staff cannot be expected to be critical of their own work' (Cracknell, 1982). We have come a long way since then and most UN agencies now have very effective and independent evaluation units of their own. The Operations Evaluation Department of the World Bank, together with the Office of Evaluation of USAID, have also both had a significant influence on the development of the subject. The World Bank Conference on Evaluation and Development in 1994, organised by the Operations Evaluation Department, was a milestone in the development of the subject and is a good example of how the Bank fulfils its role as a focal point for new ideas and methodologies.

Synthesis Seminars

As the trend towards syntheses began to replace the old one-off project evaluations during the 1980s, so a new kind of cooperation came into vogue—the synthesis seminar. So much concerted evaluation work goes into the production of a synthesis report, and its findings are so relevant to policy for the sector as a whole, that donors have found it appropriate to organise seminars, sometimes lasting several days, where the synthesis report is the main document discussed. It is common for evaluators from other countries, or other aid agencies, to be invited to these seminars, some of which have had a seminal influence on the way policy has evolved in certain sectors. The USAID has been particularly prominent in this field, but other aid donors have also organised seminars. Some donors, like Sida, have organised such seminars in the developing countries themselves, which serves to bring the developing countries more fully into the experience.

Help to Donors with Rapidly Growing Aid Programmes

The excellent donor cooperation that exists in this field has been of particular value to those countries whose aid programmes increased rapidly over a short period of time, such as Italy (some years ago), and especially Japan, now one of the world's largest aid donors. These countries needed to establish good evaluation and project management systems quickly, and they have both been able to make good use of the expertise available through the various organs of donor cooperation. Both have recently adopted the logical framework system, whilst the Japanese have just produced, with the help of a Norwegian consultant, one of the most up-to-date manuals of project management in use anywhere in the world (FASID, 1993).

Creation of New Evaluation Societies and Professional Journals

Mention has already been made, in the introduction to this book, of the emergence in recent years of evaluation societies in many countries, and also the establishment of new professional evaluation journals. This has been a very important development, in that it has helped to widen the horizons of development aid evaluators. Until recently they tended to work within the narrow confines of their own subject, and there was little cross-fertilisation of ideas with evaluators working in other sectors. Today that isolation has been much reduced. The UK journal *evaluation*, which was launched in 1995, contains articles dealing with many different sectors, including development aid, and it provides an invaluable vehicle for the exchange of information and ideas on evaluation methodologies and practice. As the editor said, in his first editorial, the field of evaluation was having to face up to 'the process of globalization', and he stressed that the new journal (and this goes for the UK Evaluation Society as well) was intended to act as a bridge. This would be a bridge not only between evaluators in different parts of the world and working in different sectors, but even more, a bridge between evaluators whose background has been mainly in academic-based evaluation research (specialising in methodology), and those evaluators whose background has been in the actual administration of policies (specialising in the more practical aspects), and who are also often involved in the commissioning of evaluations.

Not only was the new journal intended to be a bridge, but it was also meant to provide a platform and a forum for the growing professionalism within the evaluation community, and eventually perhaps for the establishment of standards of quality such as other professional bodies have. Although the journal has been in existence for only a short time it has already established itself as a serious professional journal, and a glance at the articles published so far will confirm that it is certainly achieving its objective of building bridges.

A few evaluation societies have already come into being in the developing countries, and the hope must be that this trend gathers momentum in the years ahead, and that these organisations, and the journals that may eventually emanate from them, will help to bring together evaluators from both the donor and recipient sides in a mutually supportive 'evaluation community'.

Note

1. Brian van Arkadie has given a telling personal example of the burden of unco-ordinated evaluation missions on the recipient countries: 'I recently led a mission for an international agency to one small least-developed country, only to find a mission in place from a sister agency with essentially the same terms of reference. On completing the mission, I left, only to encounter a third mission with overlapping interests from yet another agency' (Arkadie, 1986). He is not alone. I have had many similar experiences.

Evaluation as Viewed by the Beneficiary Stakeholders

'Experience is the name everyone gives to their mistakes'
(Lady Windermere's Fan, *Oscar Wilde*)

'The man who makes no mistakes does not usually make anything'
(E.J. Phelps, Speech at Mansion House, 24 January 1899)

'A good scare is worth more to a man than advice'
(Ed Howe)

Correcting the Imbalance

Up to now this book has been concerned with evaluation as seen from the donor perspective, but these last four chapters try to correct this imbalance by switching the focus to the other stakeholders and especially the direct beneficiaries. In this chapter we remind ourselves that the beneficiaries do not necessarily see things in the same way as the donors (Cracknell, 1985). There are differences arising from the cultural divide, asymmetries of power, and divergences of view about what evaluation is all about. It is important to understand these differences if the current movement towards more stakeholder analysis, and participation, is to have any chance of success.

Evaluation is still a relatively new topic, even in the developed world, but in many countries of the developing world it is still in its infancy. It was estimated in 1994 (and the number must have risen since) that about 100 developing countries now perform some kind of regular monitoring and evaluation activities (Valadez and Bamberger, 1994). However, apart from a number of relatively large developing countries in Asia, such as India, which has a large and very experienced evaluation service that grew up mainly in response to the needs of central planning after Independence in 1947 (Shah, 1984), Pakistan, Bangladesh, Malaysia, the Philippines and Indonesia, evaluation in the Third World has still not yet become firmly established. This is especially the case with the smaller countries in Africa. It was with a view to stimulating the more rapid growth of evaluation among the beneficiary countries that the Expert Group on Aid Evaluation of the DAC organised a two-and-a-half day seminar in Paris in 1987 (OECD, 1988); this was followed by regional seminars in Abidjan, Ivory Coast, in 1990 (OECD, 1991b), Kuala Lumpur, Malaysia, in 1992, and Quito, Ecuador, in 1993 (OECD/IDB, 1994). In June, 1995, the Asian Development Bank (ADB) organised a Workshop on Feedback in the Asian and Pacific Region, in Manila (ADB, 1995), and in 1996 the UNDP organised an Asian and Pacific Regional Workshop on Exploring New Dimensions in Monitoring and Evaluation. These various seminars have revealed some important differences of perspective and emphasis between donors and recipients.

Basic Differences in Perspective

Perhaps the main difference in perspective, until recently at least, has been the fact that the developing countries have generally regarded evaluation as something imposed on them by the donors to satisfy their own accountability needs. Often, as stated earlier (Chapter 2) they have tended to regard evaluation and audit as virtually the same thing. Sometimes they regard evaluation as simply a means whereby the donor checks what the recipient is doing. To quote the report on a Dutch Workshop in Islamabad: 'It was felt that project authorities often think evaluation to be a policing activity' (Frerks et al., 1990). A recent overview of recipient countries' attitudes to evaluation concludes that 'they continue to regard evaluation as a donor-driven activity providing them with few benefits' (Khan, 1998). The recipients have therefore cooperated somewhat reluctantly, fearing that if the evaluations reveal weaknesses or deficiencies, no matter how understandable in the circumstances, the result could be a reduction in the flow of aid. Fortunately there are now some signs that this reluctance is beginning to disappear as the developing countries are beginning to realise that evaluation is as essential for their own internal budgetary purposes and for accountability as it is to the donor.

As indicated in the previous chapter, the aid recipients have also suffered from a lack of appreciation, on the part of the donors, of the additional burden on hard pressed officials that evaluation missions represent. This is especially irksome when the absence of donor coordination often means that there are an unreasonable number of evaluation missions in the country at any one time, whilst all too often they require information that is virtually the same as that sought by other missions.

Even more importantly, it has become evident over time that there are some major differences in perspective between the two sides regarding the objectives of the evaluations, the criteria for assessing success or failure, and between the implicit value systems that each side is using. For example, the donor tends to be seeking an answer to the question 'Have our projects been cost-effective, and do they survive when the aid comes to an end?' But the recipients are far more interested in trying to ensure that on-going projects are being implemented successfully, that is, they focus more on project monitoring and mid-term evaluation than on ex post evaluation, and they are more interested in the evaluation of sectoral programmes than of individual projects. They complain that the donors concentrate too much on whether the projects were completed within the forecast budget, and on time, and that they are excessively interested in the meeting of implementation targets rather than on the achievement of broader sectoral targets. To quote the ADB Report 'In most developing member countries, postevaluation, and the development of evaluation capacity, is seen more as a donor-driven activity, largely because postevaluation, more often than not, has been carried out by external agencies' (ADB, 1995). No doubt the situation has improved in recent years as the donors have moved more towards impact evaluation, and as they pay increasing regard to the socio-cultural and environmental factors, but it remains true that the donor often has to take too narrow a focus because his involvement relates to only one project in the sector. The trend towards sector and programme aid should help to narrow this gap.

Another contrast in perspectives relates to the skill base and professionalism of the staff involved on the two sides. Evaluators engaged by donor agencies tend to be highly professional and often very well qualified technically, but inevitably they are likely to have only a superficial understanding of the local politics or the socio-cultural environment of the project. By contrast, the evaluators from the beneficiary country may not be so well qualified technically, but they are very well aware of the politico-social factors (maybe almost too well aware!), and they know from experience that these have to be taken into account in any assessment of a project's success or failure, especially when it comes to sustainability. Few projects are without their political overtones: a project may have been chosen in the first place because it lay in a minister's constituency, or because it would bring help to a deprived area that threatens to cause political unrest; or it may have owed its origin, or the particular shape it took, to initial rivalries between different ministries. The possibilities are legion. Generally speaking, the evaluators from the donor side tend to ignore such factors because they are sensitive, but the evaluators from the developing country cannot side-step them so readily.

The two seminars referred to earlier clearly demonstrated that the recipients are more concerned about ensuring that projects are well designed in the first place than in learning about what happened to them much later on. They have discovered from bitter experience, as indeed have the donors, that unless great care is taken at the project appraisal stage to take into account the likely impact of the project on, for example, employment, health, education, the role of women, and the environment, the projects are likely to run into difficulties. By the same token, they are more interested in the monitoring of on-going projects, and in mid-term evaluation, because there is still time to correct faults as they became apparent, whereas at the ex post evaluation stage it is too late.

So far as ex post evaluations are concerned, there are also some significant differences in perception that can have a significant influence on the judgement of the evaluators. Those from the donor side are likely to lay the main emphasis on the economic realised rate of return, usually measured in terms of border prices and shadow wage rates. The recipients, however, while also attaching importance to the realised rate of return, will attach great importance to other factors, such as the extent to which the project represented an opportunity for their personnel to acquire precious management experience (even if some mistakes were made in the process), and also whether their staff were given good training as part of the project, and whether the institutions in the country were strengthened as a result. The donors generally want to avoid making mistakes because these could have significant repercussions on the flow of aid. They sometimes go to considerable lengths to avoid this happening, such as appointing expatriate managers, and setting up enclave administrations to manage projects. These may indeed help to ensure a good economic rate of return, but in the eyes of the recipients they rob them of the opportunity to 'learn-by-doing'. Happily this syndrome is less common than it once was, and the donors have now mostly accepted that passing on a skill can be as important as leaving behind an economically viable enterprise.

One topic, which immediately separates evaluators from the donor side from those on the recipient side, is the question of tied aid. British evaluators, for instance, do not normally consider this topic because it is assumed to be an integral part of British aid, and nothing can be done about it when it comes to any one specific project. So it is simply ignored. But the recipients are not prepared to ignore it. They are acutely aware that aid tying severely restricts their freedom of choice, and may lead to them having to import more expensive goods from the donor country than they could obtain elsewhere. This applies equally to technical cooperation personnel. All experts supplied by the UK, for example, have to be British, apart from minor exceptions, even though it might be possible to find experts from elsewhere at a fraction of the cost. So it is not surprising if the recipients are not prepared to join the unwritten agreement that aid tying is ignored in project evaluations.

Another topic that divides the two kinds of evaluators is the 'brain drain', that is, trainees staying back in the developed countries after their training rather than returning home. The evaluators of training on the donor side tend to shrug this off as something beyond their control, and for which they are not responsible. Or they assume that eventually the trainees may return home and will take back with them the additional skills they have acquired through practising them in the West. Or they may argue that remittances sent back by these people counteract the adverse effects of the brain drain. But more commonly they tend to ignore the problem. However, to the evaluators from the developing countries this can be a decisive factor since a trainee who does not return represents a serious loss of scarce skilled manpower, and the developing countries seek if they can to discourage these trainees from staying overseas.

An important difference in the way evaluation is perceived in the developed countries compared with the developing countries, is that in the former it is increasingly seen as a means of ensuring transparency, of informing the public, of stimulating policy reform, and indeed as a tool of democracy. However, in the developing countries it is seldom seen in that light: it is regarded more as an internal means of informing policy-makers of the results of their decisions, and is not something to be shared with a wider public (OECD/IDB, 1994). In India the tradition has been that the evaluators are there to check on the efficiency with which government measures are implemented, and it has not been part of their role to comment on the policies themselves (Shah, 1984). According to Eisendrath (1988), the main problem with the Indian evaluation system is that the authorities feel no obligation to take any notice of the evaluation findings, so they may be less effective than they might otherwise be.

It is a fact that sometimes the leaders of the developing countries have their own reasons for requesting types of aid that the donors do not consider to be appropriate for development. For example, they may prefer large and well equipped hospitals located in the bigger towns and cities to a network of rural clinics, because one day they may need hospital attention themselves. Or they may prefer, for reasons of prestige, or because opportunities for sharing in some of the financial benefits are greater, to go for modern Western technology rather than trying to up-grade the traditional crafts. Where such sensitivities exist it is clearly something of a minefield for the evaluators, whether they represent the donor side or the recipient side.

More Subtle Differences in Perspective

There may also be more subtle differences in perception. For instance, I was surprised to discover, during the course of a collaboration with a group of East African universities on donor-funded training, that some of the African countries were very worried that the trainees they were sending to Britain might pick up the wrong kind of social mores, for example, a tendency to look down on manual work. In their eyes this could seriously diminish the value of the technical training they might receive, but it is not something that British evaluators would be likely even to think of. I experienced another subtle difference in perception when I evaluated training given to Bangladeshi trainees in Britain. Rather than commenting on the technical content of what they had learned, they tended to discount this (presumably because they could have obtained something similar at home), and instead they focused on behavioural factors, such as an employer going to speak with one of his staff at the latter's desk, a thing unheard of in Bangladesh: or a university professor helping some students to move some chairs, again this would never be seen in their own country as the professor would instantly lose face. It was experiences like this that were for them among the most valuable, or at any rate the most memorable, results of their training, yet they could easily be overlooked (Cracknell, 1985).

I have taken part in many evaluations, sometimes as a member of a donor team, and sometimes as a member of a joint donor/recipient team, and my experience has been that the latter are always more satisfactory, because even without realising it in a conscious way, the developing country representatives adopt a distinctive viewpoint which is often markedly different from that adopted (equally unconsciously) by the donor representatives. There is no blame to be attached to either side: it is merely a matter of an instinctive response being influenced by one's background. The conclusion has to be that it is only by adopting joint teams that the risk of serious bias can be avoided.

Attempts to Reduce Donor Bias

The donor agencies have attempted to meet the criticisms of donor bias by liaising more closely with the recipients, in the selection of the projects to be evaluated, in the drawing up of the terms of reference, and in trying to get representatives from the recipient side onto their evaluation teams. Their success rate with the latter has not so far been very high, because there is often a dearth of skilled people who can be spared from their desks (often they have to continue their official duties whilst participating in evaluations), and the donors recognise that in such circumstances they should not bring too much pressure to bear on the recipients to find evaluators.

A recent analysis of the extent to which personnel from the recipient countries have been involved in USAID evaluations (see Figure 18.1), shows that in more than half those evaluations for which the data were available there were no local participants. Most USAID evaluations are carried out by American consultants who fly in for a few weeks, and fly out again, and so 'the evaluation experience will leave the poor country in the plane which carries the consultant to the next assignment' (Snyder and Doan, 1995). The opportunity has thus been lost to help build an evaluation capacity in the developing country, which does not in any way 'own' the resulting evaluation report. 'Even where the funding agency has multiple evaluations in the same country, there is no discernible

Figure 18.1   Involvement of Personnel from Developing Countries in USAID-Sponsored Evaluation Activities

	Type of Personnel Involved							
	Indigenous Personnel				No Indigenous Personnel (only US contractors and/or donor staff)			
	Implementing Agency		Other Personnel				No Data Available	
	%	(n)	%	(n)	%	(n)	%	(n)
Audience/ stakeholder	17.5	(31)	7.9	(14)	33.4	(59)	41.2	(73)
Member of interim evaluation team	24.5	(26)	16.0	(17)	59.4	(63)	–	–
Member of final evaluation team	26.8	(19)	19.7	(14)	53.5	(38)	–	–
Oral briefing or recipient of report	22.6	(40)	10.2	(18)	16.4	(29)	50.8	(90)

Source: Snyder and Doan (1995).

pattern or strategy to develop the capacity of any local entity to pursue evaluation as an important means of assessing performance through involvement in the evaluation process' (Snyder and Doan, 1995).

USAID is certainly not alone in its failure to achieve a significant involvement by the beneficiaries in evaluations—indeed there are good reasons for thinking that it has tried harder than other aid agencies to foster local participation. It is simply that the rhetoric has run ahead of the actual arrangements for evaluation on the ground. Despite the exhortations in the in-house guidance manuals about the need to involve the local people, the practice of engaging American consultants, and giving them a short period in which to complete their work, virtually rules out the possibility of genuine local participation: 'Given the staffing constraints in USAID, and an administrative culture which encourages contracting out most research and evaluation work, it is likely that American contractors will continue to lead many of the evaluation teams in the short term' (ibid.:149). The disturbing thing is that, for all their brave words in favour of more participatory methods in evaluation, most donor agencies are still conducting their evaluations in a way that very much diminishes the possibilities of this actually happening. Things do not seem to have changed much since I wrote the following words in 1990:

Most donor agencies, although they pay lip service to the need to work co-operatively with the recipient countries, in fact seldom do so. Indeed they instinctively see evaluation as basically a defensive mechanism to assure their Treasuries that aid funds are being spent well—they do not really see it primarily as a means of encouraging the recipients to carry out self-evaluation so that they can more effectively learn the lessons for themselves (Cracknell, 1990).

So what can be done, assuming that there are administrative constraints that cannot be removed easily? Better advance planning of evaluations by the donors, working in close coordination with recipients, might help. Another approach might be for donors to make it a condition of the contract that local personnel, such as consultants, staff of research institutions, or academics, should be appointed as integral members of evaluation teams. This would help to build up a reservoir of people with good skills in evaluation work. However, probably the most important requirement of all would be for the donors to incorporate financial provision into their evaluation budgeting to fund the involvement of representatives from the developing countries in the evaluations. The result might be rather more expensive, and therefore fewer, evaluations, but at least they would be more representative of the beneficiary stakeholders. It would also help if the evaluation reports could be translated into the official language of the recipient country where it differs from that of the donor.

Problems of Establishing an Evaluation Culture in Developing Countries

Evaluation is now so well established in the donor agencies that it is easy to forget how difficult it was in the early days, two or three decades ago, to build up an evaluation culture in the face of considerable scepticism. What really made the difference was powerful support from the top echelons of management (who in turn were usually responding to strong external pressures). Many developing countries are now passing through this same phase, and it is therefore not surprising to find that the ADB Report of 1995 states that 'the degree of political commitment to evaluation initially determines the scope and focus of the evaluation infrastructure';

or that the first item in the 'agenda for action' that emerged from the Workshop was the need to ensure support for evaluation feedback at the highest level: 'The participants feel that advocacy at the political level, as well as the higher echelons of government, is important for the introduction and institutionalisation of postevaluation systems in developing member countries' (ADB, 1995). The agenda goes on to mention the need for adequate legislative backing, professional training, and a good career structure for evaluators, as well as sufficient resources. The agenda continues: 'concerted efforts need to be made to modify the culture of the public sector to incorporate this activity (i.e., evaluation) into the overall framework of public administration'. A recent review of evaluation capacity building in developing countries concludes that a pre-condition is the building of awareness of the benefits of evaluation within the governments of those countries. It also stresses the need for full commitment from the top political leadership (Khan, 1998).

One of the problems in getting evaluation locally established is that the monitoring and evaluation units established in connection with rural development projects, and other such major interventions, often cease to exist when the donor departs. It is important that these monitoring and evaluation capabilities be transferred, before the project's institutional structure folds up, to somewhere else in the local administration. On the basis of his experience with a large DANIDA-funded rural development project in Bangladesh, Nielsen regards this 'institutional anchoring' of the monitoring and evaluation capability somewhere outside the project to be of vital importance: 'It is necessary to secure its institutional sustainability, i.e. anchor it somehow outside a project context' (Nielsen, 1990).

Feedback from the Beneficiary Perspective

As already discussed in Chapter 11, one problem that is common to both donor and recipient is that of poor feedback of the results of evaluations to improve future activities. The problems may be even greater in the recipient countries because of the sensitivity of evaluation findings in the local situation. Many interested parties have to be consulted, and often a delicate balancing act has to take place between conflicting social and political viewpoints, before an evaluation report can be issued, and by that time its effectiveness may be limited. But an even bigger problem is the fact that the monitoring and evaluation units are often administratively located a long way from the operational departments, so that it is very difficult to feed back the evaluation findings into the project cycle of future projects. The ADB Report states that 'even where postevaluation units have been established, the absence of an effective framework to support the communication of lessons learned back into the project cycle, frustrates the unit's ability to make effective contributions to the planning process'. To cope with this problem, one Asian country, the Philippines, has decided to locate its monitoring and evaluation unit inside the organisation responsible for project planning, so that evaluation findings can be fed directly into the project cycle at an early stage.

The situation is made even worse by a serious lack of information networking in the developing countries, and so there are inadequate communication linkages between the embryonic evaluation units and the staff working at the local and operational level, or even sometimes with senior management. The developing countries need to evolve feedback systems for disseminating evaluation findings (their own and those of the donors), such as one-page summaries, seminars, and in-depth briefings of evaluation teams. No doubt more could, and should, be done by the donor evaluators to help their counterparts in the Third World to improve their feedback mechanisms. It remains the height of irony that while the donor evaluators are all the time refining and improving their internal feedback mechanisms, they are virtually ignoring feedback at the level where the findings could have most immediate impact—the project level in the developing country itself.

Sustainability from the Beneficiary Perspective

Another topic where there is a lot of common ground is sustainability. The recipients are just as anxious as the donors to ensure that a project survives the ending of the aid, and they will generally have a much better idea of what the key factors that will determine sustainability are. The recipients are keen to persuade donors not to cut off their aid too abruptly. The point has already been made earlier that a cliff-edge in aid can be highly dangerous—especially in the often difficult fiscal and financial circumstances that pertain in many developing countries. The recipient countries are continually urging the donors to run down their aid more gradually, rather than drastically, when the main capital phase of a project has been completed, thus enabling a continued flow of funds for small items of essential maintenance, repair or training, and to enable a watching brief to be maintained on a joint basis. Unfortunately, the way many donor agencies operate their aid budgets often makes it difficult for them to keep small sums in the project budget over an extended period: in this respect the European Union's Lome arrangements were superior because the funds could be disbursed over a much longer period. Sustainability is less of a problem with revenue-producing projects than it is with socially-oriented projects such as health or education, where governments often suffer from chronic shortages of funds. One solution here may be for the donors to incorporate more provision for switching the funding of such projects from project aid to sector or programme aid and structural adjustment financing.

Relevance of Shift to Sector/Programme Aid

The major shift over recent years in donor emphasis from project aid to sector/programme aid and structural adjustment financing, gives a valuable flexibility to recipient governments to help them to manage their economies more effectively. At the same time, it reduces the risk that donors will continue to fund new projects that the recipients will never be able to maintain adequately. However, they are far more difficult to evaluate than projects, and techniques for doing this are still being evolved. These are of particular importance for the developing countries because, as suggested earlier, they are even more interested in the evaluation of sector/programme aid than they are in project aid.

The different perceptions, and degrees of emphasis, between donor and recipient, outlined above, are summarised in Figure 18.2.

Need for Developing Countries to have an Independent Approach to Evaluation

Enough has been said earlier to prove the point that when it comes to evaluation 'beauty is in the eye of the beholder'. It all depends on the background and value-system of the evaluator. One cannot avoid asking

Figure 18.2   Contrasts in Evaluation Criteria and Emphases between Donor and Recipient

Donor Viewpoint	*Recipient Viewpoint*
• Often focuses on one-off projects	• Generally more interested in the effectiveness of sectoral policies or programmes
• Is anxious to avoid mistakes or failures of any kind	• Accepts that making mistakes can be positive if it helps people to learn how to do better
• Wants to maximise economic rate of return e.g. by using expatriate managers and setting up enclave project administrations	• Is equally interested in skill transfer, acquiring management expertise, and strengthening of institutions
• Tends to underplay significance of political factors and to emphasise cost-effectiveness timeliness, and technical efficiency.	• Is acutely aware of importance of political and social factors and is better equipped to cope with them.
• Is especially interested in sustainability and impact on target groups	• Is more concerned with good project design and successful project implementation
• Tends to ignore, or downplay, such aspects as aid tying, brain drain, and the problems of cross-cultural transfer of skills	• Is very concerned about these aspects of the aid relationship, and aware of the possible of adverse effects
• Sees evaluation as a means of informing the public, and as a tool of democracy	• Sees evaluation more as an internal policy management tool: criticism of policies not encouraged.

the question of every aid evaluation: 'From whose viewpoint is this activity being evaluated—from that of the donor, or that of the recipient, or perhaps from some composite viewpoint?' Because the recipients will always have a different perspective from the donor, it is crucially important that they do not passively take on board the mind-set, methodologies and approaches of the donors. By all means they can learn a lot from the donors, especially as regards the practical techniques for evaluation, but ultimately they must work out for themselves how to evaluate their own projects and programmes, and must decide the relative weights they wish to attach to the various elements involved. They cannot safely borrow these unthinkingly from the donors. The differences in perception between donor and recipient do not represent just a superficial divide—they are more fundamental than that. As the DAC Expert Group on Aid

Evaluation commented in 1986, 'the purpose of developing an evaluation capacity within recipient countries should not be to transfer the donor's evaluation responsibilities to the recipients. Rather it should promote the recipients' capabilities, regardless of how these have been financed' (OECD, 1986). I have always been a stout advocate of the developing countries working out their own salvation when it comes to evaluation, rather than slavishly copying what the donors do. I was Chairman of the Expert Group when it produced the report quoted earlier, and in the foreword I made clear the Group's position on this topic:

> The DAC Expert Group hopes that this compendium will be found useful by those donor agencies that are in the process of setting up evaluation activity. But also, and perhaps I might say especially, the Group hopes that it will be useful to the increasing number of developing countries that are also in this position. Not that they should copy what the donors have done. Their needs and circumstances are different and they will have to work out the evaluation system that suits them best (OECD, 1986).

Reports and seminars like those discussed in this chapter can perform a vital role in enhancing dialogue and the sharing of understandings and perceptions; and hopefully the future will see less donor bias and a more genuinely shared approach.

Main Weaknesses of Evaluation Systems in Developing Countries

The seminars held in recent years, in Africa, Asia, Latin America and the Caribbean, provide a useful insight into the difficulties being encountered by the developing countries, and these can be summarised as follows:

(a) The monitoring and evaluation units were mostly set up as a result of pressure from the donor agencies, and have concentrated overwhelmingly on the monitoring of implementation. Thus little experience has been gained so far in the conduct of impact evaluations.

(*b*) These monitoring and evaluation units tend to be located centrally, usually in or near the main planning ministries. This certainly enhances their influence at the strategy level, but it makes feedback of lessons at the project or programme level very difficult. Experience shows that they are only effective if they have strong political backing.

(*c*) There is still an unfortunate tendency for failures, when they are reported in evaluations, to be followed by reprimands, with the inevitable result that project managers are reluctant to make adverse reports and the credibility of the whole evaluation process is thus undermined.

(*d*) There is a general lack of resources for monitoring and evaluation, a lack of training, and poor career structures for evaluators. Even when staff have received training they are often transferred to other work soon afterwards and the skills are soon lost (Khan, 1998).

(*e*) There is a tendency, notably in the Latin American/Caribbean region but also elsewhere, for governments to be reluctant to encourage transparency and openness in the evaluation process: they tend to see it as serving the internal decision-making needs of government rather than as a means of ensuring accountability. It is increasingly coming to be recognised that there is often a close link between effective monitoring and evaluation and good governance (see, for instance, OECD, 1997). As Khan says 'democratization of political processes, freedom of expression, and other relevant political and bureaucratic reforms, are indeed essential pre-requisites of successful monitoring and evaluation' (Khan, 1998).

(*f*) Feedback arrangements are poorly developed, and monitoring and evaluation units rarely have any direct involvement in the planning of new development activities.

As a general comment, the countries that have a democratic background have gone further down the road of sustainability monitoring and impact evaluation than have the countries with more authoritarian regimes. Rather curiously, the more dependent a country is on foreign aid, the less stress seems to be placed on sustainability and impact assessment. Presumably this is because the donors have in the past put implementation monitoring at the top of their priorities, and the recent trend towards more impact evaluation has not yet worked itself through to the developing countries' own evaluation activities.

So far as the development banks are concerned, there is a growing appreciation of the value of systematic project cycle management techniques, and the logical framework is now firmly established in them. There is also a growing awareness of the need to introduce an incentive structure within the banks to encourage staff to take quality-improvement more seriously. To quote the ADB Report: 'until recently the "approval culture" that prevailed in the Bank did not provide incentives for rigorous processing of projects, and consequently discouraged longer processing time.... Since 1994, ADB has taken major steps to move to a culture of improving project quality, increasing opportunities and incentives for intensive use of postevaluation results during project processing' (ADB, 1995).

A weakness of some development banks is the lack of any systematic way of ensuring that action is taken on the recommendations in evaluation reports, or of subsequently monitoring whatever action is taken. The ADB Report comments that 'because of the lack of follow-up to ensure that recommended remedial actions are pursued and steps taken to improve performance, valuable assets created under the projects could deteriorate and become unproductive (ADB, 1995).'

Finally, one of the concluding comments in the ADB Report stresses a vital factor that would apply equally to all three regional development banks, and this is the supreme importance of local 'ownership' of the evaluation function, that is, it should not be seen by the developing countries as a donor initiative only, but increasingly as something they need for its own sake. The Report puts it this way: 'The lack of demand for, and ownership of, evaluation is slowly changing, although ownership is likely to remain the major constraint in most countries. Similarly, political commitment and institutionalisation of the evaluation and feedback processes largely remain as an unionised agenda, requiring further support at the political level' (ADB, 1995). Evaluation in the developing countries has come a long way in the last five years, but it still has a long way to go before it is fully established.

Empowerment and the Stakeholder Approach

'Economists have come to feel,
What can't be measured isn't real.
The truth is always an amount,
Count numbers, only numbers count'
(Whose Reality Counts? Putting the First Last, *R. Chambers*).

'You can't create experience. You must undergo it'
(Albert Camus)

The Stakeholder Approach

If there is one trend common to all development evaluation units (and
indeed to many evaluators working in other sectors) it is the movement
towards involving all the stakeholders (sometimes called the 'actors')
more fully in evaluations. By 'stakeholders' is meant all those people
who have an interest in the project, either as direct beneficiaries or as
those who are responsible for funding and implementing the projects
(e.g., government officials, private sector, non-governmental organisations, and people on the donor side).[1] Because the donor stakeholders
fund the evaluations of 'their' projects, their interests are already fully

covered. What is now lacking is an adequate representation of the beneficiary stakeholders in the evaluation process. The stakeholder approach can possibly be seen as an interim stage in the progress towards full participatory monitoring and evaluation (discussed in the next chapter), although whether the donors that have enthusiastically embraced it will in fact move on to the next stage only time will tell.

At one time the idea of involving the beneficiary stakeholders directly in evaluations would have been anathema to evaluators as it offends the usual convention that people directly involved in a project should not take part in its evaluation. Why then has this idea gained ground in the way it has? The reason is clear. It is because the whole emphasis of aid evaluation work has shifted from issues related to aid delivery (i.e., what the donor does) towards issues of impact on the beneficiaries (i.e., how it affects the target populations). A major concern now is to find ways of measuring impact more effectively. And evaluators have quickly come to realise that there is no way of measuring the impact of development aid on people without their being closely involved in the whole process. Yet it is not enough merely to involve them as respondents to questionnaires, or to seek their views through occasional interviews or group meetings. The difficulties of establishing what the impact of a project has really been on the stakeholders are so formidable that the evaluators have no option but to try to enter into the mindsets of the beneficiaries themselves: the term 'participatory evaluation' has come into use to refer to this process. The evaluators have to try to see things from the viewpoint of the beneficiaries (Charyulu and Seetharam, 1990).

This movement towards the closer involvement of the stakeholders has mainly grown out of the unsatisfactory experiences of evaluations of social development projects and programmes in the past, using conventional evaluation approaches. Because the evaluation of welfare schemes is a major concern in the United States it is not surprising that these new ideas have emerged particularly strongly there. In the field of development aid, the initiative for them has been mainly taken by the NGOs, but official aid agencies are now also adopting them, as described in the following section.

Fourth Generation Evaluation

In the United States there has been a lot of discussion about the emergence of what has been called a 'fourth generation' of evaluators (Guba and Lincoln, 1989).[2] The new emphasis is on the role of the stakeholders in the aid relationship. To quote Patton: 'the best way to be sure that evaluation is targeted at the personal concerns of the stakeholders is to involve them actively at every stage of the evaluation' (Patton, 1997). The new approach is based on the concept of 'value-pluralism', that is, the recognition that various categories of stakeholders will have their own value systems, and each of these is significant and cannot be ignored. One of the distinguishing features of fourth generation evaluation thinking is the introduction of the concept of 'negotiation'. The evaluator still has most of his/her former roles (technician, describer, assessor), but with a difference; now he/she has to take on a number of other roles, such as collaborator, learner/teacher, reality shaper (catalyst), and mediator or change agent. Of these, the new role of negotiator-cum-change agent, is the most important one. Richardson, Kuipers and Soeters have pointed out that the evaluator 'has to switch continuously between distance and involvement, reflection and receptivity, reservation and frankness' (Richardson et al., 1996). They also stress that the evaluator is constantly playing different roles, and that 'each researcher, consciously or unconsciously, makes continuous decisions about how much emphasis to give to each role' (Stake, 1995). With this new kind of approach, evaluation and feedback cease to be separate stages but become intertwined and take place simultaneously. It is a shared learning process, and evaluation is as much a consequence of feedback as a cause of it.

Social Development Aid Projects

As mentioned already, in Europe it has been the NGOs that have pioneered new approaches to the evaluation of social development projects, and they have gone further down the road of involving the beneficiary stakeholders than have the official aid agencies.

Evaluating projects with quantifiable costs and benefits is relatively straightforward. But evaluating social development projects with mainly social and non-material (and therefore largely unquantifiable) objectives, such as community development, promotion of self-awareness, developing leadership capacities, or fostering group solidarity, presents very difficult problems. Some agencies, like the World Bank, have demonstrated that it is possible to go further in the direction of quantification (e.g., vis-à-vis the costs and benefits of education or health) than has been generally realised, but there still remains a huge area where quantification is either very unreliable or simply impossible. Moreover, it is now generally agreed that it is not just a matter of measurement, but more fundamentally a question of how such projects should be evaluated, and by whom.

In September 1989, a path-breaking four-day conference was held at the University of Swansea to debate these issues, and to come up with solutions and methodologies. In June 1990, a report was published which summarised the main conclusions (Marsden and Oakley, 1990). In his foreword, Brian Platt of OXFAM, who chaired some of the sessions, described the purpose of the conference as follows: 'the move towards development in terms of empowerment, social democracy, and popular participation required an approach to evaluation which went far beyond the traditional and limited methods which stressed simple quantitative indices of activity, impact, results and achievements'. The conference sought to find a consensus on a new 'non-traditional' approach to the evaluation of social development projects.

Empowerment

It is no accident that of the 80 participants at the Swansea Conference, a high proportion were representatives of NGOs. In fact, only two represented bilateral aid donors (one representative was from the ODA, despite the fact that ODA had given strong financial support to the conference, and one from another agency). This highlights the fact that it is the NGOs that have taken the lead in developing new participatory approaches to social development evaluation. The main reasons are that (*a*) they operate very much nearer to the 'work-face' in the developing countries than the big donors do (*b*) their projects are small and are located right at the grass-roots (*c*) they have staff working alongside the beneficiaries in a genuinely participative way (*d*) they understand the day-to-day problems that poor people face, and appreciate the need to adapt conventional evaluation methods to these conditions and (*e*) they are highly motivated (because of the ethos of equity to be found in most aid charities) to foster participatory methods. Although the big donors seek to give priority to aid projects aimed at helping the poor, they are seldom able to implement this objective in a direct way because they operate on a government-to-government basis. One might also add that some of them have a pressing need to find ways of spending the aid funds within given time periods because of the way treasury financial controls operate, so they often cannot afford to give too great an emphasis to time-consuming poverty-oriented projects. But with the NGOs it is different. They have a basic concern to help the poor and the powerless. They speak constantly of 'empowerment' as a key objective of the aid they give, a concept that is seldom explicitly encountered in evaluations carried out by the bilateral donors. Empowerment means enabling poor people, who lack power, to acquire self-confidence and to learn how to work together to enhance their bargaining position in relation to the existing power structures. It is sometimes called 'solidarity', another term often encountered in NGO evaluations but seldom in public sector ones.

The concept of empowerment may well be seen by established hierarchies in the developing countries as a threat to the status quo; there is undoubtedly a political overtone to the word that the NGOs are comfortable with, but officials are not.

Selecting Indicators

The approach of the big donors to the evaluation of social projects has been mainly centred on the search for suitable qualitative indicators that can attempt to measure such objectives as poverty alleviation, health, education, nutrition, etc. But the NGOs have in effect moved the goalposts. Instead of accepting these 'basic needs' objectives as the important ones, they are beginning to argue that these are not necessarily the kind of benefits that poor people themselves give priority to, as was suggested in Chapter 16, and that what poor people want is often more closely linked to the building up of self-confidence, development of self-education, guidance on how to organise themselves more effectively, and ways of developing community awareness. To quote the Swansea Report again: 'While funders are interested in combating poverty, expressed in terms of material deprivation, so-called beneficiaries might be much more concerned with...moral and personal deprivations—degrading conditions which diminish their status and self-esteem'. Thus the primary aims of poor people may well be to acquire for themselves more dignity and acceptance in society; to be treated more as equals; to be able to have more self-respect; in fact, everything that is embodied in the following quotation which introduces one of the chapters in the Report: 'Today for the first time the tribal labourers of this area are going on strike, stopping work on their own initiative. This may result in a wage rise of say 100 rupees per year, or 50 rupees per year. What is important to us however is that we are asserting that we too are human beings' (Ambarsing Suruwanyi, a tribal leader in Maharastra, India, 1 May 1972).

Drawing together these themes, the experts at the Swansea Conference identified the following as typical qualitative indicators that would measure what the poor people themselves really want:

- more general access for poor people to the resources necessary for development: greater distribution of resources available;
- greater expression of self-identity by poor people, and the right to full involvement in national life;
- movement towards greater social equality, measured through the strengthening of non-hierarchical relationships among poor people;
- improved levels of caring and concern for others at national level;
- overall improvements in physical well-being and security;
- reduction of dependency relationships among poor people;
- the development of organizational capacity among poor people;
- the creation of awareness.

Since the Swansea Conference the debate has focused on these kinds of issues, and on how to devise indicators that measure not merely basic needs in the conventional sense, but progress towards achieving all aspects of human dignity. Many interesting ideas for qualitative indicators have been put forward, and Figure 19.1 illustrates two examples of these. They show how a qualitative indicator can be given a quantitative dimension. As the Swansea Report says: 'the debate should not be between quantitative and qualitative measurements. You can put a number on anything if you wish to: it is the interpretation of that number which is important'.

Practical Experience with the Stakeholder Approach

The Swansea Conference was an important milestone, and it greatly boosted the influence of the social development advisers in the ODA, for instance, who proceeded to build on the ideas developed there for

Figure 19.1   Examples of Questions and Scoring in the Evaluation of
Social Development

---

1. STYLE OF MANAGEMENT: How are group activities managed?

3 = decisions are **always** made with all members' knowledge and participation

2 = decisions are **usually** made with all members' knowledge and participation

1 = decisions are **sometimes** made with all members' knowledge and participation

0 = decisions are **never** made with all members' knowledge and participation

2. INDEPENDENCE FROM GROUP PROMOTER: How able is the group to operate without direction or intervention from the group promoter?

3 = Group **always** tries to solve a problem by itself before taking it up with the group promoter

2 = Group **often** tries to solve a problem by itself before seeking the help of the group promoter

1 = Group **occasionally** tries to solve a problem by itself

0 = Group **never** tries to solve a problem by itself.

Source: Uphoff (1989).

enhanced stakeholder analysis. However, it also brought to the surface some deep divisions of opinion regarding how far down the line towards full participation the evaluator should go. The official donor agencies were very reluctant to move too fast in the direction represented by the 'fourth generation' school: they accepted the need for improved stakeholder analysis, and set about that task with real motivation, but they were not able to embrace the full gospel of the evaluator as a negotiator or mediator—that was too fundamental a change and appeared to fly in the face of the accountability objective that was still deemed to be very important. The rest of this chapter is concerned with the way stakeholder analysis has evolved since Swansea. The next chapter takes up the issue of participatory monitoring and evaluation.

As indicated earlier, the public sector aid donors took the view that even if the circumstances do not permit a wholly integrated participatory monitoring and evaluation system to be adopted, it should still be possible to take certain steps to make sure that the stakeholders are fully informed as to what is happening, and that they have a sense of 'owner-ship'. These steps should include at least the following:

- clarifying at the outset who the main stakeholders are (a similar process to the 'participation analysis' in the problem tree ap-proach) and deciding what their respective roles and interests are;
- drawing up a plan for ensuring maximum communication between the stakeholders as the implementation proceeds, and especially when it comes to feedback, both on-going and at completion or expost; and
- making sure that key information, such as the formal project doc-umentation used by the donor and recipient officials, is made available to the other stakeholders.

Following the Swansea Conference, the ODA set about implementing some of the ideas for improved stakeholder analysis. It set up a major study to investigate the possibility of making greater use of participatory methods (participatory approaches to learning study—PALS) and to pro-duce guidelines and training materials. At the same time it took practical measures to help staff to implement the new ideas on stakeholder analy-sis. Three booklets were issued in 1995 concerning how to enhance stake-holder participation (ODA, April 1995); how to carry out stakeholder analysis (ODA, July 1995); and how to devise indicators for measuring and assessing primary stakeholder participation (ODA, July 1995). Since then a body of literature has been accumulating based on experience in the application of these guidelines and in the stakeholder approach gen-erally. MacArthur, at the Development and Project Planning Centre, Uni-versity of Bradford, has applied the ODA guidelines to two projects and his findings are summarised in Box 19.1.

MacArthur certainly found the stakeholder approach useful, despite the difficulties he encountered, but he suggests that it need not be consid-ered as an essential requirement for all projects, especially those where the main stakeholders are reasonably few and self-evident and are obvi-ously heavily involved already. He thought it would be particularly use-ful for process approach projects where the nature of the project changes over time in response to stakeholder preferences. He quotes Gass, Biggs, and Kelly (1997) as having described stakeholder analysis as a 'heavily top–down planning tool', which seems a rather surprising description

Box 19.1   Applying ODA Guidelines on Stakeholder Analysis
to Two Projects

MacArthur, of the Development and Project Planning Centre, University of Bradford, has applied the ODA's Guidance Notes on Stakeholder Analysis (ODA April and July, 1995) to two projects. His findings provide useful feedback on the value of this approach.

He first classified the stakeholders into 3 categories, namely, primary (direct beneficiaries), secondary (others directly involved), and external (others involved but not directly). He then applied the ODA guidelines. His general conclusion was that the approach was useful, and not too difficult to apply in practice. The main problems he encountered were:

- there were so many stakeholders (28 in one project and 10 in the other) that it was difficult to be sure one had identified them all, and to decide just how far upstream and downstream of the project one should go;
- it was difficult to establish what each stakeholder's actual stake was (and also identifying who in fact makes this decision in practice);
- it was difficult to select a suitable system of ranking of the different stakes.

MacArthur emphasised the importance of classifying the stakeholders into three categories and giving priority to the primary stakeholders since otherwise the number could quickly become unwieldy. He suggested that the primary stakeholders should have priority since they were the people for whom the project was mainly intended. It is interesting that another evaluator with a lot of experience in stakeholder analysis has also emphasised the importance of narrowing the list of potential stakeholders to a more specific group of primary 'intended users' (Patton, 1997).

MacArthur's general conclusion is that stakeholder analysis is useful, but it is not essential for every project, and exaggerated expectations of its potential value should be avoided.

Source: MacArthur (1997).

considering that it was intended to counter the previous donor-dominated approach. In short, MacArthur rather plays down what he obviously thinks are exaggerated expectations of what stakeholder analysis can achieve: 'Not too much should be expected. This is no new Logical Framework in terms of its potential value and expected effects on thinking in the development community' (MacArthur, 1997).

Another researcher who has been experimenting with the stakeholder approach in general is Rebien, a Danish evaluator. He devotes half his recent book (Rebien, 1996) to the results from applying it to four case studies. Like MacArthur he also found it to be a useful approach despite the difficulties he too encountered. His findings are summarised in Box 19.2.

Box 19.2   Applying the Stakeholder Approach to Four Case Studies

A Danish evaluator, Rebien, devoted half his book, published in 1996, to a description of how he attempted to apply the stakeholder approach to four projects, in East Africa, Zambia, Southern Africa and Bangladesh.

Like MacArthur (Box 19.1) Rebien found the approach generally useful, but he also encountered difficulties. The main ones were:

- he had difficulty in identifying who the stakeholders were and trying to ensure a fair representation of all of them;
- he found a great variation in the degree of genuine participation on the part of different stakeholders;
- he also found a great variation in stakeholders' resources and negotiating power;
- he had difficulty in deciding how to cope with the conflicts and antagonisms between the stakeholders.

Encouraging features of his experience were that he found the stakeholders to be effective participants, well capable of defending their corner and flexible enough to adapt to changing circumstances as they arose. He noted that if they were given the opportunity of being fully involved as participants in the project they tended to lose their former defensiveness and were keen to co-operate; in fact they greatly valued being part of the monitoring and evaluation process, and their own awareness and knowledge was enhanced as a result. Contrary to expectations he found that the process did not take up a lot of the consultants' time because there was such a substantial input from the local project staff and the beneficiaries themselves.

Source: Rebien (1996).

Rebien's main aim was rather more ambitious than MacArthur's. He wanted to test out the participatory approach in its full rigour, and his findings on those aspects will be taken up again in the next chapter.

The new emphasis on the beneficiary stakeholders is having a spin-off effect on the evaluation of development aid in general. It is further reducing the emphasis on economic methods of evaluation of the cost-benefit analysis and cost-effectiveness type (although cash-flow aspects are still seen as very important because they affect the beneficiaries directly); it is leading to great stress on practical options, and on the presentation of recommendations; and it is further strengthening the move towards more impact evaluation. It is also having an effect on the involvement of evaluators in feedback, in that the evaluators are now seen as having a more positive role to play. To quote an American evaluation researcher 'Evaluators must learn to sell their research' (Schneider, 1990)

To sum up, stakeholder analysis has already established itself and is here to stay. The interesting question now is whether stakeholder analysis is an end in itself or merely a staging post on the road to full participatory monitoring and evaluation, but that is the subject matter of the next chapter.

Notes

1. Rebien found that the term 'stakeholder' was not well understood by the beneficiaries and he wondered whether some alternative such as 'partner' might not be preferable (Rebien, 1996). Another term sometimes used is 'gatekeepers' (Guba and Lincoln, 1989), but this could also easily be misunderstood, and it has an unfortunate 'custodial' flavour about it. The term 'stakeholder' was coined at the Stamford Research Institute in 1963 to describe people who were not directly stockholders in a company but 'without whose support the firm would cease to exist' (Mendelow, 1987, quoted in Patton, 1997).
2. The previous three generations were measurement, description and judgement-oriented.

Participatory Monitoring and Evaluation: Is this the Ultimate Destination?

> 'All powerful uppers think they know,
> What's right and real for those below,
> At least each upper so believes,
> But all are wrong: all power deceives'
> (Whose Reality Counts? Putting the First Last, R. Chambers)

> 'Participatory approaches have gained a new legitimacy: even some would say an orthodoxy. Success has conferred respectability: what was radical yesterday has become conventional today. For better or for worse, participation in development is in process of becoming institutionalized'
> (Who Changes? Institutionalizing Participation in Development, J. Blackburn with J. Holland)

A Fault Line

As was stated in the last chapter, to many people stakeholder analysis is but a staging post on the way to the ultimate destination, which is participatory monitoring and evaluation. But this next step is one which raises fundamental issues on which the evaluation community is deeply divided. In the next chapter I will be discussing the so-called 'paradigm wars' that have dogged the profession in the USA, separating those who favour the evaluator remaining as detached as possible from the object being evaluated to ensure impartiality, from those who lean towards the fourth generation standpoint and who argue that by staying detached the evaluator merely ensures that he can never really understand what is going on in terms of the beneficiaries themselves and their aspirations, that is, the evaluator has to become involved. So far the evaluation profession in Europe has been largely spared the ravages of this kind of intellectual warfare, but the same fault line is there and it could shake the foundations at any time.[1] That is why this chapter may be the most important in the book.

I have used the word 'participation' repeatedly in previous chapters, assuming that the reader has a general idea what the word means. But perhaps the time has come, before we begin this important debate, to define the term more precisely. The DAC Expert Group on Aid Evaluation's *Synthesis Report* (OECD, 1997a) quotes the two following definitions:

IBRD: A process by which people, especially disadvantaged people, influence decisions that affect them

DAC: A process by which people take an active and influential hand in shaping decisions that affect their lives.

Both definitions emphasise the key fact that participation is not a passive state (e.g., people being merely consulted) but an active one (i.e., people having a genuine part to play in influencing whatever happens that may affect their lives). Passive participation is now commonplace, but active participation is still quite rare.

The growth of interest in the participatory approach over the last decade has been quite remarkable. In part it owes its origin to the impact of *Fourth Generation Evaluation* thinking in the USA (surely the most quoted evaluation book ever written), but it also has other origins. A parallel stream in the USA has been the work of John Gaventa (Gaventa, 1980) and of the Highlander Research and Training Institute in Appalachia, empowering poor communities to conduct their own appraisals, and take their own action. In the 1990s, this led to 'citizen learning teams' who monitored and evaluated a large US government programme for community revitalisation of distressed areas. In Europe, another stream has been at work from the latter 1970s onwards on rapid rural appraisal (RRA), participatory rural appraisal (PRA), and now participatory methodologies more generally. Robert Chambers at the Institute of Development Studies (IDS) at the University of Sussex, played a part in this through fieldwork, networking, workshops and writing (e.g., Chambers, 1997). IDS now has a participation reading room and a participation group including Chambers and led by Gaventa (see Guijt and Gaventa, 1998). Most of the innovation has, though, been the less visible work of professionals in countries of the South. An important milestone was reached when an International Workshop on Participatory Monitoring and Evaluation was held at the International Institute for Rural Reconstruction (IIRR) in Manila in November 1997, bringing together Southern innovators and their experience (Estrella et al., forthcoming).

Uppers and Lowers

To draw attention to the existing imbalances and power asymmetries, Chambers talks about 'uppers' and 'lowers'—those who are privileged and powerful and those who are neither of these things. His primary purpose is to get donors to recognise that their actions tend to reinforce these imbalances and to accept that they need to adopt a different working style. Instead of thrusting their own ideas down the throats of the beneficiaries, he wants them to listen more to what the lowers have to say, through genuine participation. Note the parallel between his ideas and the new project cycle, with its emphasis on listening and piloting, described in Chapter 5. He argues that instead of creating their own 'realities', the donors, if they listen more, will become increasingly aware of the realities of the lowers: 'How much is the reality we perceive our own creation as uppers? What are the realities of lowers and how can they be expressed?' Chambers describes the process of affirming multiple realities as 'the new high ground', and he argues that only if we look for, and find, the realities of others (especially the lowers) can we really learn. He wants donor-funded experts to be 'on tap' rather than 'on top' (a phrase which he borrowed from Tony Gibson [1996]). He sums up his main argument as follows:

> Our personal and professional concepts, values, methods and behaviour, have prevented our learning. Our beliefs, behaviour and

attitudes, have been similar all over the world. Agricultural scientists, medical staff, teachers, officials, extension agents and others, have believed their knowledge to be superior and that of farmers and rural people to be inferior: and even when the richness and validity of much local knowledge began to be recognised we still believed that we had to be the ones who did the analysis. (Chambers, 1997).

Chambers' philosophy, like that of his mentor Friere (Friere, 1972), is basically one of empowerment of the lowers. In terms of monitoring and evaluation, he wants them to have the opportunity of carrying out these functions for themselves. He envisages them as setting their own indicators, evaluating their own achievements against their own criteria of success. He wants to see genuine participatory methods being substituted for existing donor-dominated practices A whole range of new evaluation techniques may be needed to facilitate this new approach. These might include (in addition to the accepted techniques of participatory rural appraisal) such things as: theatre puppetry, story telling, role simulation, and communal meetings (simulated or real). Poor people may be illiterate, but they can be enabled, by the use of such methods, to participate fully in what is happening and become an active part of it. To quote the report of the Swansea conference again: 'Evaluation is much more than providing useful information to decision-takers; it is learning from people about their own methods of evaluation, and incorporating that learning into a redesigned practice' (Marsden and Oakley, 1990). Chambers argues that the logical framework conflicts with the flexibility needed for participation: 'Participatory development cannot be planned in this way: it's course is not foreseeable: it is a sea voyage not a Swiss train journey' (Chambers, 1997). In short he is set on a collision course with those who favour what he considers to be over-rigid project management techniques, and who put accountability in evaluation above lesson-learning.[3]

Accountability and Participatory Methods

The participatory approach is not just a short step onwards from stakeholder analysis—it is a giant leap into new territory, and it presents aid donors with some fundamental problems over accountability. If we take fourth generation evaluation as being representative of the genre, the participatory approach constitutes a shift from the old measurement-oriented, description-oriented, judgement-oriented, mode of evaluation to a new level 'whose key dynamic is negotiation' (Guba and Lincoln, 1989). This implies a number of basic changes in evaluation attitudes and practice as follows:

(a) Evaluation findings are no longer to be regarded as 'facts' in some ultimate sense, but instead (to quote Guba and Lincoln [1989]) 'are literally "created" through an interactive process that includes the evaluator as well as the many stakeholders that are put at risk by the evaluation. What emerges from this process is one or more "constructions" that ARE the realities of the case'.

(b) Everything is value-laden and evaluators cannot avoid having to take different value positions into account.

(c) People's values and 'constructions' are formed in the environment in which they find themselves, and they achieve a kind of working consensus in that context, that is, it becomes their 'reality', but it might not have any relevance for others in other situations.

(d) Traditional donor-driven evaluation methods can disfranchise stakeholders, for example, by giving them little or no say in how the evaluation is conducted, or by ignoring their interests in favour of those of the donor, or by selective dissemination of the evaluation findings. The donors call the shots, and the powerless can be robbed of even the little power they have.

(e) Participants in evaluations should be treated as humans and their aspirations and objectives taken seriously: they should not be treated simply as objects of study.

(f) If evaluation is to lead to follow-up action which carries the support of the stakeholders then they need to be involved through a process of negotiation that respects their plural value systems: 'The evaluators must play a larger role by far than simply that of technician-gathering-information: instead he or she must be the orchestrator of the negotiation process which in the final analysis is the guts of the evaluation' (Guba and Lincoln, 1989).

Voyage of Discovery

These six points constitute the kernel of the participatory approach with its two key elements of responsive focusing and constructivist methodology. What is envisaged is a continuous learning process between evaluator and stakeholder, each learning from the other, so that the process does not simply reveal something that already exists but actually brings into being something new. It is a voyage of discovery the end destination of which is unknown and which will only emerge as the voyage proceeds. Figure 20.1 illustrates the differences between donor-focused evaluations and beneficiary-focused ones.

The success of the participatory approach depends above all on the establishment of a situation of absolute trust between the evaluator and the stakeholders. This building of mutual trust goes beyond the traditional concept of 'validity' and calls for what Finne, Levin and Nilssen have called 'credibility' (Finne et al., 1995). This is characterised by a multiplicity of methods since the crucial thing is to seek out whatever method enables the evaluator to get close to the beneficiaries and it will not always be the same one. But credibility does not relate only to the way the evaluations are carried out. It relates also to the use that is made of the results. There cannot be mutual trust if the stakeholders perceive the findings as being the exclusive property of the donor (as tends to be the case today). Only if the stakeholders have a major role in producing the findings, and in whatever follow-up action may take place, is there likely to be mutual trust. To quote Frerks, Thomas and Tomesen: 'The main factor determining whether the results of evaluations are used is the degree to which different "actors" agree with the monitoring and evaluation system. This means that both at the design, the implementation and the final phase, communication between evaluators, project staff, beneficiaries, sponsors, and executing agents, is essential' (Frerks et al., 1990).

The participatory approach, in its full rigour, is clearly incompatible with the traditional approach to aid evaluation based on a three or four week mission, travelling out from the host country on the assumption that there are 'facts' out there to be discovered and reported upon. Guba and Lincoln state this categorically: 'We have argued that no accommodation is possible between positivist and constructivist belief systems as they are now formulated' (Guba and Lincoln, 1989). Here lies the dilemma. The participatory approach does not seem to allow any scope for objectivity, yet objectivity has hitherto been regarded as essential for accountability in evaluation.

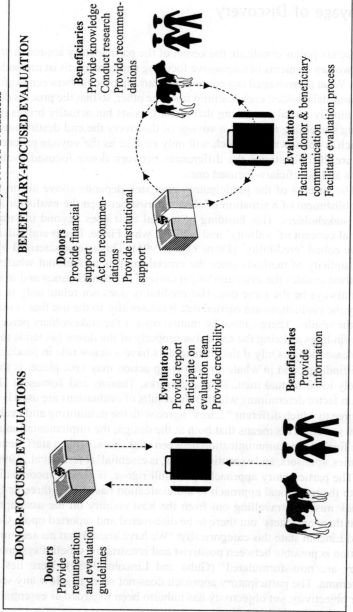

Figure 20.1 Comparison between Donor-Focused and Beneficiary-Focused Evaluations

DONOR-FOCUSED EVALUATIONS

Donors
Provide remuneration and evaluation guidelines

Evaluators
Provide report
Participate on evaluation team
Provide credibility

Beneficiaries
Provide information

BENEFICIARY-FOCUSED EVALUATION

Beneficiaries
Provide knowledge
Conduct research
Provide recommendations

Evaluators
Facilitate donor & beneficiary communication
Facilitate evaluation process

Donors
Provide financial support
Act on recommendations
Provide institutional support

Source: Freedman (1994).

The Problems of Objectivity

Some commentators regard objectivity in evaluation as so important that they reject the participatory approach completely. For example, Rein and White (1978) comment that 'transferring authority for negotiation to stakeholders is going beyond their professional competence and is improper' (Rein and White, 1978). In the USA, Scriven, an arch exponent of the concept of 'goal-free evaluation', is a stout defender of objectivity and a fierce critic of the 'cosy relationship' between evaluator and object implied by the fourth generation advocates (Scriven, 1993). There are many other evaluators who are worried about the loss of objectivity; and some, like Pawson and Tilley (1997), who disagree with Guba and Lincoln's view that there is no reality other than what the stakeholders and the evaluator construct for themselves. The donors in particular are likely to be worried that if the evaluators get too close to the stakeholders, even to the point of actually negotiating with them, they will cease to be objective and impartial. Their evaluation reports would be suspect and the accountability responsibility unfulfilled. I have noticed that the more closely linked those commissioning evaluations are to the policy-makers, the more reluctant they are to see the element of objectivity in evaluations set aside and the more they insist on a degree of distancing. One of the most experienced and policy-linked evaluators in the USA, Eleanor Chelimsky, one-time Assistant Comptroller General for Program Evaluation, was surely speaking for many official aid agency evaluators when she commented that 'distancing has its price, but involvement risks the whole capital' (Chelimsky and Shadish, 1997). Chelimsky has also commented that the failing of interactive evaluators is 'their belief in their incorruptible objectivity'. Attracted as I am by the participatory approach, a sense of realism tells me that many official aid evaluators will echo these comments.

Of course it is always possible that the donors' fears on this score may not be wholly justified. Is it perhaps possible for experienced evaluators to become two persons in one body—to both engage whole-heartedly in participatory evaluation processes while at the same time still retaining a degree of independence? So far as Finne, Levin and Nilssen were concerned, they found that they were able to participate fully with the stakeholders in the evaluation of a major Norwegian scheme to help small and medium-sized enterprises, while still retaining their personal objectivity:

'From our perspective the major challenge is to substitute objectivity with honesty, critical distance, integrity and avoidance of conflict of interests. The evaluator's task is to design a process whereby the outside stakeholders can become able to understand and decide these alternate criteria for external credibility' (Finne et al., 1995). Smith also found, after studying three cases (one of them the Norwegian one mentioned above) where participatory methods had been used, that it was possible to combine the two approaches (Smith, 1998). However, it must surely call for an unusual degree of flexibility for evaluators to be both objective and fully participatory. The issue is still an open one, and it is just possible that some workable compromise may be found that will go some way towards meeting both objectives.

Another aspect to this question is the undeniable fact that the evaluators in the past did not really possess absolute objectivity in any case. They approached their task with not only their own preconceived ideas, but also with values acquired (probably without even realising it) from the donor agency, which has its own criteria of success, often embodied in the terms of reference (however obliquely). To quote Stokke: 'It may seem to be an illusion that an evaluator can be totally impartial. That being the case, it may be more important that they truly mirror the aspirations and viewpoints of all the stakeholders' (Stokke, 1991c). A recent article has commented on 'the demise of the evaluator as "neutral and external actor"436' (Radaelli and Dente, 1996).

Some might criticise the new approach on the grounds that it may be very difficult for the evaluator to write a report that is other than a bland description of the different viewpoints of the stakeholders. This is because of the need to trade off the vested interests of different stakeholders in order to arrive at any consensus at all. An ODA synthesis study of a substantial number of NGO evaluations found that the conflicting interests among the local stakeholders, which 'might not be consistent with those of the intended beneficiaries' (Surr, 1995) was a real problem. The study concluded: 'effective stakeholder participation is not only difficult to achieve, but also difficult in many contexts, to define in the first place' (ibid.:20). How far the evaluator can go in trying to resolve such conflicts of interest is an open question, but at least it should become the practice, in evaluation reports of social development projects, to frankly discuss the different views expressed by the stakeholders, rather than feeling that a consensus has to be achieved every time.

Another criticism of the new approach is that so long as the participation by the beneficiary stakeholders is funded by the donor there is always a risk of bias. They would be unlikely to be willing to bite the hand that is feeding them. However, this might be avoided if the funds for the evaluation process were not treated separately but were regarded as an integral part of the project funding, and if the evaluation process begins from the moment the project starts up. Nevertheless, the possibility of bias will always be there if the donor is paying for it. The authors of *The Political Economy of Evaluation*, conclude with a powerful recommendation for what they call a new 'toolbox' of evaluation methods centred on the need to involve all the stakeholders, with the aim of making the evaluation function 'more democratic'. However, they add, as their final comment on the evaluation/aid process in general that 'even if we construct a better evaluation function, and sharpen our analytical tools to fit the requirements of aid projects, it will never be possible to get round the fundamental problem inherent in aid...there is one who gives, and one who receives, and the difficulties of receiving sometimes overshadow the problems of giving' (Carlsson et al., 1994).

Other Problems with the Participatory Approach

In 1995, the ILO governing body discussed the results of a detailed study of evaluation reports of 13 selected projects which had been carried out with a view to testing whether ILO had been successful in promoting participation (ILO, 1995). The concept of participation has always been basic to the tripartite structure of the ILO (i.e., workers, employers and government), so ILO has been in the business of fostering participation for longer than most other aid agencies: not only participation by the direct beneficiaries, but by the other local stakeholders as well.

The main finding of this meta-evaluation, in the words of the report, was that 'the participatory approach has developed into an indispensable tool', and that it 'improves the effectiveness and ensures the relevance of the project's activities, increases overall efficiency during implementation, and enhances the sustainability of the results after the projects have terminated'.

However, it is interesting to note that the ILO experience has not been wholly positive: they have run into some problems as well. These do not in any way invalidate the overall conclusion, but they can act as a warning to others of likely pitfalls in implementing the participatory approach.

The first problem they encountered was that many actors were illiterate and inexperienced, and so the participatory approach had perforce to be limited to trying to help these disadvantaged people to organise themselves better (a good example was an ILO project in India that tried to help poor rural women to acquire collective access to wastelands).[4]

Another important lesson is that the original concept of participatory development has had to be extended. At first it was seen exclusively as something directed only at the target groups themselves—the direct beneficiaries. But now it is realised that a successful project usually depends on the thorough involvement of the other parties as well. This is an important finding because there is a widespread tendency to associate participatory methods only with the needs of the rural poor, to the exclusion of the other actors. In this context it is noteworthy that the ODA synthesis study referred to earlier found that some of the NGOs regarded participation as 'participation of beneficiaries only' (Surr, 1995). Recent ILO projects have taken this lesson to heart, and full attention is now being given to the role of supporting agencies, for example, in such fields as training, and dissemination of information. The ILO report identifies four main groups of stakeholders at the local level as follows:

- intended beneficiaries—usually groups of individuals who have not yet organised themselves effectively;
- social actors—representatives of workers' or employers' organisations, and government officials;
- membership organisations of intended beneficiaries, such as co-operatives, community or women's organisations; and
- service organisations at all levels supporting specific population groups.

A third problem sometimes encountered was a lack of commitment on the part of partner institutions and supporting service organisations, and differences in understanding as to what participation was all about. In some ILO projects, people at the operational level were not prepared to participate effectively. One important lesson was that the more all the stakeholders were involved in the initial project preparation, sorting out what the problem was and what was the best solution, and then being involved in the on-going monitoring, the more they were willing to adopt participatory methods in a genuine way. However, the report comments that it is important that the representatives of intended beneficiaries, when they are consulted in the early stages of a project, can 'show a sufficient degree of independence and freedom of expression in meetings with the participating officials of governments and implementing agencies' (ILO, 1995). If they are too easily overawed by the (often) superior education and social status of the other actors they may not be able to promote adequately the interests of the people they represent. Sometimes they are even hijacked by the other powerful stakeholders. To quote the ODA study again, 'groups of beneficiaries have sometimes reflected those existing power structures which often prejudice the project against the very groups it was intended to help' (Surr, 1995).

Fourthly, participatory approaches have often fallen victim to the outside pressures they have to contend with. These include: donor agencies having excessive expectations of quick results; centralised bureaucratic decision-making procedures in counterpart institutions; and technocratic monitoring and evaluation systems, often controlled by the project management. ILO experience suggests that there may be an inherent contradiction between the top–down approach of many bureaucracies, and technocrats, on the one hand, and the bottom–up approach that is characterised by dialogue, information exchange, power sharing and redistribution, on the other.

Finally, the evaluation found that in some projects it is still the case that inadequate attention is paid to the participation of women, while in others the cultural and physical constraints on their participation, and measures taken to counteract them are not being adequately taken into account. There are cases where men have undertaken, as a condition of the funding, to look after the interests of the women, but then failed to do so. The solution is for women's representatives to be involved in project planning right from the beginning.

The findings in the ODA synthesis study were very consistent with the ILO ones discussed here. In addition, the ODA study commented on the lack of clarity and precision about what the term 'participation' actually covers. It can be used to refer to a process whereby, for example, a group of villagers come together, at the instigation of the donors, to dig a well; or it can be used to refer to more sophisticated community organisation-based projects. Sometimes it refers to more politically-oriented projects aimed at good governance, and at other times it has a more economic context, for example, where the aim is to empower poor people by establishing market-based systems. It might help to systematise future activities in this field if the different types of participation could be better understood and classified.

The ODA study also makes the point that beneficiary involvement was not always the most important factor in relation to project success or failure. It quotes cases where projects failed because of weak management or a hostile environment, and also cases of successful projects where there was good management but little participation: 'An enterprising and energetic project management team, with a shrewd idea of the requirements of poor people, can produce services that people require without formal beneficiary participation' (Surr, 1995).

None of the problems discussed here are insuperable, and as more experience is gained in the participatory approach some of them at least should fall away. The key is to ensure full participation of all the stakeholders right from the start of the project's life—not as a form of tokenism but simply in recognition of the fact that unless the primary stakeholders are fully involved, progress could be slow and success problematic.

Should Participatory Monitoring and Evaluation Render Traditional Evaluation Methods Obsolete?

The point that was made earlier in this chapter was that up to now participatory methods have not been much used in monitoring and evaluation, and there is little hard evidence of how successful they would be in that context. In their summing up of the findings of an IDS Workshop on Participation, Blackburn and Holland commented:

> The use of PRA in monitoring and evaluation is on the increase, often as the logical outcome of a participatory baseline study aimed at generating relevant indicators which can be compared and explored further as the project's life extends. But we are still a long way from understanding how to devise appropriate mechanisms to sustain participation in the often arduous process of negotiation, and resulting conflicts of interest, which invariably arise in the day-to-day management of a project (Blackburn with Holland, 1998).

With all this in mind, we come now to the key question. Is participatory monitoring and evaluation to be viewed merely as an alternative approach in those circumstances (possibly rather rare) where it seems to be particularly appropriate, or is it to be seen as ultimately the only acceptable method, eventually ousting the traditional methods?

The first point to make is that the participatory approach is extremely unlikely to render the traditional methods completely obsolete, if only because there are often difficult technical components that are involved in evaluations, even some of the people-centred ones, and these need to be evaluated by those with adequate technical knowledge. Reference was made in the previous chapter to the work of Rebien who has applied participatory methods to four projects. He also makes the point that there were technical aspects to these projects (which he calls 'hard' to distinguish them from the 'soft' or social aspects of the project) that required a technical input into the evaluations. He points out that even if the participatory method is used for the soft aspects it will still be necessary to use technical evaluators for the hard aspects (Rebien, 1996).

As there has been much discussion of the potential for applying participatory methods to monitoring and evaluation but as yet little real evidence from the ground, Rebien's pioneering work is of particular interest. He identifies the principal characteristic of participatory monitoring and evaluation as 'a continuous dialectic chain of questioning, answering, analysing, requestioning, reanalysing, and so on, leading to a common construction of reality by the observer and the observed'. This is an almost perfect description of the iterative 'listening-piloting-demonstrating' process based on the process approach and the new project cycle that I was trying to depict in Figure 8.3 in Chapter 8.

Rebien addresses directly the question whether this new method should supersede the old traditional methods. He tackles it in two ways. First he points out that in the situation of asymmetries of power that currently exist between donor and recipient the participatory approach cannot be expected to work properly. This is such an important issue for official aid agencies that his comments are worth quoting in full:

Although a participatory evaluation is undertaken in the spirit of providing democratic access to decision-making and is based on the assumption that the people actually involved in the intervention also know its weaknesses and how it should be changed, the evaluation still takes place within the structural framework of a donor-recipient relationship, which is not easily changed and which ultimately determines the fate of major evaluation recommendations. The question arises whether structural conditions and the asymmetric relation of power between donor and recipient do not actually obstruct the potential of participatory evaluation to an extent that it remains a somewhat naive and idealistic notion (Rebien, 1996).

Rebien's second response to the question is to quote Swantz (presumably because he agrees with her), a Finnish researcher with unparalleled experience in the evaluation of people-centred projects using participatory methods: 'Once (the participatory approach is) established as a regular process, the number of necessary conventional external evaluation missions could be reduced. The focus of external evaluation would change accordingly to become assessments of long term project impact' (Swantz, 1992). Swantz obviously sees the participatory approach as complementary to conventional aid evaluation, not as a substitute for it. Other writers (e.g., Feuerstein, 1986) also take this view, and it is one that I would wholeheartedly endorse. I cannot see how the participatory approach can entirely replace traditional evaluations, if only because of the accountability imperative, but there can be no doubt that only if some kind of participatory methods are used can there be any prospect of getting really useful feedback about what makes for success or failure in people-centred projects. The old-style three-week mission simply will not provide this kind of information. This is not to say that one has to go the whole hog of the evaluator as a negotiator, and even if participatory methods are used there will still need to be some element of objectivity if possible. It may have to be left to the NGOs to continue to develop the full gospel of the participatory approach since their need for accountability seems to be rather less. It is significant that Rebien concludes his review of the literature on participatory monitoring and evaluation by commenting that 'accountability and field implementation goals cannot both be pursued in the same evaluation: they are distinctly different purposes, serving different masters, and should be kept apart'. We seem to be facing a period of experimentation ahead, with NGOs probably leading the field in participatory methods but official agencies adopting such aspects as they can without prejudicing their accountability requirements. It promises to be an interesting phase in the development of our subject.

Project Cost Empowerment

Unlike the situation with the logical framework, where it was the evaluators who took the lead, it seems to have been the social development advisers in DFID, working closely with the NGOs and interested academics, who have been the main motivators of stakeholder analysis and participatory methods in the UK. However, the DFID evaluators have not been inactive. Not only have they conducted evaluations with stakeholder analysis and participatory methods very much in their sights but they have also developed evaluation techniques that give more emphasis to the role of the stakeholders. One of these is the project cost empowerment system described in Box 20.1. However, this has been somewhat overtaken by the trend, throughout the DFID, towards greater use of participatory methods, and especially the growing realisation that participation is most useful if it is not tacked onto the end of the project cycle as part of evaluation but used at all stages of project implementation.

Box 20.1   The Project Cost Empowerment System of Evaluation

DFID is pioneering a new approach to the evaluation of people-centred projects which involves participation by the individuals directly affected by the projects.

The basic idea is that it is possible for individuals to make meaningful judgements about project decisions that have been taken, and which have affected them directly. The key decisions in any project relate of course to the pattern of expenditure, so the first step is to calculate the annual cost of the project and express it "per recipient" or "per household". Secondly, the participants are asked to describe what the impact of the project has been, using Participatory Rural Appraisal (PRA) techniques. Thirdly, the cost of the project, or service, is translated into a form that is most likely to be meaningful to the recipients, e.g. "cost per day's supply of water per household". Finally the participants are asked to make a judgement as to whether they think the benefits were clearly worth more than the cost, or less, or whether it is too difficult to say.

This participatory approach (which is similar to the "Revealed Preference" technique) can empower recipients (hence the title), and can be used to assess the success or failure of people-centred projects.

Source: Aidwatch, Nov–Dec, 1995, No. 5.

Notes

1. The first shots in the European version of the American 'paradigm wars' may have already been fired. As mentioned earlier, a backlash against the overselling of the participatory approach has been developing, and a forum for the discussion of these issues was provided by a conference, in November 1998, at the University of Manchester with the title 'Participation—The New Tyranny?', in which I participated. It turned out that most participants were not rejecting the basic arguments in favour of the participatory approach, but they

thought there should be a greater appreciation of the difficulties and problems associated with it, including those I have discussed in this chapter (Cleaver, 1998; Mohan—1998, and Mosse—1998). There was also some criticism of the almost messianic fervour with which the adherents of the participatory approach tend to promote their ideas (Henkel and Stirrat, 1998).

2. An outstanding pioneer of participatory monitoring and evaluation has been Sam Joseph from India, working for Action Aid in Somaliland, where community-based organisations have conducted their own evaluations of Action Aid programmes using their own appraisals, knowledge and indicators (Sanaag community-based organisation, 1999).

3. Gasper reports that some people are attempting to use the logical framework in a participatory way, but instead of calling the process 'project cycle management' they call it 'participatory co-operation management' (Gasper, 1997).

4. Rebien found the same problem: 'What about the destitute, who might also be stakeholders but who by definition cannot exercise agency?' (Rebien, 1996).

Part 5

The Wider Horizon
and
the Way Ahead

The Conference on Evaluation organised by the World Bank in 1994 has been quoted many times in this book. The editors of the Proceedings, Picciotto and Rist, take a look at what the future holds for aid evaluation:

Given the more exacting and diverse goals of development, the structure of demand for evaluation is changing fast. Evaluation will need to be retooled in order to sustain its credibility and enhance its usefulness. Among the improvements proposed for development evaluation are: greater focus by evaluators on relevant policy questions, speedier and more cost-effective responses to emerging needs, and more open and participatory evaluation processes, more focus on evaluation dissemination, and greater responsiveness to the capacity development needs of developing countries. Such changes are expected to lead to more effective links between evaluation and research...the cultural gap that still exists between evaluators and decision-makers should be bridged. To quote Sylvia Escobar Gomez: "The only way to improve development is to improve public management, and the only way to improve public management is to create an evaluation culture.

The Wider Horizon and the Way Ahead—A Look at Tomorrow's Evaluation World

'I see the Past, Present and Future existing all at once'
(Jerusalem, William Blake)

'A state without the means of some change is without the means of its conservation'
(Reflections on the Revolution in France, *Edmund Burke*)

'Evaluation in the next century will be far more diverse than it is today. So we must face the discomfort of stirring ourselves if we are to avoid being left behind'
(Evaluation for the 21st Century, *Eleanor Chelimsky and William Shadish*)

The Wider Horizon

As I remarked in the Introduction to this book, aid evaluators lived very much in a world of their own until quite recently, with little contact with evaluators working in other fields. But today that is changing fast, and now aid evaluators are engaging in fruitful dialogue with their fellow evaluators in other sectors. Each has a lot to learn from the other, but inevitably, in view of the relatively small size of the aid sector, the traffic in ideas has been mainly inwards from other sectors rather than outwards. The first part of the chapter reviews the nature of this two-way traffic, and the second part looks at the directions in which aid evaluators are likely to move in the years ahead.

Paradigm Wars in the USA

The last two decades have been characterised in the USA by the 'paradigm wars' mentioned briefly in Chapters 19 and 20. On one side stood the conventional evaluators represented by Rossi and Freeman, who gave great emphasis to the need for scientific method, particularly the use of controlled experiments, as the basic tool of evaluation: this is often called the positivist approach. And on the other side stood the Fourth Generation Evaluation adherents who rejected the validity of the experimental approach in the evaluation of human resource projects and instead advocated full involvement by the evaluator: this is often called the constructivist approach. At the same time, there was another major debate taking place in the USA between those evaluators who tended to regard themselves as researchers and took little interest in what the client needed or in how their results were going to be used, and those, like Patton and Chelimsky, who go almost to the other extreme and argue that only if an evaluation meets a felt need, and is in fact used, is it worth doing. The latter school was not too concerned about the precise method being used so long as it produced the goods—they certainly were not committed to the experimental approach.

Seen from the European standpoint, the passions and intellectual fury aroused by these debates seem surprising and indeed rather pointless. This is particularly the case if one's own speciality is aid evaluation because the controlled experiment has seldom, if ever, been practical in relation to projects thousands of miles away and under the control of a sovereign state. Moreover, aid evaluators have always operated very close to the policy-makers and decision-takers, so that there has never been any doubt in their minds about the need to ensure that the evaluations meet the needs of clients and that they are utilised. Patton would be preaching to the converted because virtually all aid evaluation is utilisation-focused. However, the storm in the USA now seems to have blown over, or to revert to the military metaphor, a peace treaty has come into effect (Patton says the argument has 'run out of steam' [Patton, 1997]). Most people now accept that the pluralist approach is the right one that is, the use of a number of different techniques and methods, is the right one, as may seem appropriate, rather than just focusing on one; whilst the need to gear evaluations to meet the needs of clients ('intended use by intended users' to quote Patton's favourite slogan) is now generally accepted.

Cross-Fertilisation of Ideas

If European evaluators do not have much to learn from the history of the paradigm wars does this mean that they have little to learn from American evaluation experience in general? Certainly not. Although the authors of fourth generation evaluation undoubtedly carry their case to extremes, and can easily be criticised for this (see, for example, Pawson and Tilley, 1997), the fact is that the basic ideas developed in that book resonate closely with the parallel trend in European thinking that originated with rapid rural appraisal, and has now become participatory reflection and action. The work of Chambers at the Institute of Development Studies in this connection has already been referred to in the previous chapter. There is now a substantial body of literature in Europe concerning the participatory approach in aid evaluation, and as we saw in the previous chapter, European evaluators such as Rebien, Carlsson, Kohlin, Ekbom, Forss, Samset, MacArthur and others,[1] are now actively researching into the impact of these ideas. My own proposals in Chapter 8 for a more participatory approach to monitoring and evaluation represent an attempt to extend these ideas a stage further.

Evaluation and the Learning Organisation

Another area where European evaluators have learned a lot from American experience has been organisational learning. Many of the key texts (e.g., Argyris and Schon, 1978) are American, and it is from America that the most innovative ideas about knowledge generation and sharing are emanating. For example, the President of the World Bank, Mr Wolfensen, has declared that he intends to make the Bank more of a 'learning organization'. He has reorganised the Bank's internal administrative structures to give greater scope for mutual learning, and he has created a new cadre of learning officers. He has also given a huge boost (in money and staff) to the World Bank Institute so that it can become what he calls 'the learning arm of the Bank'. However, there has also been a growing interest in this subject in Europe as demonstrated by the decision of the newly created Swedish Expert Group on Development Issues to commission the study of organisational learning discussed in Chapter 9; and also by the recent decision by DFID to set up a Knowledge Policy Unit.

Realistic Evaluation

One of the most influential books on evaluation that has appeared in Europe in recent years is Pawson and Tilley's *Realistic Evaluation*. The authors reject any excessive emphasis on the experimental approach, although they cannot accept the assumption of the Fourth Generation school that there is no reality outside whatever emerges from the interaction between stakeholders and evaluators. They take issue with that school on the grounds that they ignore the asymmetries of power that exist in the real world, and also that their approach is unlikely to generate practically useful results that the commissioners of evaluations can use. Pawson and Tilley stress the supreme importance of taking into account in every evaluation the context in which the projects or programmes are implemented, and they express this in the form of an equation: 'M (i.e., mechanism) + C (i.e., content) = O (i.e., outcome). For them the key question that evaluators have to try to answer is 'What works, for whom, in what circumstances? (the three Ws)'. It is this emphasis on studying the context that represents the 'realism' in the book's title. In other words, the evaluator is not only interested in what has happened after an intervention of some kind has taken place, he/she also wants to know **why** people reacted as they did. It is this knowledge that can add enormously to the practical value of the evaluation results for decision-takers.

I suspect that to most evaluators working in the aid evaluation field, these arguments may seem all rather obvious since context has always been regarded as a vital component in aid evaluations. Perhaps this is because we were hardly ever able to use the experimental approach, in the way that many academic evaluation researchers working on welfare schemes and the like were, so that we had nothing to 'unlearn'. However, for those evaluators who were working on UK welfare projects, attribution was a key objective, that is, being able to distinguish with some confidence what outcomes could be attributed to what packages of assistance, and this task consumed so many resources that there was a tendency to ignore the reasons why people acted as they did. In the development field there was generally a much closer relationship between the evaluators (many of whom were ministry staff) and the decision-takers than would normally be the case when evaluations were carried out wholly by academic institutions. Aid evaluators (many of whom are only temporarily working in the evaluation field and soon return to tasks involving aid implementation) have always been acutely conscious of the need to produce practically useful evaluation results—which implies examining contexts as well as mechanisms.

Reverse Flow of Ideas and Experience from Aid Evaluation to Other Sectors

Not all the flow of ideas and experience has been in one direction only. In recent years there has been movement in the opposite direction. I was delighted, for instance, when the UK Treasury invited me to address a conference they were holding on evaluation in the UK public sector (Cracknell, 1994a). My participation led eventually to an article on this subject in a professional journal (Cracknell, 1994b). One of my successors as Head of the Evaluation Department in the ODA was a founder-member of the committee of the UK Evaluation Society. I mention these facts simply as an indication that aid evaluators are beginning to find a place in the wider evaluation community, and this is surely to be welcomed.

There is one area in particular where the traffic in ideas and methodologies has been strongly in the reverse direction, that is, from aid evaluation to other sectors. I am referring to the logical framework approach which was first developed by the American aid agency USAID, and was then taken up not only by other aid donors but more widely by some public sectors, including Canada, UK and others. The technique has had such a tremendous impact on the efficiency of aid administration that I am puzzled that it does not seem to have spread even more widely outside the aid field. It is seldom indeed, when one reads the pages of *Evaluation*, or the works of American evaluators, that one comes across any reference to the logical framework, or indeed to the whole topic of project cycle management. One reason for this may be that the difficulties of administering aid programmes located outside one's own borders, and often through very ill-equipped and inexperienced agencies in the developing world, are so acute that some kind of systematic project management is almost a necessity, whereas it may not appear so essential within a domestic situation. Another contributory factor may be that domestic evaluations are typically carried out by academic evaluators who do not have direct responsibility for the way their reports are utilised, and who in any case have only limited opportunities of informing themselves about the internal administrative arrangements of the ministries or bodies that commission them. The apparent lack of interest in project cycle management issues in the evaluation field generally is surely a weakness, and maybe aid evaluators could do more to pass on their experience in this area.

The broadening of horizons over the last five years or so has been a tremendously exciting and encouraging development for aid evaluators in Europe. Whether this has happened in other parts of the world to the same extent I cannot judge, although the proliferation of national, regional and international evaluation societies, and the contributions to evaluation journals that are coming from all over the world, suggest that it has. There is plenty of scope for this process to continue, and hopefully it will become more of a two-way traffic, with evaluators working in other sectors becoming more aware of the contributions that aid evaluators have to make and willing to enter into a constructive dialogue.

The Way Ahead: A Look at Tomorrow's Aid Evaluation World

It seems appropriate to round off this review of the issues, problems and solutions in aid evaluation with a glance at what may lie ahead. Where are we heading towards in aid evaluation? Let me throw some straws in the wind.

Search for a Modus Vivendi between Traditional Evaluation and the Participatory Approach

This will surely be the most dominant issue in the years ahead. Stakeholder analysis will be still further developed in the direction of a more participatory approach, although still falling well short of the 'negotiation' mode, but it will remain complementary to the existing conventional methods rather than being a substitute for them. The trend towards more participation will itself be strengthened by the continuing decentralisation of aid from the headquarters to the field, with a concomitant extension of the process approach with its greater flexibility and scope for local autonomy. The DAC Expert Group on Aid Evaluation Synthesis Report recommends that participation needs to be mainstreamed by donor agencies into their operations, and that evaluation tools need to be further developed in this area (OECD, 1997a).

Strengthening Evaluation Capacity in the Developing Countries

As part of the trend towards more participation, the need to beef up the evaluation capacities of the recipients will become ever more obvious. How can they be genuine participants in the evaluation process unless they have received some training in evaluation methodologies? The OECD/DAC Expert Group on Aid Evaluation has already given a strong lead in this direction but it cannot all be left to them and evaluation units in all the main donor countries will need to take on their share of the responsibility.[2]

More Flexible Application of the Logical Framework Technique

I remain a committed advocate of the logical framework in general, but I can see that the pressures are building up for it to be applied in a more flexible fashion, and in a few special cases it may even have to be jettisoned in favour of a participatory system of project management. It should be used in a dynamic fashion, being amended frequently, but even so the more widely the process approach comes into use (and it is now the dominant project management mode in DFID, especially now that poverty alleviation has become the priority aid objective) the less appropriate is the matrix approach. What is the point of labouring to produce excellent matrices, including indicators of progress, if the project itself is constantly being changed to meet the wishes of the stakeholders? With people-centred projects the emphasis will certainly have to change from the logical framework approach towards the more flexible system I suggested in Figure 8.3. These are new and uncharted waters, but they hold out promise of more successful project implementation where people are the principal actors.

A difficult issue is whether the logical framework approach is suitable for the developing countries, or whether it is too closely linked to a Western way of thinking. I had some doubts on that score myself when the National Productivity Council of India invited me in 1992 to run a series of training courses on the logical framework technique in three Indian cities. But in the event I need not have worried. I found that those who attended (admittedly some were of very high calibre being senior members of the Indian Administrative Service) quickly grasped the method and produced matrices (of ODA projects in India) that were of excellent quality. I came away with the impression that the technique is ideally suited to the Indian mentality, with its love of debate and reasoned argument. I have also run a similar workshop in Nairobi for UNEP, attended mostly by Africans, and again the results were very good. However, I realise that it may not suit other cultures so well, and I realise that there have been other cases where participants from developing countries have been resistant to the method.

More Effective Feedback

The trend towards more participatory monitoring and evaluation will also have repercussions in terms of feedback. The great weakness of feedback in the past has been at the policy or strategy level, but now the situation is changing as aid agencies continue to decentralise and to allow more local autonomy. Today most project-level aid decisions in DFID (and in many other aid organisations also, although not the European Commission) are taken in the field without any reference to headquarters. The pattern now is for project level findings from evaluations to be taken on board as an integral part of on-going project management activity. There will still need to be feedback at the regional level of lessons that others working in the same region (or others working on similar types of projects elsewhere in the organisation) need to be informed about, but this can best be achieved locally rather than through the central evaluation unit. This means that the central evaluation unit has to be responsible only for the macro lessons. This task may be more difficult than hitherto since there will be fewer of the traditional type of evaluation reports, and therefore less scope to pick up the macro lessons. Evaluation units may need to think of fresh ways of synthesising the macro lessons (such as they are) that may be emerging from the project work in the field.

From Vertical Information Flows to Horizontal

The trends outlined also have implications for organisational learning. I have already mentioned (Chapter 9) that when I carried out the review of evaluation practice in several aid agencies as a member of the team commissioned by the Swedish Ministry of Foreign Affairs, I discovered that a number of aid agencies are adopting internal management structures that facilitate horizontal rather than vertical learning flows. In other words, whereas in the past information tended to be passed vertically up the line from the field operational level to the headquarters, and vice versa, now, for the reasons set out earlier, the tendency is for information to be passed sideways to others working in the same region or in the same area of specialisation. Aid agencies are establishing regional centres of information, holding more local and regional seminars and arranging meetings of subject matter specialists not necessarily at the headquarters but at any convenient location to suit the people concerned, often regionally rather than centrally. The old-style vertical flows were linked to the need for command and control, but that top–down planning process has largely been superseded. The more the aid agencies adopt poverty alleviation as their priority target the more these trends are likely to be reinforced. There is still a major learning task to be accomplished, but it will be learning-by-listening, learning-by-doing, and learning-by-sharing, rather than learning from the book or from instructions issuing from some central source.

More Qualitative rather than Quantitative Information Flows

As regards management information systems, the present trend towards more computerised data systems will undoubtedly continue (if only because there will be new developments in information technology), but at the same time the weaknesses of these systems will become increasingly apparent and new methods of storing, retrieving and sharing data will be sought which will involve more face-to-face contact. There will be a move away from more and more quantified data towards a more selective flow of qualitative information. However, aid agencies are finding that the usefulness of such information can be very much reduced if it is divorced from its origins. It is not much use being given the bare facts that an intervention in an African country produced a certain reaction on the part of the beneficiaries. One needs to know precisely what the intervention was, where and when it took place and what the circumstances were at the time, and also something about the informant (partly in case there was any possibility of bias or undue influence, but mainly because those who receive the information may well need to consult the source of it face-to-face). Some aid agencies are already beginning to experiment with new kinds of information systems along these lines, aiming to put the seekers after information into touch with those who might have it.

New Evaluation Techniques to Cope with New Kinds of Aid

The movement away from project aid towards non-project aid, such as sector and programme aid and structural adjustment assistance and programmes addressing such issues as poverty alleviation, good governance, environment, gender, community empowerment and institution building, has already put pressure on evaluators to come up with new methodologies, new criteria of success, and new types of indicators. There is an increasing flow of research papers addressing these issues, whilst agencies like USAID that have begun to accumulate experience in handling sector-level performance indicators, and other agencies that have acquired special experience in certain areas, will need to share it more widely, through the aegis of the DAC Expert Group on Aid Evaluation (which should have plenty of work to keep it going for a good many years yet). The trend towards non-project aid (i.e., in the macro direction) is running the opposite way from the trend towards more participatory methods (i.e., in the micro direction), but both will be continue to take place concurrently.

The evaluation of such politically sensitive matters as structural adjustment, good governance and sector aid, will inevitably mean more involvement by evaluators from the recipient countries, and this will be another factor reinforcing the need for donor evaluators to help train them.

Further Broadening of Horizons

The process of aid evaluators 'coming in from the cold' and enjoying closer relationships with evaluators working in other sectors is a very healthy one and will hopefully continue. I hope I have been able to demonstrate that aid evaluators have a useful contribution to make to the general world of evaluation and they should seize every opportunity that offers—and start creating a few of their own! Unfortunately, their day-to-day work seldom brings them into contact with civil servants working in other ministries, so they tend to become a little isolated within the government structure. They need to cultivate official contacts with fellow evaluators working elsewhere in the public sector, as well as participating in seminars and conferences as much as possible.

More Participation in On-going Debates Regarding the Future of the Evaluation Profession

As an extension of the previous point, aid evaluators should surely play a greater role in the debates taking place in the wider evaluation community regarding the future of the profession. Should it move in the direction of setting standards for evaluation, with entry qualifications as a mandatory feature, and possibly with rewards for outstanding achievements? Should there be some system of centralised training for evaluators, and if so what part can aid evaluators play? Is there a case for a national register of evaluators, and a library of completed reports? What should be the role of the commissioners of evaluations within the profession? How can aid evaluators best inform themselves about the new ideas and new methodologies emerging in other parts of the profession? Is there a case for a newsletter or a 'best practices' information system of some kind? There is a lot of scope for interchange on such issues. These are exciting times to be alive for evaluators. There is a buzz in the air, and a sense of being in at the beginning of some important developments. I hope my book has reflected some of this sense of excitement and that it may have made a small contribution to the ferment of ideas that so enlivens the evaluation profession.

Notes

1. The contribution to European aid evaluation literature coming from Scandinavian evaluators is remarkable. Forss, Carlsson Kohlin and Ekbom, are from Sweden; Stokke and Samset from Norway; Rebien from Denmark; and Swantz from Finland. A number of them have cooperated together on research and consultancy projects and this has proved to be a very fruitful relationship.
2. A study of evaluation capacity building among the main donor agencies, carried out by the DAC Expert Group on Aid Evaluation in 1997, found that the Directorate General for International Cooperation in the Netherlands was one of the very few bilateral agencies that had formulated a policy on support of evaluation capacity building (OECD, 1997a).

References

Ackroyd, D. (1995) 'Steps Towards the Adoption of the Logical Framework Approach in the African Development Bank', *Project Appraisal*, 10 (1).

Action Aid (1987) *Poverty-Focused Aid: The Lessons of Experience*, Action Aid, Chard, Somerset.

———. (1990) *The Effectiveness of British Aid for Training*, Action Aid, Chard, Somerset.

———. (1999) Action Aid Impact Assessment Workshop, 30 November–4 December 1998, Isle of Thorns, Sussex (report and collected papers), Action Aid, Hamlyn House, MacDonald Road, Archway, London.

ADB (Asian Development Bank) (1981) *Guidelines on Logical Framework Planning and Project* Benefit Monitoring and Evaluation, ADB, Bangkok.

———. (Asian Development Bank) (1995) Postevaluation and Feedback: Realities and Challenges in the Asian and Pacific Region. Proceedings of the Regional Workshop on Strengthening Postevaluation Feedback Systems.

Argyris, C. and **D. Schon** (1978) *Organizational Learning: A Theory of Action Perspective*, Jossey-Bass, San Francisco.

Arkadie, B. van, (1986) 'Aid Management and Co-ordination: Some Dilemmas' *IDS Bulletin*, 17 (2): 28–31.

Asian Institute of Technology (1978) Tracer Study and Employer Survey, AIT, Bangkok.

Bacha, E. (1990) 'A Three-Gap Model of Foreign Transfers and the GDP Growth Rate in Developing Countries', *Journal of Development Economics*, 32 (2): 279–96.

Baulch, B. (1995) 'Different Methods for Measuring the Dimensions of Poverty', in *Seminar Report: Methods for Evaluation of Poverty Oriented Interventions*, Appendix 7, DANIDA, Copenhagen.

Baum, W.C. (1970) 'The Project Cycle', *Finance and Development* (World Bank, Washington DC), 7 (2): 2–13.

———. (1978) 'The World Bank Project Cycle', *Finance and Development* (World Bank, Washington DC), 15 (4): 10–18.

Bell, C., P. Hazel, and **R. Slade** (1972) *Project Evaluation in a Regional Perspective*, World Bank, Washington DC.

Blackburn, J. with **J. Holland** (1998) *Who Changes? Institutionalizing Participation in Development*, Intermediate Technology, London.

Branson, W.H. and **C. Jayarajah** (1995) 'A Framework for Evaluating Policy Adjustment Programmes: Lessons from a Cross-Country Evaluation', in Robert Picciotto and Ray C. Rist (eds), *Evaluation and Development: Proceedings of the 1994 World Bank Conference*, World Bank, Washington DC, pp. 61–80.

Browning, R. (1984) 'Evaluation in the ODA: A View from the Inside', *Public Administration and Development*, 4: 133–39.

Buch-Hansen, P. (1995) 'Poverty Alleviation Evaluation: Approaches and Methodology', in *Seminar Report: Methods for Evaluation of Poverty Oriented Aid Interventions, Appendix 4*, DANIDA, Copenhagen.

Cameron, J. (1993) 'The Challenges for Monitoring and Evaluation in the 1990s', *Project Appraisal*, 8 (2): 91–96.

Cameron, C. and **J. Cocking** (1991) The Evaluation of NGO Activities, Organization Methodology and Results. Discussion draft, ODA, London.

Carlsson, J., G. Kohlin, and **A. Ekbom** (1994) *The Political Economy of Evaluations: International Aid Agencies and the Effectiveness of Aid*, Macmillan Press, Basingstoke

Carvalho, S. (1995) *Appendix 6, Seminar Report: Methods for Evaluation of Poverty Oriented Aid Interventions*, DANIDA, Copenhagen

Casley, D. and **D.A. Lury**, (1981) *Monitoring and Evaluation of Agriculture and Rural Development Projects*, Johns Hopkins Press, Baltimore.

Casley, D. and **K. Kumar**, (1986) *Project Monitoring and Evaluation in Agriculture*, World Bank, Washington DC.

Cassen, R. and associates (1986) *Does Aid Work?*, Clarendon Press, Oxford.

CFTC (1985) *CFTC Evaluation System*, Commonwealth Secretariat, London.

Chambers, R. (1988) *Farmer-First: A Practical Paradigm for Third World Agriculture*, Institute of Development Studies, Brighton, Sussex, UK.

——. (1997) *Whose Reality Counts? Putting the First Last*, Intermediate Technology, London.

Chambers, R., A. Pacey and **L.A. Thrupp** (1989) *Farmer First: Farmer Innovation and Agricultural Research*, Intermediate Technology Publications, London.

Charyulu, U.V.N. and **M. Seetharam** (1990) 'Participatory Evaluation of People's Development Projects—A Case Study', *Journal of Rural Development* (NIRD, Hyderabad, India), 9: 391–96.

Chelimsky, E. (1994) *Where We Stand Today in the Practice of Evaluation: Some Reflections*, World Bank, Washington DC, pp. 3–11.

——. (1995) New Dimensions in Evaluation, in *Evaluation and Development: Proceedings of the 1994 World Bank Conference*, World Bank, Washington DC.

——. (1996) Politics, Policy and Research Synthesis, *Evaluation*, 1 (1): 97–104.

Chelimsky, E. and **W.R. Shadish** (1997) *Evaluation for the 21st Century*, Sage, Thousand Oaks.

Choksi, A.M. (1995) 'Evaluation in the Bank: Taking Stock of 50 Years of Development Work', in Robert Picciotto and Ray C. Rist (eds), *Evaluation and Development: Proceedings of the 1994 World Bank Conference*, World Bank, Washington DC, pp. 15–20.

Clague, C. (1995) 'Comments on "Assessing Institutional Development: The Legal Framework that Shapes Public Institutions" by T.H. Stanton', in Robert Picciotto and Ray C. Rist (eds), *Evaluation and Development: Proceedings of the 1994 World Bank Conference*, World Bank, Washington DC.

Cleaver, F. (1998) Paradoxes for Participation: A Critique of Participatory Approaches to Development. Paper prepared for 'Participation—The New Tyranny?' Conference at the University of Manchester.

Clift, C. (1998) Knowledge Policy Unit, *Forum*, 57 (Summer): 2.

Colclough, C. (1990) Technical Co-operation: Assessment of a Leviathan. Paper delivered to workshop at Lysebu, organised under the auspices of the European Association of Development, Research and Training Institutes, Norwegian Institute of International Affairs, Oslo.

Coleman, G. (1987) Logical Framework Approach to the Monitoring and Evaluation of Agricultural and Rural Development Projects, *Project Appraisal*, 2 (4): 231–39.

Collister, P., J. Carstairs, L. Mountford, A. Hall and **J. Kehler** (1979) *Mid-term Review of ODA's Aid to the Allama Iqbal Open University, Pakistan*, ODA Evaluation Department, London.

Conlin, S., Butcher, D., and **R. Chambers** (1985) *Process Planning and Rural Development*, Institute of Development Studies at the University of Sussex, Brighton, Sussex.

Cordingley, D. (1995) Integrating the Logical Framework into the Management of Technical Co-operation Projects. *Project Appraisal*, 10 (2): 103–12.

Cracknell, B.E. (1982) Evaluation in the UN System and Elsewhere, as Viewed by the UK. Unpublished paper presented to an informal inter-agency meeting in Geneva.

——. (1984a) 'Learning Lessons from Experience: The Role of Evaluation in the Administration of the UK Aid Programme', *Public Administration and Development*, 4: 15–20.

——. (1984b) *The Evaluation of Aid Projects and Programmes*, HMSO, London.

——. (1985), It Looks Different from the Other Side: Project Evaluation from the Perspective of the Developing Countries. Unpublished paper delivered to the annual conference of the Development Economics Study Group of the Economic and Social Research Council.

——. (1986) 'European and International Aid Agencies' Approaches to Evaluation: A Bird's-eye View', *Bulletin of EADI* (June): 1–13.

Cracknell, B.E. (1988a) 'Evaluating Development Assistance: A Review of the Literature', *Public Administration and Development*, 8: 75–83.

——. (1988b) 'The Role of an Evaluation Unit: Functions and Constraints. With Particular Reference to the Feedback of Evaluation Findings'. Paper prepared for a workshop at Lysebu, Oslo, organised by the European Association of Development Institutes.

——. (1989) 'Evaluating the Effectiveness of the Logical Framework System in Practice', *Project Appraisal*, 4 (3): 163–67.

——. (1990) 'Evaluation: A Code of Good Practice, *Development Journal* (February): 8–10.

——. (1991) 'The Evaluation Policy and Performance of Britain', in O. Stokke (ed.) *Evaluating Development Assistance: Policies and Performance*, Frank Cass, London.

——. (1993) 'Evaluation Feedback: So Important yet so Neglected!', *Project Appraisal*, 8 (2): 77–82.

——. (1994a) Use of Evaluation by Overseas Governments. Unpublished paper presented at the Treasury Conference on Evaluation.

——. (1994b) 'Monitoring and Evaluation of Public Sector Investment in the UK', *Project Appraisal*, 9 (4): 222–30.

Cracknell, B.E. and **J. Rednall** (1986) *Defining Objectives and Measuring Performance in Aid Projects and Programmes*, Evaluation Department, ODA, London

Cracknell, B.E., Forss, K. and **K. Samset** (1994a) 'Evaluation Systems when Aid Policies are Changing', *Project Appraisal*, 9 (1): 29–36.

Cracknell, B.E., Miranda, W.A.D., and **F.G. Miranda** (1989) *Evaluation of EEC Aid to Botswana (1976–1989)*, Evaluation Unit, EEC.

Cracknell, B.E., Kaulule, R., Kiiskinen A., and **R. Tembo** (1994b) *Practical Subjects in Zambia: Study of the Impact of Practical Subjects Teaching on those most Directly Affected, i.e. Teachers, Ex-Pupils, Parents and Employers, Report 1994: 2*, FINNIDA, Helsinki.

Crapper, D., Thomas, D., and **A. Handyside** (1997) *Contraceptive Social Marketing in Northern India, Evaluation Report EV 601*, Evaluation Department, ODA.

DANIDA (1995) *Seminar Report: Methods for Evaluation of Poverty Oriented Aid Interventions*, DANIDA, Copenhagen.

Development Journal (1990) 'DAC's Feedback Database under Evaluation', Issue no. 3: 22–25. Paris.

Duran, P., Monnier E. and **A. Smith** (1995) 'Evaluation à la Francaise: Towards a New Relationship Between Social Science and Public Action', *Evaluation*, 1 (1): 45–63.

Dyer, N. and **A. Bartholomew** (1994) *Project Completion Reports, Synthesis*, ODA, London.

EEC (1988) *Semi-annual Programme/Project Report*. Internal document.

Eggers, H. (1992) 'The Integrated Approach to Project Cycle Management', *Project Appraisal*, 7 (1): 3–10.

Eisendrath, A. (1988) 'The Use of Development Project Evaluation Information: A Study of the State Agencies in India', Ph.D. thesis, University of Wisconsin, Madison, Ann Arbor, IUMI Quoted in O. Stokke (ed.) (1991) *Evaluating Development Assistance*, Frank Cass, London.

Estrella, M. and **J. Gaventa** (1998) 'Who Counts Reality? Participatory Monitoring and Evaluation: A Literature Review'. Working paper no. 70, August, 1998, IDS, Brighton, Sussex.

Estrella, Marisol with **Jutta Blauert**, Dindo Campilan, John Gaventa, Julian Gonsalves, Irene Guijt, Debra A. Johnson and Roger Ricafort, eds (forthcoming), Learning from Change: Issues and Experiences in Participatory Monitoring and Evaluation, Intermediate Technology Publications, London.

Eyken, W. van de, Goulden, D. and **M. Crossley** (1995) Evaluating Educational Reform in a Small State, *Evaluation*, 1 (1): 33–44.

FASID (1993) *Project Cycle Management: Management Tool for Development Assistance*, FASID, Tokyo.

Feachem, R. et al. (1978) *Water, Health and Development: An Interdisciplinary Evaluation*, Tri-Med Books, London.

Feuerstein, M-T. (1986) *Partners in Evaluation: Evaluating Development and Community Programmes with Participants*, Macmillan, London.

Finne, H., M. Levin, and **T. Nilssen** (1995) 'Trailing Research: A Model for Useful Program Evaluation', *Evaluation*, 1 (1): 11–31.

FAO (Food and Agricultural Organisation) (1984) *Review of Field Programmes 1982–4*, FAO, Rome.

Forss, K. (1985) *Planning and Evaluation in Aid Organizations*, Economic Research Institute, Stockholm School of Economics.

Forss, K., B.E. Cracknell, and **K. Samset** (1994) Can Evaluation Help an Organization to Learn?, *Evaluation Review*, 18 (5).

Forss, K. and **J. Carlsson** (1997) The Quest for Quality—Or Can Evaluation Findings be Trusted?, *Evaluation*, 3(4): 481–501.

Forss, K., B.E. Cracknell, and **N. Stromquist** (1998) 'Organizational Learning in Development Co-operation: How Knowledge is Generated and Used'. Working paper 1998: 3, Swedish Ministry for Foreign Affairs, Expert Group on Development Issues.

Forster, R. (ed.) (1996) *ZOPP Marries PRA? Participatory Learning and Action—A Challenge for our Services and Institutions*, GTZ, Frankfurt.

Foulkes, G. (1998) 'Evaluation and International Development: A British Perspective', *Evaluation*, 4 (3): 359–62.

Freedman, J. (1994) Participatory Evaluations: Making Projects Work. Technical paper no. TP 94/2, Division of International Development, International Centre, University of Calgary, Canada.

Freeman, H.E., Rossi, P.H., and **Sonia Wright** (1979) *Evaluating Social Projects in Developing Countries*, OECD, Paris.

Frerks, G.E., H. Thomas, and **L.B.M. Tomesen** (1990) *Effect Monitoring and Impact Evaluation: Report of a Workshop*, Royal Netherlands Embassy, Islamabad.

Freudenthal, S. and **J. Narrowe** (1992), *Baseline Study Handbook—Focus on the Field*, Evaluation Unit, Swedish International Development Authority, Avebury.

Friere, P. (1972) *Pedagogy of the Oppressed*, Penguin Books.

Gasper, D. (1997) Logical Frameworks: A Critical Assessment: Managerial Theory, Pluralistic Practice, Working paper no. 264, Institute of Development Studies, The Hague.

———. (1998) The Logical Framework Approach and the Planning and Evaluation of Humanitarian (Complex) Emergency Assistance. Paper presented to the Development Studies Association Conference, Bradford.

Gass, G., S. Biggs, and **A. Kelly** (1997) *Stakeholders, Science and Decision-Making for Poverty-focused Rural Mechanisation Research and Development*, 25(1).

Gaventa, J. (1980) *Power and Powerlessness: Rebellion and Quiescence in an Appalachian Valley*, University of Illinois Press, Chicago.

Georghiou L. (1995) 'Assessing the Framework Programmes—A Meta-evaluation', *Evaluation*, 1 (2): 171–88.

Gibson, T. (1996) *The Power in Our Hands: Neighbourhood-based World Shaking*, Jan Carpenter Publishing, Charlbury, Oxfordshire.

Goyder, H. (1995) 'New Approaches to Participatory Impact Assessment', in *Seminar Report: Methods for Evaluation of Poverty Oriented Aid Interventions*, DANIDA, Copenhagen.

GTZ (1989) *Indicatorbank for Rural Regional Development Programmes*, GTZ, Frankfurt.

Guba, E.G. and **Y.S. Lincoln** (1989) *Fourth Generation Evaluation*, Sage, Thousand Oaks.

Guerrero, P. (1995) 'Evaluating Development Results: Methods and Procedures', in Robert Picciotto and Ray C. Rist (eds), Evaluation and Development: Proceedings of the 1994 World Bank Conference.

Guijt, I. and **J. Gaventa** (1998) Participatory Monitoring and Evaluation: Learning from Change, IDS Policy Briefing No. 12, IDS, Sussex.

Hashemi, S.M. and **D.S.P. Das** (1994) *The Noakhali Integrated Rural Development Project: A Rapid Rural Assessment*, DANIDA, Copenhagen.

Healey, J. and **M. Robinson** (1992) *Democracy, Governance and Economic Policy*, Overseas Development Institute, London.

Henkel, H. and **R.L. Stirrat** (1998) Participation as Spiritual Duty: The Religious Roots of the New Development Orthodoxy. Paper prepared for the 'Participation—The New Tyranny?' Conference at the University of Manchester.

Hewitt, A. (1986) 'Anatomy of a Non-Profit Evaluation: Stabex Operations 1975–9', *Bulletin of the EADI* (June): 15–27.

Higginbottom, A.C. (1990) *Lessons from Evaluations, 1980–1989: An EVSUM Synthesis, ODA Evaluation Report, EV 510*, ODA, London.

Higginbottom, A. and **S. Henderson** (1990) *Project Completion Reports: Synthesis Study, ODA Evaluation Report 444*, ODA, London.

Hill, R.G. (1982) *A Synthesis of Rural Road Evaluations*. Occasional Paper No. 127. Transport and Road Research Laboratory (Overseas Unit).

Hirschman, A.O. (1967) *Development Projects Observed*, Washington DC, Brookings Institution, Washington DC.

Holtham, G., and **A. Hazlewood** (1976) *Aid and Inequality in Kenya*, ODI, London.

House of Commons (1981) *Fourth Report from the Committee of Public Accounts, Session 1980–81, ODA*, HMSO London.

———. (1987) *Foreign Affairs Committee Session 1986–7, ODA Bilateral Country Programmes*, Minutes of Evidence, 17th December 1986, and 27th January, 1987, HMSO London.

Hume, D. (1990) *The Effectiveness of British Aid for Training*, Action Aid, Chard, Somerset.

IBRD (1972) *Project Evaluation in a Regional Perspective: A Study of an Irrigation Project in North West Malaysia*, C. Bell, P. Hazell, and R. Slade, World Bank, Washington DC.

———. (1979) *Operations Evaluation—World Bank Standards and Procedures*, World Bank, Washington, DC.

IDRC (1996) 'The IDRC Evaluation Unit: Its Work and Organization', *Evaluation*, 2(3): 349–61.

IDS (1995) Can Aid Promote Good Governance? Policy briefing paper.

ILO (1993) *Report on the Study of the Usage of the Evaluation Database*, ILO, Geneva.

———. (1995) *Participatory Elements of Technical Co-operation Programmes and Projects*: An Assessment, ILO, Geneva.

Imboden, N. (1978) *A Management Approach to Project Appraisal and Evaluation, with Special Reference to Non Directly Productive Projects*, OECD Development Centre Studies, OECD, Paris.

Ingersoll, J. (1988) 'The Evaluation Process and Human Factors', *Advisory Council on Development Co-operation: Irish Bilateral Aid—The Evaluation Process*, Advisory Council on Development Cooperation, Dublin.

IFAD (International Fund for Agricultural Development) (n.d.) *Operational Guidelines on Monitoring and Evaluation*, IFAD, Rome.

Jennings, A. (1990) Measuring the Success or Failure of Aid: An Experiment in the Scoring Method for Aid Evaluation. Paper to workshop in Lysebu, Oslo, organised under the auspices of the Norwegian Institute of International Affairs, Oslo.

Jones, D. (1977) *British Aid to Botswana, Lesotho, and Swaziland*, Overseas Development Institute, London.

Khan, M.A. (1998) 'Evaluation Capacity Building: An Overview of Current Status, Issues and Options', *Evaluation*, 4 (3): 310–28.

Klitgaard, R. (1995) 'Including Culture in Evaluation Research', in Robert Picciotto and Ray C. Rist (eds), Evaluation and Development: Proceedings of the 1994 World Bank Conference, pp. 189–216.

van de Knapp, P. (1995) 'Policy Evaluation and Learning', *Evaluation*, 1 (2): 189–216

Kumar, K. (1995) 'Measuring the Performance of Agricultural and Rural Development Programmes', in Robert Picciotto and Ray C. Rist (eds), Evaluation and Development: Proceedings of the 1994 World Bank Conference, World Bank, Washington DC.

Lewin E. (1994) *Evaluation Manual for SIDA*, SIDA, Stockholm.

Little, I.M.D., and **J.R. Mirrlees** (1974) *Project Appraisal and Planning for Developing Countries*, Heinemann, London.

———. (1990) 'Project Appraisal and Planning Twenty Years On'. Proceedings of the World Bank Annual Conference on Development Economics, 1990, Washington DC, IMF/IBRD 1991.

Lowcock, M., and **D. Watson** (1988), *Evaluation of an ODA-funded Programme of Assistance to the Indonesia Institute of Public Administration, 1972–86, Evaluation Report EV 442*, ODA, London.

MacArthur, J. (1997) 'Stakeholder Analysis in Project Planning: Origins, Applications and Refinements', *Project Appraisal*, 12 (4): 251–65.

MacArthur, J.D. (1994) 'The Project Sequence: A Composite View of the Project Cycle', in MacArthur, J. and J. Weiss (ed.) *Agriculture, Projects and Development*, Avebury.

———. (1995) *The Evaluation of Development Projects: A Review of the Approaches and Experiences of Donor Agencies*, Development and Project Planning Centre, University of Bradford.

Maddock, N. (1993) 'Has Project Monitoring and Evaluation Worked?', *Project Appraisal*, 8 (3): 188–92.

Marsden, D. and **P. Oakley** (1990) *Evaluating Social Development Projects*, OXFAM, Oxford.

Mendelow, A.L. (1987) 'Stakeholder Analysis for Strategic Planning and Implementation', in W.R. King, and D.L. Cleland (eds) *Strategic Planning and Management Handbook*, Van Nostrand Reinhold, New York, pp. 177–78.

von Metzsch (1995) 'Implications for Evaluation: Structures and Processes' in Robert Picciotto and Ray C. Rist (eds), Evaluation and Development: Proceedings of the 1994 World Bank Conference.

Mohan, G. (1998) Beyond Participation: Strategies for Deeper Empowerment. Paper prepared for the 'Participation—The New Tyranny?' Conference at the University of Manchester.

Morris, J., and **M. Lowcock** (1990) 'Evaluation of Technical Co-operation—The Difficulties of Quantifying the Outcome', in *The Effectiveness of British Aid for Training*', Action Aid, Chard, Somerset.

Morton, K. (1975) *Aid and Dependence*, Croom Helm, London.

Moser, C.O.N. (1995) Evaluating Gender Impacts in, Robert Picciotto and Ray C. Rist (eds), *Evaluation and Development: Proceedings of the 1994 World Bank Conference*, World Bank, Washington DC.

Mosley, P. (1981) Aid for the Poorest: Some Early Lessons of UK Experience, *Journal of Development Studies* (January): 214–25.

——. (1983) The Politics of Evaluation: A Comparative Study of World Bank and UK (ODA) Evaluation Procedures. Unpublished paper, University of Bath, UK.

——. (1986) 'Aid Effectiveness: the Micro-Macro Paradox', *Institute of Development Studies Bulletin*, 17 (2).

——. (1987) *Poverty Focused Aid: The Lessons of Experience*, Action Aid, London.

——. (1990) Evaluating the Effectiveness of Technical Co-operation Expenditures. Paper to workshop at Lysebu, Oslo, organised under the auspices of EADI

Mosley, P. and **J. Toye** (1991) *Aid and Power: The World Bank Policy-Based Lending*, Vol 1, London, Routledge.

Mosley, P. et al. (1984), *Peru: The Cajamarca Agriculture and Livestock Development Project—Baseline Study*, ODA, London.

Mosse, D. (1998) The Making and Marketing of Participatory Development: A Sceptical Note. Paper prepared for the 'Participation—The New Tyranny? Conference, University of Manchester.

Musto, S.A. (1988) Evaluation Policy and Performance in the Federal Republic of Germany. Paper to workshop at Lysebu, Oslo, organised under the auspices of EADI.

Neefjes, K. (1993) *Participatory Environmental Assessment and Planning for Development*, OXFAM.

Nielsen, H.A. (1989) *Monitoring Rural Development in Bangladesh*, Development Research Group, Aarlborg University, Denmark.

——. (1990) *Monitoring the Development Intervention: An Alternative Approach to Impact Evaluation*, Aalborg University, Denmark.

——. (1998) Decentralising the Monitoring of Development Intervention: From Donor-Supervision to Local Government Impact-Monitoring, Development Research Series, Research Center on Development and International Relations (DIR). Working Paper No. 63, University of Aalborg, Denmark.

ODA (1975) *A Guide to the Economic Appraisal of Projects in Developing Countries*, HMSO, London.

——. (1979a) *Evaluation of the North Sumatra Sprinkler Irrigation Project*, EV 103.

——. (1979b) *Tunisian Text-books Project 1969–77*, OECD, London.

——. (1980) *Songea-Makambako Road, Tanzania: Baseline Study*, EV 140, OECD, London.

——. (1982) *Indo-British Technical Co-operation Training Programme*, ODA Evaluation Department, London.

ODA (1983) *The Control of Sheep Scab in Lesotho, and the Control of Foot and Mouth and Tick-Transmitted Diseases in Malawi*, OECD, London.

——. (1985) *Rural Development in Africa: A Synthesis of Project Experience*, OECD, London.

——. (1989) *Interim Evaluation of the Songea-Makambako Road, Tanzania*, EV439, OECD, London.

——. (1992) *Action for the Environment*, London.

——. (1994) *A Guide to the ODA Evaluation System*, OECD, London.

——. (April 1995) *Note on How to Enhance Stakeholder Participation*, OECD, London.

——. (July 1995) *Guidance Note on How to Carry Out Stakeholder Analysis*, OECD, London.

——. (July 1995) *Guidance Note on How to Devise Indicators for Measuring and Assessing Primary Stakeholder Participation*, OECD, London.

——. (1995) Project Reporting, Monitoring and Reviews. Unpublished document.

——. (1996) *The Role of Rating Systems in Aid Management: Experience of DAC Member Organizations*, Operation Review Unit IDGIS, Ministry of Foreign Affairs, the Netherlands and Evaluation Department.

ODI (1979) *Food Aid and the Developing World*, C. Stevens, Croom Helm and ODI, London.

OECD (1969) *The Evaluation of Technical Assistance*, OECD, London.

——. (1984) *Lessons of Experience*, DAC Expert Group on Aid Evaluation, OECD, London.

——. (1986) *Methods and Procedures in Aid Evaluation*, DAC Expert Group on Aid Evaluation, OECD, London.

——. (1987) *Evaluation of Non-Project Aid*, DAC(87)28.

——. (1988) *Evaluation in Developing Countries: A Step in a Dialogue*, DAC Expert Group on Aid Evaluation, OECD, London.

——. (1989a) *Sustainability in Development Programmes: A Compendium of Evaluation Experience*. Selected Issues in Aid Evaluation, No 1, DAC Expert Group on Aid Evaluation.

——. (1989b) *The Environmental Impact of Development Projects*. Selected Issues in Aid Evaluation, No 2, DAC Expert Group on Aid Evaluation.

——. (1989c) *Women as Agents and Beneficiaries in Development Projects*, Selected Issues in Aid Evaluation, No 3, DAC Expert Group on Aid Evaluation.

——. (1990) *A Review of Donors' Systems for Feedback from Aid Evaluation*. Selected Issues in Aid Evaluation, No 4, DAC Expert Group on Aid Evaluation.

——. (1991a) *Principles for Evaluation of Development Assistance*, OECD, London.

——. (1991b), *Evaluation in Africa: Report on the Regional Seminar on Evaluation in Africa Held in May 1990*. Selected Issues in Aid Evaluation, No 5, DAC Expert Group on Aid Evaluation.

OECD (1993) *A History of the DAC Expert Group on Aid Evaluation*. Selected Issues in Aid Evaluation, No 7, DAC Expert Group on Aid Evaluation.

——. (1997a) *Evaluation of Programs Promoting Participatory Development and Good Governance: Synthesis Report*, DAC Expert Group on Aid Evaluation, OECD, London.

——. (1997b) *Synthesis Review of NGO Evaluations*, DAC Expert Group on Aid Evaluation, OECD, London.

OECD/IDB (1994) *Regional Seminar on Monitoring and Evaluation in Latin America and the Caribbean*, OECD, London.

OECD/CIDA (1994) *Assessment of DAC Members' WID Policies and Programmes: Work Carried out under the Auspices of the DAC Expert Group on Aid Evaluation*, Overall Report.

ORU/DGIS/ODA (1996) *The Role of Rating Systems in Aid Management: Experiences of DAC Member Organizations*.

Overseas Development Group, UEA (1977) *The Effects of Roads in West Central Nepal*, P. Blaikie, J. Cameron, and D. Seddon, University of East Anglia.

Parot, R. (1993) Cost-Benefit Analysis: Reassessing its Role in Development Assistance. Unpublished paper, Inter American Development Bank.

Partridge, W. (1995) 'Comments on *Including Culture in Evaluation Research* by R. Klitgaard' in Evaluation and Development: Proceedings of the 1994 World Bank Conference.

Patton, M.Q. (1997) *Utilization-Focused Evaluation: The New Century Text*, Sage, London.

Pawson, R. and **N. Tilley** (1997) *Realistic Evaluation*, Sage, London.

Penalver, M. (1995) Comments on Evaluating the Effectiveness of Poverty Alleviation Programmes by L. Squire, in Evaluation and Development: Proceedings of the 1994 World Bank Conference.

Picciotto, R. (1994) 'The New Role of Development Evaluation', in *Rethinking the Development Experience. Essays Provoked by the Work of Albert O. Hirschman*, Rodwin, L. and D.A. Schon (eds), Brookings Institution and Lincoln Institute of Land Policy, pp. 210–30.

——. (1995a) 'Postscript' in Evaluation and Development: Proceedings of the 1994 World Bank Conference.

——. (1995b) *Evaluation in the World Bank: Antecedents, Processes and Concepts*, World Bank, Washington DC.

——. (1999) 'Towards an Economics of Evaluation', *Evaluation*, January, 5 (1): 7–22.

Picciotto, R. and **R. Weaving** (1994) 'A New Project Cycle for the World Bank?' *Finance and Development*, Vol 31 (4): 42–44.

Pohl and **Minaljek**, 'Uncertainty and the Discrepancy Between Rate-of-return Estimates', World Bank Policy Research and External Affairs Working Paper 761, World Bank, Washington DC, cited in Carlsson, J. Kohlin G. and

A. Ekbom, (1994) *The Political Economy of Evaluation: International Aid Agencies and the Effectiveness of Aid*, Macmillan Press, Basingstoke.

Practical Concepts Incorporated (1979) *Project Management Systems (PMS): An Integrated Systems Approach to Managing the Project Cycle*, Washington DC. Quoted in: Carlsson, J. Kohlin G. and A. Ekbom (1994) *The Political Economy of Evaluation*, Macmillan Press, Basingstoke.

Psacharopoulos, G. (1995) 'Using Evaluation Indicators to Track the Performance of Education Programs', in *Evaluation and Development: Proceedings of the 1994 World Bank Conference.*

Quesnel, J. (1995) 'Implications for Evaluation: Structures and Processes', in *Evaluation and Development: Proceedings of the 1994 World Bank Conference.*

Radaelli, C.M. and **B. Dente** (1996) 'Evaluation Strategies and Analysis of the Policy Process', *Evaluation* 2 (1): 51–66.

Rebien, C.C. (1996) *Evaluating Development Assistance in Theory and Practice*, Avebury Aldershot, Hampshire, England.

Rein, M. and **S. White** (1978) 'Can Policy Research Help Policy?', *Evaluation Studies Review Annual*, Vol 3, Quoted in Stokke (1991).

Renard, R. and **L. Berlage** (1990) The Rise and Fall of Cost-Benefit Analysis in Developing Countries. Paper to workshop, Lysebu, organised under the auspices of EADI

Richardson, R., H. Kuipers, and **J.L. Soeters** (1996) 'Evaluation of Organizational Changes in the Dutch Armed Forces', *Evaluation* 2 (1): 7–22.

Riddell, R. (1987) *Foreign Aid Reconsidered*, Overseas Development Institute, London.

——. (1990) Judging Success. Evaluating NGO Approaches to Alleviating Poverty in Developing Countries, Overseas Development Institute, London.

Rodwin, L. and **D.A. Schon** (eds.) (1994) *Rethinking the Development Experience. Essays Provoked by the Work of Albert O. Hirschman*, Brookings Institution and Lincoln Institute of Land Policy.

Rondinelli, D.A. (1987) *Development Administration and US Foreign Aid Policy*, Lynne Rienner Publishers, Boulder and London.

Rossi, P.H. and **H.E. Freeman** (1993) *Evaluation: A Systematic Approach*, Sage, London.

Salmen, L.F. (1995) 'The Listening Dimension of Evaluation', in *Evaluation and Development: Proceedings of the 1994 World Bank Conference.*

Samset, K. (1992) Norwegian ODA: Testing the Integrated Approach to Planning, Evaluation and Quality Management. (Unpublished paper.)

Samset, K., Forss, K., and **O. Hauglin** (1992) *Learning from Experience in the Royal Norwegian Ministry of Foreign Affairs*, Royal Norwegian Ministry of Foreign Affairs.

Samset, K., Forss, K., and **B.E. Cracknell** (1994) 'Evaluation Systems When Aid Policies are Changing', *Project Appraisal* 9 (1): 29–36.

Sanaag Community-based Organisation (1999) *Action Aid Somaliland Programme Review, June 1999*, Action Aid, Hamlyn House, Archway, London.

Scanteam International (1993) *Internal Learning from Evaluations and Reviews*, Royal Norwegian Ministry of Foreign Affairs (Report No. 1.93).

Schaumburg-Muller, H. (1988) The Evaluation Policy and Performance of Denmark. Paper to workshop at Lysebu, Oslo, organised under the auspices of EADI.

Schneider, S.K. (1990) 'Review of Four Books on Evaluation Program Research', *Public Administration Review*, May/June 50 (3): 393–95.

Scott, J.M., Lambie, G. and **H. Wedgwood** (1987) *An Evaluation of Bilateral Project Monitoring*, EV 408, Overseas Development Administration, London.

Scriven, M. (1972) 'Pros and Cons about Goal-Free Evaluation', Evaluation Comment, *Journal of Educational Evaluation*, Centre for the Study of Evaluation, UCLA 3 (4): 1–7.

Scriven, M. (1993) *Hardwon Lessons in Program Evaluation*, New Directions for Program Evaluation, No. 58, San Francisco, Jossey-Bass.

Sensi, D. and **B.E. Cracknell** (1991) Inquiry into Evaluation Practices in the Commission, Service de Developpement et d'Evaluation de Programmes de Formation. Unpublished report.

Shah, S.M. (1984) 'The Indian Evaluation System' in Cracknell, B.E. (ed.) (1984).

SIDA (1994a) *Evaluation Manual for SIDA* (author: E. Lewin).

——. (1994b) 'The Economic Efficiency of Project Development Assistance', in *SIDA Annual Report*, SIDA, Stockholm.

Silvert, F. (1990) *Knowledge Bank: A Model for Project Monitoring and Impact Assessment*, UNIFEM, New York.

Smillie, I. (1995) NGO Learning, Evaluation and Results: Life in a Three-Ring Circus. paper prepared for the DAC Expert Group on Aid Evaluation.

Smith, N.L. (1998) 'Designing Investigative Evaluations', *Evaluation* 4 (2): 117–29.

Snyder, N.M. and **P.L. Doan** (1995) 'Who participates in the Evaluation of International Development Aid?', *Evaluation Practice* 16 (2): 141–52.

Sommerland, E. (1995) 'Self Evaluation and the Practitioner Evaluator', Book Review, *Evaluation* 1 (1): 106–10.

Squire, L. (1995) 'Evaluating the Effectiveness of Poverty Alleviation Programs', in Evaluation and Development: Proceedings of the 1994 World Bank Conference.

Stake, R. (1995) *The Art of Case Study Research*, Thousand Oaks, CA, Sage.

Stern, E. (1995) Editorial, *Evaluation* 1 (1): 5–9.

Stokke, O. (1991a) 'The Evaluation Policy and Performance of Norway', in Stokke, O. (ed.) (1991) *Evaluating Development Assistance: Policies and Performance*, EADI Book Series No. 12, Frank Cass, London.

Stokke, O. (1991b) 'Policies, Performance, Trends and Challenges in Aid Evaluation', in Stokke, O. (ed).

——. (ed) (1991c) 'Evaluating Development Assistance', in Stokke, O. (ed).

Stufflebeam, D.L. (1980) 'An Interview with D.L. Stufflebeam', *Educational and Policy Analysis* 2 (4): 90–92.

Sugden, R. (1987) The Use of Cost-Benefit Analysis in Post-Project Evaluation. Unpublished notes of lectures delivered to the Civil Service College, Sunningdale, England.

Surr, M. (1995) *Evaluation of Non-Government Organizations (NGOs) Projects: Synthesis Report*, ODA, Evaluation Report, EV 554.

Swantz, M-L. (1992) *Participatory Research and the Evaluation of the Effects of Aid on Women*. Paper prepared for workshop at Lysebu, Oslo, organised under the auspices of EADI.

Taylor, L. (1990) *Foreign Resource Flows and Developing Country Growth*, World Institute for Development Economics Research, Helsinki, Finland.

Team Technologies Inc. (1990) *Logical Framework, Trainers Guide*, Team Technologies, Chontilly, Virginia, USA.

Toulemonde, J., Fontaine, C., Laudren, E., and **P. Vincke** (1998) 'Evaluation in Partnership', *Evaluation* 4 (2): 171–88.

Treasury, H.M. (1985) *Policy Work and the FMI: Report by the Cabinet Office (MPO)/ Treasury Financial Management Unit*, HMSO, London.

——. (1988) *Policy Evaluation: A Guide for Managers*, HMSO, London

Turner, P.J. et al. (1980) *India: Bagging of Fertilizers*, ODA, Evaluation Report No. EV 282.

United Nations (1976) *Glossary of Evaluation Terms*, Joint Inspection Unit, Geneva.

——. (1980) *Report of the Director-General for Development and International Economic Co-operation*, United Nations, New York.

University of East Anglia (1976), *The Effects of Roads in West Central Nepal*, ODA, Evaluation Report No. EV 1.

Uphoff, H. (1989) A Field Methodology for Participatory Self-Evaluation of PPP Group and Inter-Group Association Performance. Paper submitted to the Conference on The Evaluation of Social Development Projects in the Third World, Swansea.

USAID (1986) Flexible Project Design Approaches. AID Occasional Paper, No 3.

——. (1990) *The USAID Evaluation System. Past Performance and Future Directions*, USAID, Washington DC.

Valadez, J. and **M. Bamberger** (1994) *Monitoring and Evaluating Social Programs in Developing Countries*, World Bank, Washington DC.

Vernon, R. (1992) *Review of Information Management in Geographical Projects and Programmes*, ODA, London.

Wheatley, C., G. Arnold, J. Leckscheidt, and **A. Adade** (1985) Assessment and Interpretation of Development Aid Success: A Proposed Scoring System for Application by the EEC and Other Development Agencies, Integration, Frankfurt am Main. Unpublished report.

Widstrand, C. (1990) Approaches and Methods in the Evaluation of Aid. Paper to workshop at Lysebu, Oslo, organised under the auspices of EADI.

Wiggins, S. and **D. Shields** (1995) 'Clarifying the Logical Framework as a Tool for Planning and Managing Development Projects', *Project Appraisal* 10 (1): 2–12.

Williams, P.R.C. (1985) *They Came to Train*, ODA, London.

Winkel, K. (1990) 'What DAC's Expert Group is Doing', *Development Journal*, Issue 3: 15–16.

Winpenny, J. (1984) Development Projects Re-observed: An Aid Practitioner's Assessment of Albert Hirschman after Fifteen years. Unpublished paper.

——. (1991) *Values for the Environment: A Guide to Economic Appraisal*, Overseas Development Institute, London.

——. (1995) 'Evaluating Environmental Impacts: The Process of Unnatural Selection', in Robert Picciotto and Ray C. Rist (eds), *Evaluation and Development: Proceedings of the 1994 World Bank Conference*, World Bank, Washington DC.

World Bank (1979) *Operations Evaluation: World Bank Standards and Procedures*, World Bank, Washington DC.

——. (1985) *Annual Report of Project Performance Results*, Report No 5859, OED, Washington DC.

——. (1990) *Evaluation Results for 1988*, World Bank Washington, DC.

——. (1991) *Annual Review of Evaluation Results, 1990*, Report No 9870, Operations Evaluation Department, Washington, DC.

——. (1993) *Expanding OED's Program of Impact Evaluations: Proposed Principles and Procedures*, Report of Interim Working Group, World Bank, Washington DC.

——. (1994) *Assessing Development Effectiveness: Evaluation in the World Bank and the International Finance Corporation*, World Bank, Washington DC.

——. (1995) *Evaluation and Development: Proceedings of the 1994 World Bank Conference*, World Bank, Washington DC.

——. (1996) *Participation Sourcebook*, World Bank, Washington DC.

Index

About the Author

Basil Edward Cracknell lives in the village of Kingston-near-Lewes, in East Sussex (a mere stone's throw away from the Institute of Development Studies at the University of Sussex and its splendid development studies library) having moved there from Surrey when he left the ODA in 1985 and began a new career as an evaluation consultant. Since then he has carried out consultancies for over 30 clients, including the World Bank, the European Union, OECD, ILO, ODA, OXFAM, the Commonwealth Secretariat, and many others. He joined the ODA in 1969 and was responsible for establishing the newly created Evaluation Department: he saw it grow from one man and his dog to a staff of 9 people and a budget for commissioned evaluations of over £0.5 million per annum.

Dr Cracknell was Chairman of the OECD/DAC Expert Group on Aid Evaluation, 1983-85, and he reckons that this experience was invaluable in opening up new horizons of evaluation activity for him, especially the need to involve the beneficiaries more. He was able to build on this experience when he became a consultant and found himself working for many different clients, including governments of some developing countries. He also reckons that it is pretty rare for an evaluator to have first hand experience both of commissioning evaluations and of being a consultant carrying them out–gamekeeper turned poacher! He greatly values the opportunity of having been on both sides of the fence. Over the last 30 years he has covered all types of evaluation activity, and all the main sectors. He is especially interested in project cycle management, including the logical framework technique which he helped to introduce into the ODA, and subsequently other organisations, including the Global Environment Facility of the World Bank and the European Union.

Dr Cracknell is a founder member of both the UK and the European Evaluation Societies, a member of the Development Studies

Association, the Society for International Development, the Plunkett Foundation and the Agricultural Economics Society. He has run training courses in evaluation techniques for the European Union, OECD/DAC, Government of India, Commonwealth Secretariat, and SIDA. He has written over 30 articles on evaluation in professional journals, and has also edited a book on the subject. He is co-author of a book on organisational learning published by the Swedish Ministry of Foreign Affairs in 1998.

He has visited all parts of the developing world, and says that one of the joys of being an aid evaluator is that you get to see the world! Another joy, he says, is that you get to meet so many interesting people from other cultures. He suggests that it is probably this that most distinguishes aid evaluation from other types of evaluation, and which lends a special poignancy to the ever-present tension between participation and accountability that is one of the principal themes addressed in the book.

of related interest

Organisations and Development

Strategies, Structures and Processes

Reidar Dale

The theme of this book is organisation analysis pertaining to societal development. Reidar Dale explores the concept of development bringing terms and ideas from the academic fields of development studies, planning, public administration and management. Among the topics covered are: the types and forms of development organisations; formulating strategies for development work; modes of development planning; people's participation in development work; organisation and institution building; and evaluation of development work.

The author provides innovative perspectives and interpretations on several topics, including, a typology of development organisations, perspectives on strategy formulation, a typology of organisational forms in the development field, coordination mechanisms relating to development work, and a basic evaluation model.

Lucidly written and supported by illustrations, this book is a must for all those in the field of development.

CONTENTS: *List of Figures, Tables and Boxes/Foreword* by Hands Detlef Kommeier/*Preface*/1. Conceptualising Development/ 2. Organisations in Development/3. Strategy Formulation for Development/4. Organisational Features and Work Categories/ 5. Participation, Empowerment and Capacity-Building/6. Evaluating Development Organisations and Their Work/*References/Index/About the Author*

220mm × 180mm/Hb/Pb/Forthcoming

Sage Publications
New Delhi/Thousand Oaks/London